IN DEFENSE OF
THE LIFEWORLD

SUNY Series, Empowerment and School Reform
Henry A. Giroux and Peter L. McLaren, editors

IN DEFENSE OF THE LIFEWORLD

Critical Perspectives on Adult Learning

edited by
Michael R. Welton

STATE UNIVERSITY OF NEW YORK PRESS

Published by
State University of New York Press, Albany

For information, address State University of New York Press,
State University Plaza, Albany, N.Y., 12246

Production by Christine Lynch
Marketing by Dana E. Yanulavich

Library of Congress Cataloging-in-Publication Data

In defense of the lifeworld : critical perspectives on adult learning
    / edited by Michael R. Welton.
        p.   cm. — (SUNY series, teacher empowerment and school
    reform)
        Includes bibliographical references and index.
        ISBN 0–7914–2539–8 (acid-free paper). — ISBN 0–7914–2540–1 (pbk.
    : acid-free paper)
        1. Adult education—North America. 2. Critical pedagogy—North
    America. 3. Adult learning—North America. I. Welton, Michael
    Robert, 1942– . II. Series: Teacher empowerment and school
    reform.
    LC5251.I54   1995
    374'.97—dc20   94–31396
                                                                       CIP

10 9 8 7 6 5 4 3 2 1

C O N T E N T S

Introduction

Michael R. Welton

OUR MOTIVATION IN WRITING THIS TEXT

This particular text emerged, as many others no doubt do, from conversations among colleagues and friends during the exhilaration of conference meetings. All of us had completed major texts (Mezirow, 1991; Hart, 1992; Collins, 1991; Welton, 1991; Plumb, 1989), and it appeared to us that our work had a kind of elective affinity. Our work appeared to occupy a common theoretical space on the North American adult education scene. Though "critical perspectives on adult learning" were making some inroads into the discourse and practice of adult education in North America, we thought that it was the right moment to bring our ideas together in a single volume and to see where we stood with our field and one another. We were also intensely aware that this book, the work of five persons, would not address itself to every important issue pressing in upon us like water from a broken dike. One reviewer, for instance, wondered about the absence of African-American or Hispanic voices. No text can accomplish everything and we admit to certain lacunae. We recognize the complexities of the politics of knowledge and certainly know how contentious debates are about the most fruitful ways to map the intricacies of exploitation and oppression in our late modern world. This text is limited in many ways, given the whiteness of all of its participants. Still, our intention is less than modest. We attempt to grapple with some of the important issues impinging upon all of us as human beings and adult educators respectively. We think it is important to grapple with those systemic forces crushing in upon all of us. We would hope that this text would be accepted as a dialogue partner by those located in many spaces and living out of ever shifting kinds of identity formations.

By bringing five perspectives together, we hoped to accomplish two purposes: (1) to provide serious students of adult education with a reasonably systematic and richly complex treatment of the impact of some critical social theories on adult education thought and research in one volume, and (2) to introduce our thinking to those with an interest in critical social theory but who may not yet be aware of arguments about the centrality of emancipatory adult learning theory to social transfor-

1

mation and human freedom. Even the "critical pedagogy" literature often associated with Henry Giroux and Peter MacLaren scarcely references any of the critical adult education literature. Educational theory exists in two solitudes as those who write about children and schools remain oblivious to important discussion on the learning of adults. This is quite puzzling, really, particularly when we all know that children do not change the world and that the powerful, formative curricular structures lie outside the walls of the classroom. We are directing this text to serious students of adult education and contemporary society. It is not really a beginner's text; it assumes some familiarity with the Marxian legacy, feminism, and postmodernism, as well as some awareness of central debates within the discipline of adult education. Readers who are steeped in critical social theory, but who are not yet familiar with critical adult education, may find our way of reading social theory provocative,with its implications for an emancipatory learning theory.

To accomplish our goals is not exactly an easy task. For one thing, there is a deep-rooted suspicion of philosophical languages within the field of adult education. Even in a recent special issue of *Studies in Continuing Education*, which was dedicated specifically to examining the theoretical foundations of adult learning, editor Griff Foley expressed his uneasiness, wondering if a serious "dealing with issues" (exploring the meaning of research paradigms, reflexivity, historiography, etc.), courted the "danger of becoming *further* separated from the practitioners and learners whose interests our work supposedly serves" (1993, p. 76; italics mine). There is a danger here, to be sure. It is hard not to feel the sting of those who maintain that social and literary theory in the late modern academy often seems remote from the gritty worlds where we live, move, and have our being. Yet, at the same time, a more serious danger for the study of adult learning lies in the direction of constituting adult education as a "normative discipline" teaching our future practitioners quickly digested and easily formulated principles of program planning and instructional design. All of the authors in this book would argue that adult education as a *field of study* requires space for the free and open inquiry into the nature of adult learning in historical and social contexts. This inquiry must permit the exploration and development of theoretically rich and complex philosophical and social languages. Indeed, academic writing ought to be lucid, simple, aesthetically pleasing. But we must distinguish bad, jargon-ridden writing from bad thinking, and understand that some difficult languages (like those of Adorno, Freire, or Habermas) hold the promise of breaking us out into new ways of seeing the meaning of adult learning and adult educational practice. Adorno was definitely on to something when he complained that in times when instrumental rationality holds the bit in our mouths the most accessible and comprehensible languages are those that bind us to what is, that press us into the mud of our common-place notions, thoroughly riddled as they are with ideological assumptions about self and world. Still, this will not satisfy everyone; perhaps part of a solution to the theory-practice divide is more serious attention both to *foundational* scholarship and to elaborating *pedagogies* that mediate theory to graduate students, who are, after all, the future leaders within the field. The fear of theory on the part of our graduate students (or general readers) must be confronted head-on, and the reasons for our resistance to particular texts and styles explored courageously. In our dreadful neo-conservative times, the university-based study of adult education is under intense pressure to abandon any kind of critical social theorizing in favour of short-term training programs for whatever "need" panic-stricken governments deem salient. It is also under intense pressure to abandon any coherent approach to the study and practice of adult education, fragmenting into multiple allegiances and specialisms. In the long-run, abandoning deep theory and celebrating the "people's knowledge" uncritically is disastrous for the radical democratic project of adult education. This is so because the longing for the not-yet is, in part, carried by theory itself. I learned that from both Adorno and Marcuse, and it is a lesson well learned for our time. Critical theory, in a very dark time, helps to preserve the sacred trust of human longing for freedom.

A second difficulty facing our project has to do with our dystopic and unsettling world. This particular text has not been written at a high-point in the history of the radical, or critical adult education movement. We are thinking about the future of a critical adult education vision and practice in an increasingly disenchanted world. There can be no doubt that what sociologist Anthony Giddens labels the "tribulations of the [late modern] self" have intensified, even in the last two or three years. The human selfhood is increasingly forced to be reflexive, which, as Jack Mezirow details, unveils learning potential to reflect on taken-for-granted assumptions about one's perspective on the world. But the "reflexive project of the self" must find its way through "numerous contextual happenings," sort out seemingly endless choices about lifestyle, steer its way between "commitment and uncertainty" and construct a "narrative of the self" in a commodified world. However, as the stable routines of life collapse and traditions within the lifeworld erode, the reflexive self is threatened with meaninglessness and dread (Giddens, 1991, p. 201ff.). In modernity, we dispute the meaning of our lives; postmodern times call into question whether meaning is anything other than our private hunches. Our uncertainty of everyday living plunges us deeper into the depths of our ontological sense of security.

It seems inescapable, to me at any rate, that we are not only confronting in quite dramatic ways the old Weberian theme of the "loss of meaning." We are also threatened by a loss of our own identities as radical intellectuals. Lenin's statues have collapsed, and along with their toppling has gone our own sense of hope. It is not that Soviet-style communism should not have been superseded; it is, rather, that along with communism's collapse in the East and the degradation of social democracy in the West has gone the old dream of a better world. Hope is in very short supply (unless it be, ironically, the hope of making a fortune now that a predatory market economy is in place in Russia, China, and elsewhere).

But, as Italian political theorist Norbert Bobbio astutely observes, "Historical communism has failed. I don't deny it. But the problems remain—those same problems which the communist utopia pointed out and held to be solvable, and which now exist, or very soon will, on a world scale. That is why one would be foolish to rejoice at the defeat and to rub one's hands saying: 'We always said so!' Do people really think that the end of historical communism (I stress the word 'historical') has put an end to poverty and the thirst for justice?" (1992, p. 5). As always, the question: what kind of society do we live in, what kind of society do we wish to promote into the twenty-first century, how will people learn their way towards a more enlightened and more just society? All of us— Mezirow, Hart, Collins, Plumb, and myself—are deeply distressed by the times we are living in and the threat posed to the critical practice of adult education. All of us affirm that viewing the multiple crises of late modern society through the social learning lens illuminates oft-neglected pedagogical dimensions of the struggle for the further democratization of our societies. We do not, however, either agree on all matters or speak with the same accent.

HOW TO READ THIS TEXT

Each of the authors of *In Defense of the Lifeworld* was invited to set out in essay form their central ideas and present preoccupations. This strategy is captured by the subtitle: "Critical Perspectives on Adult Learning," and assumes immediately that, while we are all positioned toward the radical end of the spectrum in North American adult education thought and share a number of common concerns, we have different preoccupations and are at work on different problematics.

From our perspective, the discipline of adult education (adult education is often divided in two—adult education as a field of study and practice) is in serious crisis. The "andragogical consensus" (anchoring the study of adult education in methods of teaching and understanding the individual adult learner), formulated by the custodians of orthodoxy in the American Commission of Professors in the 1950s and solidified by Malcolm Knowles and others in the 1960s and 1970s, has unravelled at the seams. For about a decade and a half, voices from the margins have been levelling four fundamental accusations against the modern practice of adult education: (1) adult education has abandoned its once vital role in fostering democratic social action; (2) the discipline of adult learning was based on a shaky foundation; (3) the contemporary modern practice of adult education is governed by an instrumental rationality that works to the advantage of business, industry, and large-scale organizations; (4) consequently, the guiding principle of the modern practice of adult education, self-directed learning, is conceptually inadequate to serve the interests of the poor, oppressed, and disenfranchised in North American society.

This theme—a discipline in crisis—when linked with its correlative—a commitment to understanding how societal structures and ideational systems hinder and impede the fullest development of humankind's potential to be self-reflective and self-determining historical actors—provides this text with its central *focus*.

The title of the book, *In Defense of the Lifeworld*, has its roots in the imagery of Jürgen Habermas. The lifeworld is the realm of intersubjective interaction and adult learning par excellence. It is within the lifeworld that we learn what life means, what binds us together as human beings and what constitutes an autonomous personality. It is in the lifeworld that we organize our common affairs through non-instrumental forms of communication, even though various traditions provide substance to our meaning perspectives and to our interactions. Critical adult education practice, we argue, has as its normative mandate the preservation of the critically reflective lifeworld (communicative distortions can be sedimented in traditional practices) and the extension of communicative action into systemic domains; thus the fate of critical adult education is tied to the fate of the lifeworld. Expressed boldly, this formulation—in defense of the lifeworld—holds the promise of replacing the old andragogical paradigm. Readers with interest in Jürgen Habermas will surely find much food for thought in this book!

We all share a common concern to articulate a critical social theory that provides both the philosophical-sociological and normative grounding for our practice as educators of adults. We do, however, have different preoccupations and have been at work over many years on different theoretical problematics. It would seem, then, that some readers will find it useful not only to see how each of the chapters of this book relates to the *central theme* of the text, but also to pursue particular *sub thematics* such as the crisis of the discipline, professionalization, feminism and adult education, the purposes of adult education, the meanings of modernity and postmodernity, the vocation of the teacher of adults, critiques of Human Resource Development (HRD) and so on. Let us now look briefly at some of the preoccupations of each of the authors.

Jack Mezirow locates himself in the social reform tradition within American adult education. Now in his early seventies, with a long history of engagement in various critical and community-based ventures, in the last several years he has been a persistent, even exasperated, critic of the modern practice of American adult education and has confronted his colleagues with pointed criticisms of their narrowed horizons and lapsed memories. Mezirow feels most at home within the American pragmatic intellectual tradition. Readers will note, in the concluding dialogue section of the book, that he distances himself somewhat from the "European" tradition of critical theory. But a close scrutiny of Habermas' work would reveal the significant impact of American thinkers like John Dewey, George Herbert Mead, and Charles Peirce (see, Diggins, 1994, p. 417ff.). It is actually quite tricky to untangle authentically "American," "Canadian," or "British" traditions from those of Europe. Although Mezirow's transformative learning theory continues to be worked and reworked (those who follow Mezirow's work carefully will have a little fun detecting what is new), he has consistently written about the ways people understand their world and the potential available to them to effect social change. He is most at home within the symbolic interactionist theoretical frame (the influence of George Herbert Mead is evident here), and has almost relentlessly pursued the cognitive dimensions of the process whereby adults transform their perspective on world, self, and others. Mezirow has argued that there is an emancipatory dimension to the developmental, maturational process, and this, like other notions of his, has precipitated spirited debates in the influential journal *Adult Education Quarterly*. Mezirow has insisted that the capacity to reflect critically on taken-for-granted assumptions is the cardinal dimension of adulthood, and he has argued persistently that this social psychological truth provides the grounding for the central task of the adult educator, namely, to foster critical reflection. This key notion provides the bridge for Mezirow to appropriate some elements of Habermas' theory of communicative action. Thus, Mezirow foregrounds the cognitive dimensions of the transformation of the individual's perspective, and the social structural framing of our lives slides into the background. This latter problematic is addressed in the concluding dialogue by myself and Plumb.

Michael Collins situates his work both in the radical tradition of adult education (Hodgkins, Tawney, Lindeman, Horton, Lovett, and Freire) and in a variety of critical theoretic traditions (he has a deep affinity to Habermas' work, but insists on being open to wider Marxian streams—Luxemburg and Gramsci—as well as to elements of phenomenology and pragmatism). Two themes persist throughout Collins' work over several decades. First, he has fiercely criticized the modern practice of adult education for its absorption into the "cult of efficiency" and its adoption of instrumental rationality as its guiding light. Reading Collins allows the reader to see how his commitment to preserve the lifeworld (Collins sometimes uses the Illichian phrase, the "commons," as a synonym) impels him to criticize competency-based approaches to education and to insist that program, or curricular, planning not close off collaborative, dialogic learning processes. Both Collins and myself, particularly, have problematized "professionalization" and the deleterious consequences of "expert cultures" on the lifeworld. Second, Collins has criticized the professionalization of the field (and its attendant dominant ideology, self-directed learning), and this has impelled him to challenge the currently fashionable idea of the adult educator as facilitator. For Collins, the turn to a social learning theory, while important, could distract attention from the importance of the ethical agency of the educator of adults. This strikes me as an important subtheme in the book: defending the lifeworld requires that we find the "courage to teach" (Collins). More than ever, adult educators ought to have something to teach and struggle against the weakening of ethical resolve. But the question of grounding the discipline of adult learning in the agency of the adult educator remains problematic.

From the early 1980s until the publication of *Working and Educating for Life* in 1992, Mechthild Hart's theoretical work has been informed by two powerful currents of critical thought: Frankfurt critical theory and several varieties of feminism. More recently, and this is reflected in her contribution to this book, she has immersed herself in literature examining racism and her feminist reading has focused primarily on works often associated with the "womanist" stream of feminist thought (Martin, 1994). This latter fact introduces a jangling note into this text as Hart wonders if her perspective is, in fact, marginalized within this text itself! Two themes stand out in the work in the early period. First, she examined how power relations distorted the relations between men and women, and offered us many insights on the learning processes within women's consciousness-raising groups. Second, like Collins, she demonstrated how the Habermasian distinction between communicative and strategic rationalities could help us understand how the organization of work and technology had been structured by an instrumental rationality. This penetrating critique of technology fed into her sharp denunciation of the way a huge segment of the American adult education field had jumped onto the HRD bandwagon. Though not as preoccupied, at least in her writing, with the practice of adult education per se, Hart demonstrated convincingly that a *critical* practice of adult education must be anchored in a socially and historical contextual analysis of specific domains of human interaction (and therefore of learning or anti-learning). This latter preoccupation is manifest in her essay for this book; however, one can see that she is at the moment more concerned with affirming the value of woman's nurturing work as moral-spiritual ground for survival in a terribly debilitating and violent world than she is in elaborating systematic, global theory, so manifest in her earlier work. Nonetheless, Hart is offering us a radical version of the defense of the lifeworld. She draws upon the selective tradition of woman's life-affirming labor to defend vulnerable and oppressed women as well to find a source of resistance to capitalism's incessant exploitation of women everywhere. There is, however, a noticeable shift in her most recent work away from the Habermasian idea (argued by myself) of the unfulfilled project of modernity towards a post-enlightenment positioning in relation to the ideology of progress. Thus, further debate between Plumb and Hart may well prove very fruitful.

Donovan Plumb is a relative newcomer to the North American adult education scene and is the most youthful of all of us. Plumb's central intellectual trait of fearlessness is manifest in his writings to date. In his own way, like Hart, Plumb is a disquieting presence in the current debates about the potential of a critical practice of adult education. In Plumb's earliest work (1989), he brought Habermas and Freire into dialogue, arguing that Freire's pedagogy needed Habermas' theory of communicative competence to place itself on a less shaky, less moralizing ground. Recently, Plumb (1994) has moved onto even more uncomfortable ground. His central project is to place the critical project of adult education in dialogue with postmodernist theorizing. Although he remains convinced that Habermas' theory of communicative action provides a better foundation for critical adult education than Freire provided, he believes that the postmodernist critique of Habermas itself raises questions about the normative foundation for critical theory.

Plumb contends that postmodernist discourses such as the commodification of culture and the undermining of hegemonic domination in favour of surveillance and seduction raise "deep doubts about critical adult education's practices" (1994, p. 2). Though Plumb argues that the critical project of adult education has not exhausted its emancipatory potential, he thinks that we must confront the *sociological* and *cultural* tendencies evident in our time. One of these tendencies is the massive cultural shift away from a discursive, verbal culture to one that is figural. This shift, he argues, pulls the floor out from under the rug of the critical project, based as it has been on Gramscian assumptions regarding the way the dominant class actually dominates subordinate sectors. Plumb's work will help us clarify the vision and theoretical resources we need to move into the twenty-first century. Is the critical project exhausted? Are the modernist, universalist ideals of freedom, justice, and equality preservable? If so, what forces are arraigned against us in our disquietude?

One of my central preoccupations in the last decade or so has been to help shift the way "adult education" has been conceptualized, namely, from an individual, psychologistic focus to one that is socially and historically contextual. Drawing upon the work of Habermas, who has executed the epochal "learning turn" in social theory, I have sought to understand learning as an intersubjective process. I have wanted to find a way of thinking about the various domains of human (adult) interaction as a social learning process. How can we understand the family and workplace, public life and social movements as learning sites? Toward this end, I have been trying to outline a way of thinking about work and politics that would enable me to understand these domains as collective learning processes.

In my contributions to *In Defense of the Lifeworld*, I attempt to reconstruct the critical theoretical tradition as a social learning theory; I argue that there is an implicit learning theory in the Marxian tradition, and that with Habermas this learning theory becomes explicit. This reading, I contend, has been marginalized in the Habermasian educational literature. In the chapter from which the book title has been taken, I try to anchor critical adult education practice, now deeply threatened by cultural and political-economic developments, in the lifeworld. Picking up on themes present in my earlier work, I choose to use Habermasian role theory as a way of tying critical adult education practice concretely to the constraints and possibilities of contemporary social organization. From time to time, I think of my work as a radical developmentalist approach to learning. Simply, I believe that human individuation requires structures that permit human beings to act autonomously with others toward the creation of a just and equal and free society.

In sum, I hope that readers will find in *In Defense of the Lifeworld* a storehouse of ideas toward the transformation of our thinking and our practices in a dangerous and unnerving time.

1

The Critical Turn in Adult Education Theory

Michael R. Welton

For more than a decade now there have been rumblings in the margins of the field that the university-based study of adult education has been professionally colonized, that the dominant paradigm, the "andragogical consensus," has crumbled. The field of adult education theory is presently occupied by an array of competing discourses. Two of the most engaging theoretical developments to appear in the last couple of years have been: (1) an anti-foundational contextualism (Usher and Bryant, 1989; Wildemeersch and Jansen, 1992; Weil and McGill, 1989), which takes it cues from phenomenology, hermeneutics, and postmodernism, and (2) a critical learning theory, which takes its direction largely from Habermas (Mezirow, 1991; Collins, 1991; Hart, 1990; Collins and Plumb, 1989; Collard and Law, 1989; Clark and Wilson, 1991). All of the authors contributing to this text have learned deeply from Habermasian critical social theory in their attempts to create a conceptual frame comprehensive enough to provide theoretical solidity to the field, and ethical guidance for all practitioners across multiple settings. The essays in this text vary in the explicitness of their engagement with Habermas and in their willingness to walk all the way down the Habermasian highway. Whether in the foreground or background, however, Habermas' giant presence casts large shadows over our texts.

This text has taken shape and direction in response to urgent questions facing global civilization and the adult education movement. In an increasingly disenchanted world bleached of spirituality and dominated by a manic market mentality, we are hungry for philosophical orientation and depth. This hunger has driven adult education from its tents in the wilderness into the depths of critical theory at a time when great aspersion has been cast upon the very notion of an emancipatory project. Crushed from one side by the brutal logic of neo-conservativism and from the other by a sceptical postmodern discourse, it appears that even those who have been friendly to a critical adult educational practice are losing their nerve (Wildemeersch, 1992a, 1992b). The question of the potency of adult education to respond to the almost endless learning challenges of our time has been called into question by the friends of critical theory, and those who are not so friendly to critical adult education appear to be having the last laugh. Nonetheless, though the capitalist restructuring of the global (dis)order may be on fast-for-ward—smashing just about everything humanly valuable in sight—it makes sense to consider carefully the legacy of critical social theory. What are its historical origins? What are its assumptions about how human beings learn to be free? How do critical theorists see the world, its agonies, problems, and possibilities?

In this chapter I would like to argue that the critical theoretical tra-dition from Marx to Habermas has much to teach us about adult learn-ing, and can provide a "foundation" for an emancipatory educational practice. A theory of emancipatory learning has always been *implicitly* present within the Marxian tradition; it is only with Habermas that we begin to see the "learning theory" become *explicit* and self-conscious. This chapter attempts to accomplish two interrelated conceptual tasks: to provide a brief history of critical social theory and to show how the critical theoretical tradition itself can be interpreted as a socially and historically grounded theory of adult learning (how adults unlearn their adherence to unfreedom and learn to be enlightened, empowered, and transformative actors in particular times, places, and spaces). This chap-ter also has a secondary intention: to provide the theoretical and histor-ical context for the collective project of reconstructing the discipline of adult learning. A critical theory of adult learning and education does not make full sense without understanding the origins and impulses of crit-ical theory.

Critical theory holds out the promise of enabling us to specify con-cretely with practical intent *how* we can think of all of society as a vast school; it also helps us to understand how a global society ruled by pred-atory corporations and dominated by a "technocratic" or "instrumental" rationality, is consciously structured to block, constrain, and contain societal-wide and historically deep collective enlightenment, empower-ment, and transformative action. Without a critical theory of society we will never know how even the individualist ideals we posit—the fulfill-ment of the individual, our commitment to "autonomous" self-directed learning—are *systemically* blocked and constrained: in our homes, workplaces, the public sphere, cultural and intellectual life, associa-tional and movement spaces. Nor will we know how our late capitalist society, with its class, gender, ethnic, and bureaucratic divisions, generates dissatisfactions (needs that cannot be met adequately within society's frame), contradictions and, periodically, massive crises, which create the potentiality for emancipatory practice. Critical theory ought to help radical adult educators to ground their "untheorized" practice.

Critical adult educators and critical theorists converge in affirming that the system reproduces itself in the subjectivity of men and women. Simply focusing upon and celebrating the learning taking place everywhere (particularly outside bad formal educational institutions [Thomas, 1991]), will blind us to the fact that in an unjust and unfree society, men, women, and children will be socialized across the life span to systematically misunderstand their identity, needs, what constitutes happiness, what is good and of value, how one should act in one's relations with others to achieve these things. Even informal and non-formal learning are pressured to conform to what Michael Ryan has called "the principle of non-contradiction: if the system is to retain legitimacy and survive, the consciousness of social agents must not contradict the presuppositions of the economy, the social network, and the state" (Ryan, 1982, p. 56). Despite this conforming pressure, critical educators and theorists argue that people are victims of causal processes that have power over them because they are unaware of the precise ways they have been implicated in the processes that oppress them. Here we have the necessary theoretical opening for understanding how an educative process might enable people to give up their illusions—"abandoning one's self-conception and the social practices that they engender and support, things people cling to because they provide [false] direction and [false] meaning in their lives" (Fay, 1987, p. 214).

Today, there can be no doubt, "critique" is a vogue word. Educators, social scientists, literary critics, and philosophers all use the word "critical"; it is by no means clear that we are all talking the same language. The tendency in contemporary educational discourse is to restrict the meaning of critical to processes of validating arguments. This approach (often labelled "critical thinking") cannot be identified with critical theory as understood in the western philosophical and Marxist tradition. Simply put, critical thinking does not understand its project as providing an analysis of the "complex of interrelations out of which capitalist crises arise in order to make it possible, through philosophical critique giving guidance to action, to eliminate politically the causes of those crises" (Honneth and Joas, 1988, p. 152). It is imperative, then, in order to understand the meaning of the critical turn in adult education theory, that we risk oversimplification and sketch the meaning of critique from antiquity to Habermas. We will discover that contemporary critical theory has emerged through a dialectical engagement with German intellectual thought (Kant, Hegel, and Marx) interplaying with the evolution of capitalism and modernity. Critical theory is a theory of history and society driven by a passionate commitment to understand how ideological systems and societal structures hinder and impede the fullest development of humankind's collective potential to be self-reflective and self-determining historical actors.

CRITIQUE FROM ANTIQUITY TO THE RENAISSANCE

Critique, like crisis, is derived from the Greek *krinein* (making distinctions: separating, judging, deciding). Between antiquity and the Renaissance "crisis" was used solely in a medical context (through into the seventeenth century). During the Renaissance the term "critic" was applied to the grammarian or the philologist. Critique became the philological criticism of literary texts. Here the task was to reconstruct the authenticity of a particular source—to rescue a text from history's decay. Reformers used philological critique to describe the art of informed judgment. This was thought to be appropriate to the study of ancient texts, whether the classics or the Bible. But critique of texts was a "double-edged weapon." As the world became increasingly disenchanted (the dissolution of all-embracing systems of world-interpretation ascribing a unique and integral meaning to human existence with reference to a transcendental being [Markus, 1986, p. xii]), the art of critique itself achieved a status independent of both Church and State. The concept of critique shifted from defending revelation to driving a wedge between reason and revelation.

This was one of the cardinal unmaskings in Western thought (Sloterdijk, 1988, p. 23ff.). Peter Bayle's *Dictionnaire historique et critique*, written in the late seventeenth century, posited "reason" and "critique" as indivisible. What Bayle accomplished was to shift critique as method (philological work *on* texts) to critique as principle: critique extends beyond philological criticism and becomes the essential activity of reason while acquiring negative and destructive connotations. All claims to authority, whether religious or other, become fair game for reason's scalpel. "La raison humaine . . . est un principe de destruction, non pas d'édification," says Bayle. Paul Connerton astutely comments:

> Critique is certainly committed to the task of seeking truth; but to a truth which has yet to be established. Whence it follows that critical activity does not yield truth directly, but indirectly. Truth is to be reached, in the first instance, through the destruction of appearances and illusions. This notion of a republic of letters presupposes the equality of all participants in the process of critical activity. . . . It is now assumed that truth flourishes, not through the illumination of human understanding by inherited traditions, but rather through the medium of a communicative struggle. (1976, p. 19)

By the mid-eighteenth century critique was becoming gradually politicized. In clubs, lodges, coffee houses, a new moral authority, the public, found its earliest institutions (Habermas, 1974; 1989b; Gouldner, 1976; Calhoun, 1992).

THE "AGE OF CRITIQUE": FROM KANT TO HEGEL

In 1781 in his preface to *Critique of Pure Reason*, Kant declared his age the "age of critique" in which neither religion nor the legislature was exempt. With Kant the model of critique characteristic of the Enlightenment underwent a basic structural change. The *philosophes* had understood critical activity as a external discussion with a partner. Reason focused on a particular object of critique, seeking through negation to discover the truth or falsity of text or institution. Now, for Kant, reason becomes both subject and object. Reason, once turned against acceptable authorities, turns on itself. His great critiques (of theoretical reason, practical-moral insight, and aesthetic judgment) are reflections on the conditions of possible knowledge, on the potential capacities of human beings possessing the faculties of knowing, speaking, and acting. Dare to know! What are the conditions of our knowledge through which modern natural science is possible and how far does this knowledge extend? Kant focused on the "rational reconstruction of the conditions which make language, cognition, and action possible" (Connerton, 1976, p. 23). The Kantian "Copernican turn" influenced one direction of Habermas' thought. But Habermas, unlike Kant, attempts to understand the fundamental forms of knowledge in the light of the problems humankind encounters in its efforts to produce its existence and reproduce its species being (Held, 1980, p. 254). Habermas places reason inside the historical process.

Kant's solution was to posit certain *a priori* categories or forms, embedded in the human subject, which allow us to constitute "things" in the factual world, now severed from the constituting subject. This idea—that a "transcendental ego" *both* constitutes the world *and* leaves "room" for the possiblity of moral freedom—precipitated endless debates about the relationship between activity and passivity, *a priori* and sense data, philosophy and psychology. In *Theory and Practice* (1973) Habermas argues that the philological criticism of the humanists understood itself as theoretical and practical critique. With the ascendancy of German idealism, critique "no longer understands itself in its correspondence to crisis" (p. 213). Critique and crisis become uncoupled in Kant. But, Habermas maintains, the Hegelian project of the early nineteenth century attempted to reconstitute "philosophy of the world as crisis," even though philosophy was not subject to the crisis itself. Hegel attempts to escape the embarrassment of Kant's ineffable "universal subject" by postulating the "absolute spirit" as the most real thing of all. Reason need not stand over against itself in *purely* critical fashion. In his classic essay, "Traditional and Critical Theory," Max Horkheimer states that reason has become affirmative in Hegel, even before reality itself is affirmed as rational. But, confronted with the persisting contradictions in human existence and with the impotence of individuals in face of situations they themselves have brought about, the Hegelian solution seems a purely individual assertion, a "personal peace treaty between the philosopher and an inhuman world"(1976, p. 217). Hegel believed that the "ought" and the "is" would coincide in history. On the surface this Hegelian move seems to dissolve the critical function of reason because the "ought" is now placed within the realm of the particular. In his sympathetic reclamation of Hegel, *Reason and Revolution* (1960), Herbert Marcuse argues correctly that Hegel's insistence that the universal is pre-eminent over the particular, signifies in the concrete that the potentialities of men and things are not exhausted in the given forms in which they actually appear (1960 [1941], pp. 113–14). This notion of potentiality is fundamental to critical theory and emancipatory educational practice in the broadest possible sense. Reality points to and strives toward its own overcoming.

MARX'S CRITICAL PROJECT:
FROM SPRINGTIME TO MATURITY

Unlike Hegel, Marx locates his principle of negation within the dynamic social order itself. Accusing his "Young Hegelian" comrades of being "mere critics" who stood outside reality and nagged it to change, Marx asserts that mere criticism is ineffectual, like a lone fog-horn calling to a ship lost in a fierce storm. He certainly does not believe that the "weapon of criticism" alone will burst asunder the chains and free the immiserated! In what way can critique become truly efficacious? By answering that theory will only become a "material force" when it has "gripped the masses" (Marx, 1975, p. 182), Marx has asked himself a historically decisive question. In fact, we might even say that modern critical theory was born at this moment. The role of theory, says Marx in the springtime of his thinking, is not to "face the world in doctrinaire fashion with a new principle, declaring 'Here is truth, kneel here!' " (Easton and Guddatt, 1967, pp. 211–15). Rather, the task is to facilitate the "collective subject" to reach its own self-consciousness— the consciousness of its latent radical needs, induced by but unsatisfiable under the existing social conditions. Revolutionary potentiality seethes within a specific complex of material conditions. Theory only awakens the emergent proletariat to its historical mission and springs it into the daylight of historical praxis.

Critique reveals itself in Marx (and later critical theorists) as being tied to the "myth of the Enlightenment." In 1784 Kant had asked himself the famous question, "What is Enlightenment?" and answered that, to the extent that reason shapes human life, human history is assured of progress, of departing from a condition of servitude. Kant had declared his age the "Age of Enlightenment." If it were to be achieved, it would be in all spheres of life (religion, politics, science, philosophy). To be enlightened was to be autonomous, to question dogma, to take responsibility for historical unfolding. Kant's ideal was the critically reflective *individual*. Nonetheless, the way was now clear for the "philosophy of history" to identify a new subject, God having being relieved of responsibility for the world. Hegel thought that the world-spirit governed history and refused to identify a historical subject. Marx replaced the world-spirit with the proletariat—the embodiment of enlightened reason (Connerton, 1980, pp. 116–18).

In his third "Thesis on Feuerbach," Marx contrasted his revolutionary theory with that of his Enlightenment and utopian socialist predecessors. "The materialist doctrine of the modifying influence of the change in conditions and education forgets that the conditions are changed by men, and that the educator himself must be educated. It is thus forced to divide society into two parts, one of which rises above the society. The coincidence of the changing of conditions and of human activity or self-transformation can only be conceived and understood rationally as *revolutionary practice*." The educator cannot stand outside people's life-situation and proclaim the truth. Either her ideas will be so removed from reality as to be false or, if derived from reality, would merely mirror it. What accounts for valid knowledge of the world? Revolutionary practice—"learning that arises from an activity which both changes the world and the person acting on the world" (Howard 1988, pp. 32–33). In *The German Ideology* (1845), Marx and Engels argue that the revolution is necessary "because the class *overthrowing* it [the dominant class] can only succeed in ridding itself of all the muck of the ages and become fitted to found society anew in revolution" (cited, Howard, 1988, p. 33). Marx and Engels recognize that the oppressive society recreates itself (or, as Freire would say, houses itself) in its victims' hearts and minds in the form of behavior patterns and attitudinal beliefs which are sustained by the normal functioning of social intercourse itself. How men and women unlearn their adherence to unfreedom and learn emancipatory subjectivity is one of the central educational questions confronting critical theoretical work, past and present (Sherover-Marcuse, 1986). There can be no "critique" without "politics," without understanding that "revolutionary praxis" is *educatively constituted* (Allman and Wallis, 1990).

Karl Korsch, who is responsible along with Georg Lukacs for the revitalization of Marxian humanism in the 1920s and 1930s (Vajda, 1972; Arato, 1972), argued that "Marx's book on capital, like Plato's book on the state, like Machiavelli's *Prince* and Rousseau's *Social Contract*, owes its tremendous and enduring impact to the fact that it grasps and articulates, at a turning point in history, the full implications of the new force breaking in upon the old form of life. . . . Karl Marx proved himself to posterity to be the great forward-looking thinker of his age, in as much as he comprehended early on how decisive these questions would be for the approaching world-historical crisis" (Korsch 1972, p. 39). In his magnum opus, *Das Kapital* (1867), subtitled "A Critical

Analysis of Capitalist Production," we see Marx's critical methodology playing itself out in his masterful analysis of the dynamics of industrial capitalism. It is important to grasp the *levels* and *complexity* of this method of critique because in contemporary discussions of critical thinking or critical educational practice the prevalent tendency has been to identify critique with a cognitive process of reflection upon an individual's taken-for-granted assumptions, values or roles and then to propose techniques for fostering individual reflectivity (Mezirow, 1990). The consequences of forgetting Marx for the construction of a critical theory of adult learning and transformative education are enormous, inevitably binding us to an individualistic model of learning—even if we label it "transformative" and add "action" as outcome (see the final chapter).

Marx's critical methodology works on three levels. On the first level, *categorical critique*, Marx does not counterpose his conceptual structure to that of classical political economy. What he does is to show that the concepts of classical political economy are logically inconsistent and self-contradictory. Marx demonstrates that acceptance of the classical definition of exchange value does not allow us to explain the actual increase in the value of capital. Rather, one must consider not the exchange process alone, but the process of the production of commodities (profits result from the exploitation of worker surplus labor power). This procedure, Benhabib observes, presents an *immanent* critique of political economy's scientific categories. "It is this discrepancy and inconsistency between categories and their objects, or concepts and their actual content, which reveals how these categories turn into their opposite" (1984, p. 287).

On a second level, Marx uses *normative critique*. Here we are on slightly more familiar ground. Marx will demonstrate that the posited norm of bourgeois society—the right of all to freedom, equality, and property—is expressed in actual social relations of "exchange between individual property owners, who are equal in their abstract right to voluntarily dispose of what belongs to each" (p. 287). Marx argues that "freedom" actually means that the worker is free to sell his or her labor-power in a relationship of unequal exchange. Thus, Marx juxtaposes the "*normative* self-understanding" of society to the "*actual* social relations prevailing in it" (p. 287). To be sure, in *Capital* Marx does not abandon his youthful philosophical critique of alienation. Now, he provides a more precise account of the nature of human alienation in terms of how

the exploitation process actually works under the conditions of capitalist production.

On the third level, Marx uses the method of *defetishizing critique*.
Marx's concern is twofold: to critique political economy as a specific
mode of theoretical and social consciousness, and as a specific mode of
social production (p. 288). Marx wants to reveal the fetishistic character
of everyday life (social relations between humans appears as a relation
between things). He believes that the categories of political economy
conceal the actual "social process of production" (p. 288) which operate
behind our backs and mystify our consciousness. Next Marx moves on
to historical territory to open out future emancipatory possibilities. He
argues, contrary to classical political economy, that the capitalist mode
of production is not a natural, eternal system. It has both "systemic as
well as social limits." The systemic limits of capital manifest themselves in economic crises (depressions, unemployment, bankruptcies)
and the social limits of capital express themselves in antagonistic struggles of classes and social groups against capitalist hegemony. It is in
these "crisis moments" that exploited men and women are particularly
open to unlearning their false self-understandings and acquiring an
emancipatory consciousness about the system's transitoriness and irra-
tionality. Marx thinks that these crises will catalyze deep insight into the
gap between the potential wealth of society (including the possibilities
of developing the many-sided individual) and the actual misery of individuals (in all spheres of human interaction).

In sum, Marx's critical method is rather complex. In *Capital* he tries
to show that capitalist society "contains within itself an unrealized
potential" (p. 290). In Benhabib's words:

> Marx's normative vision is that of an active humanity, dynamic,
> enterprising, transforming nature and unfolding its potentialities in
> the process. The bourgeoisie, which can be named the first social class
> in history to derive its legitimation from an ideology of change and
> growth rather than one of order and stability, is, on Marx's view, not
> be rejected but sublated (*aufgehoben*). For in bourgeois society the
> "true universality of individual needs, capacities and pleasures" is
> identified with a *limited* form, namely with wealth in the sense of the
> mere accumulation of material objects. What is required in the society
> of the future is to make this wealth not an end but rather a precondition
> for the development of *real human wealth*, i.e. true human universal-
> ity and individuality. (p. 291)

Nonetheless, there is an unresolved tension in Marx's critical methodology. Marx thought of class interests as objectively determined and targeted one collective actor, the proletariat, as revolutionary agent. But the determination of class interests requires a normative standpoint and there is always more than one potential collective subject.

As the nineteenth century played itself out into the terror and barbarism of the twentieth, unresolved problems in the Marxian critical project would more fully reveal themselves. The facilitative, dialogic relationship between critical theorist and collective subject, so delicately balanced by the youthful Marx, dissolved as revolutionary theory became increasingly the province of intellectuals. Critical theory, instrumentalized by communist and socialist parties, became, ironically, a standpoint outside the historical process. Moreover, Marx's "latent positivism" (Wellmer, 1971, pp. 67–119) was turned into a mechanistic explanatory system by the Marxist theoreticians of the Second International (Kautsky and Bernstein) that spoke of capitalism's inevitable transformation into socialism and the necessity of reformist politics. By the second decade of the twentieth century, Marxism was suffering from sclerosis of the will and fossilization of its theoretical categories.

HAUNTED HOUSE:
THE FRANKFURT SCHOOL OF CRITICAL THEORY

The "Frankfurt School" of critical theory (Horkheimer, Adorno, Marcuse are its main founding figures) emerged in the 1920s to conduct for its time a "searching reexamination of the very foundations of Marxist theory with the dual hope of explaining past errors and preparing for future action" (Jay, 1972, p. 226). They were doing so in an historical period that had seen the socialist centre of gravity shift eastward and the collapse of the European socialist movement. Although initially enthusiastic for the Russian Revolution, they were soon disenchanted with the Leninist derailment of socialism. Nor were they particularly enamoured with the remnants of moderate European socialism. Removing themselves from active political praxis, critical theory's "beautiful souls" (Hegel) set out to spotlight the emancipatory potential of a new and darker time. This would turn out to be a formidable task in a "century when every revolution has in some sense been betrayed, when virtually all attempts at cultural subversion have been neutralized, and when the threat of a nuclear *Aufhebung* of the dialectic of enlightenment continues unchecked" (Jay, 1984a, p. 162). Critical theory had moved into a haunted and deeply troubled phase.

The Frankfurt critical theorists were thinking in changed conditions. Capitalism had entered its monopolist phase, the government was increasing its intervention in the economy, science and technology were imbricated in the productive apparatus, and glimmerings of the "culture industry" were appearing. Most important for the inheritors of Marx's ambiguous legacy, no longer were there stirrings of a new "negative" force in society. In the 1840s an optimistic Marx had triumphantly declared that "philosophy cannot be made a reality without the abolition of the proletariat, the proletariat cannot be abolished without philosophy being made a reality" (Marx, 1975, vol. 3, p. 187). The resurrection of the proletariat would fling philosophy to its tomb. Over a hundred years later, a wiser and sadder Adorno opened *Negative Dialectics* (1973) with this riposte: "Philosophy, which once seemed obsolete, lives on because the moment to realize it was missed. The summary judgment that it had merely interpreted the world, that resignation in the face of reality had crippled it in itself, becomes a defeatism of reason after the attempt to change the world miscarries." None of the Frankfurt theorists doubted that critique should promote the enlightenment and collective development of the working class. But they had lost confidence in the "revolutionary potential of the proletariat," and were "forced into a position of 'transcendence' by the withering away of the revolutionary working class" (Jay, 1972, p. 230). This placed them in an anguished and ambivalent position. Critical theory's intended audience was unspecified. In his bleakest moments Adorno could defend the importance of critical thinking as "bottles thrown into the sea" for future addressees, identity unknown (Jay, 1984a, p. 54). It was almost as if defending reason (preserving negativity and hope) had become a form of revolutionary praxis itself.

Yet it was precisely their loss of confidence in the historical mission of the revolutionary subject that forced them to grapple with the reasons why emancipatory learning was blocked and constrained in particular social formations. The Frankfurt theorists reflected on the distorting pressures to which individuals and collectivities succumbed in the process of self-formation and collective identity construction. And they did so driven by a revulsion toward closed philosophical systems. All of their work (until Habermas) had an open-ended and provisional quality—most often expressed through dialogical critique of other thinkers (one thinks of Adorno's studies on Husserl and Kierkegaard, Marcuse on Heidegger, Fromm's engagement with Freud, Horkheimer with Schopenhauer, and Habermas' mammoth dialogue with contemporary philosophy and social science). Horkheimer and Adorno were also wary of specifying the "concrete utopia," reflecting, perhaps, the Jewish belief that the Absolute remain unnamed.

Max Horkheimer is widely recognized by historians of Frankfurt critical theory to be the dominant figure in the Institute for Social Research's development. He became the Institute's director in 1931 and developed a program of studies to demonstrate critical theory's potential for the reconstruction of philosophy, the social sciences, and cultural studies. In his essays written in the 1930s one can capture the contours of his thought. There are many important themes (his hostility to metaphysics and identity theory; his attempt to retrieve a liberatory moment from bourgeois individualism; his critique of vulgar materialism; his interest in Freud and recognition that critique had a fundamental practical interest). But the central theme that emerges is the increasing domination of natural science over men and women's lives—one of the fundamental "distorting pressures" that undermined the achievement of a rational society. Conducting a "spirited defense" of reason, Horkheimer argued that positivism (or scientism) denied the traditional idea of reason (*vernuft*, the going beyond mere appearances to a deeper truth in contrast to *verstand*, or analytical, formal logic) by reifying the social order. All "true knowledge" now aspired to the condition of "scientific, mathematical conceptualization" (Jay, 1972, p. 243; cf. Wellmer, 1971, pp. 9–65). Reason had been transformed into "instrumental rationality" obscuring the link between theory in the positive sciences and the class dynamics of the social order. Science itself had become ideological, and critical theory had to unmask its absolutist claims in order to reveal how domination was socially organized through the medium of intersubjective, albeit distorted, communication.

By the 1940s, however, critical theory twisted in a very gloomy direction. Thoroughly freaked out by the catastrophes of the 1930s and the 1940s (failure of the working-class movement to resist fascism; the unspeakable horrors of concentration camps), Horkheimer and Adorno grappled in the sombre pages of *The Dialectic of Enlightenment* (1972) with the question of "why mankind, instead of entering a truly human condition, [was] sinking into a new kind of barbarism." Domination was no longer seen as arising from any *specific* social formation but as inherent in the logic of the Enlightenment itself. This vision of technological hopelessness resonated with another theme—that capitalism was evolving into an "administered world" of one-dimensional homogeneity, rather than a true community of fulfilled subjects in a socialist society (Jay, 1984b, p. 216). Critical theory had skidded off course into the "Grand Hotel Abyss." Nonetheless, this critique of science and technology—later constructively elaborated in Habermas' theory of "knowledge-constitutive interests" *(Knowledge and Human Interests* [1972])—was an important initiative towards the building of emancipatory learning theory. Positivism rules out *a priori* the possibility of critique and rejects the Hegelian-Marxian notion of potentiality.

It was not only science and technology that constrained emancipatory learning forms and processes. In his stiletto-like critique of major Frankfurt figures, Paul Connerton (1980) finds the basis of comparability among these diverse thinkers in the "methods by which systems of social constraints became internalised" (p. 134). Their studies of the family revealed how the inability to resist Authority became sedimented in the human personality. In their analyses of the "culture industry," political propaganda and marketing psychology they demonstrated how messages reached down into areas of individual life to exploit personal conflicts or to awaken artificial needs in support of a particular social system. Horkheimer and Adorno tried to link the exploitation of external nature to the repression of man's instinctual nature. Marcuse probed, more than the others, the social constraints operative in affluent capitalism, where men and women were legally free but addicted to the commodity-form. And Habermas would analyze the internalised constraints at work in the form of a new, technocratic ideology which repressed the explicitly moral sphere.

Adorno, Horkheimer, Marcuse—all left a dazzling legacy of writings covering an extremely vast area of human experience. Yet none really attempted a systematic critical theory of society or resolved satisfactorily the relation of critique to history (how can critical theory be part of the movement of history and a means of enlightenment?) or the relationship of theory to practice (they offered a theory of the importance of fundamental social transformation which appeared to have no anchor in social struggle [Held, 1980, pp. 398–99]). It was to Jürgen Habermas, born in 1929, that the Frankfurt mantle would pass, and he would have the task of addressing himself not only to the inherited problems of the Marxian legacy but also to the blindspots of the Frankfurt School itself.

LEARNING AS CENTRAL CONCEPT:
THE CRITICAL PROJECT OF JÜRGEN HABERMAS

Like his predecessors, Habermas was thinking in changed circumstances. His attempts to interpret Marx's theory for a new time were informed by a politically motivated updating of Marxism in the 1950s. The intellectual world was rather pathetic: Soviet Stalinism had hardened into a "dialectical universal science" without ethical heart and the most creative radical currents had transformed Marxism into a philosophy of alienation without connection to a practically oriented critique of capitalism. Habermas also had to confront the changed reality of West German capitalism (a deeper intrusion of the state "steering apparatus" into the economy and lifeworld). As his critical project gathered momentum in the 1960s and 1970s, rolling like a juggernaut through the intellectual and political landscape, his work would be profoundly influenced by the political activity of the new social movements and the proliferation of oppositional thinking that erupted inside and outside of formal educational complexes. Habermas was unwilling to embrace uncritically any of these movements (New Left communitarianism, feminisms, peace, ecology), or to name the new revolutionary subject(s). But his massive theoretical undertaking cannot be understood apart from the presence of oppositional fragment-movements and other critical standpoints in late capitalist society. His project, despite its labyrinthine passageways, was consciously constructed with Marx in contest with his attempt to construct a "natural history of society," against the pessimism of Adorno and Horkheimer and toward the development of critical theory with emancipatory practical intent. Not satisfied to throw his theory to audiences unknown, and knowing all too well that one could no longer address the proletariat as singular transformative agent, Habermas addressed a multiple audience of potential transformative agents working within the social movements and without in various institutional sectors of society. The crisis tendencies within late capitalism were once again linked, albeit tenuously, to its emancipatory potential.

Habermas places learning processes at the centre of his critical project. This signifies a major shift within Western critical theory—

shall we call this the "learning turn" and think of this development as a revolution in social theory? But there can be no doubt that critical theory's missing link until Habermas was its inability to link crisis and potential to a theory of how adult learning releases this potential in particular times and places, resulting in new institutionalized forms of freedom and enhanced individual and collective competence to be self-determining historical actors. His much debated theory of knowledge-constitutive interests, his recasting of historical materialism and his recent work on the theory of communicative action—all interrelate and probe in a rich and deep philosophic manner the cognitive determinants of historical evolution and contemporary social organization. It cannot be argued that Habermas's revision of critical theory as a learning theory is in all ways satisfactory; indeed, this is not the case (see Benhabib, 1981; Cohen, 1987, pp. 203–11; Plumb, 1994). He has, however, placed crucial and complex questions on the agenda for adult educators and theoreticians struggling toward a critical theory of adult learning.

Habermas executes his revision of historical materialism in dialogue with Marx. He organizes his discussion of historical materialism around two basic concepts—"social labor" and the "history of the species," and two basic assumptions—the "theory of base and superstructure" and the "dialectic of forces and relations of production" (McCarthy, 1985, p. 237). These concepts and assumptions are familiar enough within Marxian scholarship. But, says Habermas, "whereas Marx localized the learning processes important for evolution in the dimension of the productive forces—there are in the meantime good reasons for assuming that learning processes also take place in the dimension of moral insight, practical knowledge, communicative action, and the consensual regulation of action conflicts—learning processes that are deposited in more mature forms of social integration, in new productive relations, and that in turn make possible the introduction of new productive forms" (cited, Held, 1980, p. 270). This citation capsulizes key Habermasian notions. One can still recognize the Marxian concepts of "productive forces" (the sphere of labor power, technical and organizational knowledge oriented to instrumental action on nature) and "relations of production" (institutions and social mechanisms that determine how labor power can be combined with available means of production at a given level of productive forces). Habermas is clearly emphasizing previously neglected aspects of historical evolution. Behind the objectivity of the productive forces there are certain mechanisms of cognition that reflect the deep structure of the labor process understood as instrumental action. And a "logic of growing insight" operates within social interactions and regulates the development of the relations of production as a special, and crucial, case of the latter.

Human learning, in the deepest sense, proceeds along a double axis—one fundamental knowledge-constitutive interest is guided by the interest in the instrumental disposition over nature, another by the interest in the preservation and expansion of intersubjective communication and agreement, an interest which became a necessity for the survival of the species with its dependence on language (Honneth and Joas, 1988, p. 154). The third interest, Habermas will argue, is grounded in the human capacity to "reflectively appropriate human life." Historical materialism aims, by means of theoretically guided interpretation of the history of the species, at "collective emancipation from a history of domination that heretofore has come into being and proceeded spontaneously, that is, a history that hitherto resembled a natural process in that it has not been guided by human reflection" (Honneth and Joas, 1988, p. 155).

Habermas believes that the learning process of the human species takes place through the accumulation of both technical and moral-practical knowledge. Both forms obey a "logic of growing insight," whose successive steps consist in rules of possible problem solutions. Habermas insists, however, that the "learning mechanism" within the sphere of work does not explain how these problems can be resolved. New forms of social production require knowledge of a moral-practical kind, not simply technically useful knowledge. And these two fundamental learning processes are both subsumed under a common denominator and combined in a synthetic structure, the "principle of organization" (market, global economy, administration). This principle determines the overall level of learning processes possible in a given social formation. Habermas also insists that this "principle of organization" must guarantee "social integration"—the "legitimating normative structures and principles in terms of which needs are interpreted and motivations generated within the symbolically structured life world" (Cohen, 1987, p. 203). A crisis will exist, then, if a specific steering mechanism of a society threatens social integration, or damages the consensual foundations of normative structures.

Over and over again Habermas will return to this theme: the concern for "technical control" over nature has been transferred to "those

areas of society that had become independent in the course of the indus-
trialization of labor" (1970, p. 56), namely, the family, the public
sphere, community life, and cultural expressions. The very foundation
of democracy—"institutionally secured forms of general and public
communication that deal with the practical questions of how men can
and want to live" (p. 57)—is eroding under constant battering from
technical reason. How, he asks, can the "force of technical control" be
"made subject to the consensus of acting and transacting citizens?" (p.
60). Our hope for the "rationalization of the power structure," Habermas maintains, lies in creating "conditions that favor political power for
thought developing through dialogue. The redeeming power of reflection cannot be supplanted by extension of technically exploitable
knowledge" (p. 61). Habermas believes that the systemic crisis of late
capitalist society results from the illegitimate intrusion of state and corporate steering mechanisms into the lifeworld; the social crisis manifests itself in a plethora of new social movement struggles to defend the
threatened lifeworld and its ecological substructure. This latter theme is
explored in depth in my other chapter in this volume, "In Defense of the
Lifeworld." Any adequate critical social theory of adult learning, Habermas teaches us, must be able to encompass processes of systemic
learning (the organization of learning around the reproduction of the
social order) and social revolutionary learning (the genesis and collective development of socially critical, system-bursting orientations of
action which are tied to everyday lived pain and crises). The blocked
learning capacity of the system, directed by the state and corporate
steering mechanisms, precipitates a multiplicity of oppositional forms
of learning within civil society. Are the new social struggles (ecology,
peace, women, local and personal autonomy movements) particularly
privileged sites for the organization of enlightenment and emancipatory
praxis? In our time, do they hold the potential for creating a freer and
more just social order? Habermas and his associates encourage us to ask
these questions. To what extent are the new social movements merely
defensive responses to the colonization of the lifeworld, that is, do they
"seek to stem or block the formal, organized spheres of action in favour
of communicative structures?" (Habermas, 1981, p. 34). To what extent
are they offensive global projects, impelled by commitment to universalist values toward the radical transformation of the relationship of
civil society to state and economy? (see Arato and Cohen, 1992). A critical social theory of adult learning would argue that collective protest is

best understood as a collective learning process. What are the external and internal conditions that enable critically reflective learning to occur within the movement site? What role does formal adult education play in movement formation and development? This latter question is especially salient: the historical record of the university's role in supporting social movements is not very encouraging (Welton, 1991b). Are we witnessing in our deeply troubled times, not the "workers' movement at the high-point of its historical action," but the emergence of new conflicts, new actors, new stakes, new social struggles—the "spring hidden beneath the cement"? (Touraine, 1981, p. 55; cf. Finger, 1989; and Welton, 1993b).

THE ONTOLOGICAL ASSUMPTIONS AND
CORE VALUES OF CRITICAL THEORY

It is a daunting task to specify the ontological assumptions and core values anchoring critical theory. Several very powerful intellectual currents within contemporary philosophy and social theory are skeptical of all talk of "human nature." Postmodernist thinking (Foucault, Derrida, and others) has challenged the essential beliefs of the Enlightenment (that reason, rooted in a stable, coherent self, and its "science" can provide an objective, reliable, and universalizable foundation for knowledge). Reason, they argue, is inescapably dependent upon ephemeral social relations, and the self's existence is always historically specific. Structuralist Marxism, no longer in vogue, tried to purify Marxism of all "anthropological resonances." Thinkers like Louis Althusser intepreted capitalism as a "structural process devoid of all intentionality" (Honneth and Joas, 1988, p. 30). These critical developments helped us to understand that human nature is not a timeless essence outside history, and that reactionary historical forces have often appealed to human nature to justify their repressive social and political action. However, both postmodernists and structuralists were left without: (1) a theoretical-normative basis for understanding the repression of human potentiality under particular historical conditions, and (2) a way of understanding the social learning processes that precipitate critical reflection and impel actors to change their circumstances.

Cynicism and melancholy about human possibility pervade our intellectual culture and historical epoch. The nineteenth and twentieth centuries have given us as "much terror as we can take" (Lyotard, 1984a, p. 81). We also know that many of those who promised to liberate people from oppression have turned liberation into tyranny. Instrumentalized revolutionary projects . . . cultural revolutions turned bitterly sour . . . dreams of human emancipation ending in the Gulag grin. It almost seems as if history mocks the critical tradition, turning our dreams of becoming "masters of our own destiny" into a sepulchral cliché. Historically, the left posed this alternative to humankind: socialism or barbarism. We did not imagine that "actually existing socialism" would be one of barbarism's names. But history is not at its end point; the world is full of surprises. It is easy and quite human to want to separate ourselves as critical educators from particular historical perversions in practice. We should, however, be emboldened to scrutinize carefully our ontological assumptions, core values and specificity of educational practice within our framework. We need to do so in order to create the kind of critical theory and educational practice that truly enlightens, with enlightenment leading to emancipation in which groups empowered by their new found self-understanding, can alter their social arrangements and alleviate their suffering (Fay, 1987, p. 30).

In his introduction to Honneth and Joas' exemplary study of philosophical anthropology, *Social Action and Human Nature* (1988), philosopher Charles Taylor states that the exploration of "issues of human nature" is both "terribly necessary" and "unbearably problematic." It is necessary, he says,

> because all efforts to elaborate a science of human beings, in psychology, politics, sociology, anthropology (in the narrow sense), linguistics, etc. lean on certain assumptions about what human beings are like, which are often highly questionable. Certainly the big disputes about the methods and scope of science which rage in all these disciplines reach down into such deep underlying assumptions. And what affects these sciences doesn't matter only for the intellectual world in our day: their assumptions shape public policy and widely accepted images of human life, as we can see, for instance in the present vogue for computer-based models of the mind. (1988, p. vii)

These raging disputes do not emerge primarily from the world of academics. Deep-rooted doubt about the emancipatory potential of industrial growth—as articulated by the ecological, peace, counter-cultural, and women's movements—have to do with nature: with external nature and a humane relationship to it, as well as with the inner nature of the human being and its humane development (Honneth and Joas, 1988, p. 1). Despite efforts to erase the human subject (individual and collective) from history, questions about human nature and our relationship to the external natural world, are back on the intellectual and political agenda. Are we really sinful creatures who need to be constantly monitored by authoritarian institutions? Are we really greedy creatures with insatiable appetites for consumer goods? Are we really hapless creatures who need to be ruled by expert minorities? Is nature really a limitless object for the unlimited satisfaction of human needs?

What, then, are the deep underlying assumptions upon which critical theory, as one way of seeing and being in the world, rests? In his recent work, *Critical Social Science: Liberation and its Limits* (1987), Brian Fay has provided a valuable account of the foundations of critical social science. Fay believes that the vision of existence underlying critical theorizing has a "deep history" in human thought. He calls this vision the self-estrangement myth: that is, human beings are viewed as essentially fallen but potentially redeemable creatures. He says that the self-estrangement myth is one of the most powerful stories humans have invented to account for their feeling of powerlessness before an inexplicable nature and fear before the face of death. Fay then asserts that critical theory is a secular version of this myth, of the Enlightenment ideal that "through reason humans can achieve a form of existence which is free and satisfying" (p. 3). He also places critical theory in the humanist camp—because of its notion of human possibility.

To illustrate, Fay digs into the "master narratives" that have guided Western societies—Plato's cave parable and the Jewish Exodus story. What he unearths is a vision of life which paints human reality as deeply alienated though potentially salvageable. At the core of these myths is the idea that ordinary humans live an illusory existence, that they mistake the shadows of the cave for reality, and that human beings have the capacity to learn who they are and to reshape their existence on the basis of this learning. Thus, for Plato education is the "process by which people become enlightened as to their existence and emancipated from the prison in which they have been living because of their ignorance" (p. 11). Fay reads the Exodus story in a parallel manner (not unlike Liberation theologians). This story is an account of a people whose enslavement is in part their own doing. They are ignorant of their true identity as God's chosen people. It is an account in which the Hebrews "throw off their chains partly because they acquire a self-understanding which reveals their genuine needs and possibilities. The Exodus story provides a paradigm of the process of emancipation through enlightenment" (p. 14). Fay believes that the Christian tradition is also guided by this vision which sees human beings as severed from the source of meaning and energy at life's core. Because they are unconscious of this fact, they organize their lives in self-defeating ways. But self-defeat can be overcome if human beings acquire appropriate knowledge. Within Christian conceptions of life, the way enlightenment is understood will involve knowledge of the Transcendent Other (understanding that human beings are dependent upon God and his son Jesus Christ). Empowerment means acting in accordance with one's knowledge of God's will. If "God" is understood as the one who calls us to act justly in the world, then Christians may act to rectify injustice and oppression. If, on the other hand, God is grasped as Wholly Other, commanding us to withdraw from the world and place our hope in the paradisal future, the fundamentally corrupt and unredeemable world will be abandoned.

Excavating the deep structural meaning in these myths permits Fay to make sense of the emergence of a secularized version of the self-estrangement myth in the modern world. This is the remarkable aspiration to develop theories capable of transforming human life. "Essentially the hope is that, through an abstract and general understanding of the workings of nature, society, and the mind, humans can manipulate the physical world and reorganize their social order so as to improve massively their collective existence" (p. 17). This is the Enlightenment's grand dream and represents a profound shift in human thought (see Leiss, 1974). Plato and Aristotle had understood theoretical knowledge as knowledge of the unchanging structure of things, of the basic and eternal principles that govern the cosmos. Theoretical reason revealed the true end of humankind; ethics was the practical science (or educative vehicle) showing humans how they could be transformed from what they happened-to-be to what-they-ought-to-be (MacIntyre, 1981, pp. 50–51).

Scientific knowing, renouncing the contemplative role of theory and banishing ethics from its domain, explodes into modernity brashly announcing its usefulness for a new humanity and radically redefining the function of theoretical knowledge (what constitutes knowledge, the conditions in which it is possible to achieve it, and the means to test its claims). A humanist variant of the self-estrangement myth elbows its way on to center stage, shifting emphasis from the "salvific power of enlightenment" (Fay, 1987, p. 20) toward scientifically directed action on the world. Humanism holds that on the basis of a theoretical understanding of the cosmos humans can learn how to live their own lives in a truly self-directed and more satisfactory way. Critical theory—in a *generic* sense—is a variant, therefore, of the humanist self-estrangement myth. It too seeks a theory which will simultaneously explain the social world, criticize it and empower its audience to overthrow it. But critical theory—from Marx to Habermas—gives a particular historical and substantive meaning to the myth that humans are essentially fallen but potentially redeemable.

All attempts to elaborate a science of human beings rest, Charles Taylor reminds us, on certain assumptions about what human beings are like. Critical theories of the world, or learning, are no exception. Fay argues (1987, pp. 42ff.) that the concepts theorists use reflect and embody in their meaning beliefs about how the world operates. These beliefs, often only implicit in empirical research, are ultimately tied up with a general understanding of the nature of human beings. What ontological vision lies behind the critical model of history and society? A picture, Fay answers, which portrays humans as self-interpreting beings who partially create themselves on the basis of their own self-interpretations (Giddens, 1984; Touraine, 1981; Jarvis, 1987). Human beings, critical theory assumes, are activist creatures.

What is meant by active? Fay's opening conceptual tactic is to explicate the meaning of active in terms of four fundamental dispositions of the *individual*: intelligence, curiosity, reflectiveness, and willfulness. By intelligence Fay means the disposition to alter one's beliefs and ensuing behavior on the basis of new information about the world. One either gives up an old belief or acquires a new one: both processes occur on the basis of "mental computation" in which already known bits of information are put together in novel ways. Jack Mezirow's work on "perspective transformation" (1977, 1981; see chapter 2 below) pursues several dimensions of this process. Fay thinks, however, that "epistemic passivity" is still possible. But curiosity, the disposition to seek information about one's environment, overcomes this sort of passive receptivity. Fay depicts reflectiveness (the *core* disposition for many critical theorists) as the capacity to make assessments of one's own assessments, that is, reflectiveness is the disposition to evaluate one's own desires and beliefs on the basis of particular criteria. These criteria aid in answering this question: what is the proper end of my life and what sort of person ought I to be? A reflective creature (animals do not have this capacity) can step back from its mental experiences and activity. Reflectiveness is often linked in the philosophical anthropological literature with our capacity to be self-conscious, and consciousness intimately bound up with our ability to use language (Markus, 1986; Bernstein, 1983). The final disposition is willfulness: the propensity to be and act on one's reflections. Thus, Fay concludes, an "intelligent, curious, reflective and willful being can be active towards itself as well as its environment, and so can transform its inner constitution as well as its external conditions" (p. 49).

Fay then turns the tables on himself by asserting that his story, thus far, is too individualistic. Indeed, if Fay stopped here he would be trapped where most mainstream thinking in adult education currently rests (Maslow's humanistic and individualistic theory of human dispositions has reigned supreme)—without a historical and contextual understanding of the formation and unfolding of the human potential to be active creatures. Fay immediately asserts that intelligence, reflectiveness and willfulness necessarily involve others. It is the cultural community which provides the impetus for, and substance of, the self-understandings of active creatures and their capacity to learn how to reflect on and change their behavior, ideas, desires, and principles. In becoming a member of a particular group—learning its language, acquiring its beliefs and concepts, mastering the habits of interaction—an active being forms its identity and gains the ability to reflect upon its cultural assumptions, norms and practices. Only in interaction with others do we appreciate our potentialities and inadequacies, and come to desire to realize the former and change the latter.

If we, as active "social individuals," are to change ourselves, we must also change at least part of the social world which shapes our individual and collective identity. Transformative action is *possible* because all of the elements that comprise society (ideational systems, institutions, authority relations, means of conflict resolution, status systems, etc.) are dependent upon shared values, beliefs, and preferences. Therefore, in describing the transformation of an active being one ought to replace the individualistic "I wish to become x by altering myself" with the social "We wish to become x by altering our collective arrangements in such and such a way" (p. 51). This shift is pivotal for a critical theory of adult learning (and much resisted in contemporary adult education theory and practice). In asserting that humans are active, historical creatures, Fay captures the ontological vision of the critical theoretical tradition.

> Active creatures are historical in the full-blown sense that, though pressed to behave in particular ways by their physical environment and even more by the structures of power in their social arrangements, it is they who change themselves by internalizing new conceptions of self and society, new possibilities of action, and by incorporating these in social practices and relations. The changes of truly historical creatures are self-induced and self-effected changes of their very identity. (Fay, p. 52)

This vision, baldly asserted, is too utopian and romantic: a soft-underbellied vision of humankind. For Marx and his followers insist correctly that human beings are only potentially active creatures. In the *Economic and Philosophic Manuscripts* (1844)—the inspiration for much of the current revitalization of philosophical anthropology—Marx portrays humankind as a "suffering, conditioned and limited creature" (Marx, 1975, vol. 3, p. 336). Human beings are thrown into history and enmeshed in a world created in conditions of inequality and domination. Alienated from their "species being" (Marx's phrase for human potentiality), humans do not experience the world as their own creation. In such a world the human being does not "affirm himself but denies himself, does not feel content but mortifies his body and ruins his mind" (Marx, 1975, vol. 3, p. 274). The historically rooted organization and relations of production, Marx says, makes humans "stupid and one-sided" (Marx, 1975, vol. 3, p. 300). In such a debased world activity is externally imposed—human activity is not really our own because our capacity to act reflectively is radically distorted. For Marx, the "richness of man's essential being" (Marx, 1975, vol. 3, p. 301) can only be unfolded in history by enlightened actors who are aware of their reflective capacity and consciously decide to resist those forces and structures mortifying the body and ruining their minds. The "strong thesis"—that we are always active creatures—is not required by a critical learning theory of history and society.

Fay identifies three core values which he believes are consistent with the activist conception of human beings. These values (rational self-clarity, collective autonomy, and happiness) are fundamental dimensions of the enlightenment process. A critical learning theory, therefore, radically socializes and historicizes mainstream adult education's commitment to self-directed learning. Critical learning theory preserves the commitment to enhance individual competence to act on the basis of self-reflection while maintaining that social and historical individuals can only achieve maturity through interactive learning and collective action. One of the tasks of a revitalized dialectical social psychology would be to specify the characterological preconditions for the unleashing of individual capacity to be socially attuned and active (Sullivan, 1990). Critical theorists are particularly interested in identifying those character traits that enable actors to engage openly, respectfully and actively in communicative learning processes (see chapter 2).

Fay defines rational self-clarity as the state in which, on the basis of rationally warranted grounds, people know the true nature of their existence. This notion of self-clarity is linked to the idea that it is possible to discover a coherent pattern in the affairs of people, even though the pattern may be clouded from the actors themselves. Fay believes that critical theory assumes that there is "unity in human lives" (p. 69), and that it is possible to construct a narrative that makes sense of disparate human experiences by showing how the various elements fit into a "meaningful whole" (p. 69). Fay considers the Marxian narrative of the emergence of the proletariat as paradigmatic. What Marx constructs is a narrative frame which places the "drama of the emergence of a praxis self-conscious and free, as the centerpiece of human existence" (p. 70). His narrative accounts for humankind's sorrow and hope. "The sorrow of human life has been precisely that, ignorant of what in fact they desired, humans did not organize their working lives in an orderly, fulfilling, fully expressive manner, and so the actual labour of people has given them only a truncated, ersatz form of practice" (p. 70). Emancipatory learning is triggered, then, when the proffered narrative allows a particular audience to separate "genuine" from "false" narratives. Self-clarity means that a group can learn the "genuine narrative of its life in which all its significant events are placed in their proper order, and in which the immanent direction of its genuine satisfaction is revealed" (p. 70). Fay insists that any change in self-understanding must occur as a result of rational persuasion and reflection. He cites the Nazi narrative of the meaning of human experience as a pseudo-narrative because in part it was imposed on people; in part because its "truth claims" violate norms of justice and universality. The enlightenment process must proceed dialogically (people must be free to reject the theory in an uncoerced learning setting). Enlightenment is educative and not instrumental.

The purpose of critical theory, however, is not only to enable human beings to be relatively "transparent to themselves" (p. 75). Its aim is also to help people to stop being passive victims who collude, at least partly, in their domination by external forces. Critical theory's liberating project is to name the enemies of human freedom, and to point to the possibility of freedom's enlargement. Fay conceives freedom as "self-conscious control of life," but thinks that the idea is best captured conceptually by the term autonomy. Free people are those who command their life situation in accord with laws and norms they prescribe for themselves. An autonomous being is "one which ordains for itself the principles by which it shall live, and is therefore self-governing" (p. 76). Fay argues that the idea of autonomy in which critical theory is interested in is collective autonomy, and this involves a "group of people determining on the basis of rational reflection the sorts of policies and practices it will follow and acting in accordance with them" (p. 77). He expands the notion of a collectively autonomous people to include an understanding of true interests and proper goals which are continually reassessed and reestablished as situations change. To be true masters of their own affairs, a collectively autonomous group must not be subject to forces which cause them to be other than they desire. A collectively autonomous group faces an arduous task: it must not be dominated by "natural forces," undesirable social practices inherited from the past and the "coercive intrusions" (p. 79) by other groups. Coming to this state of affairs is a long and difficult process. Thus, collective autonomy weaves two elements together: members must will to live their lives on the basis of a "rationally informed self-transparency" (p. 80) and have the power to express their enlightened wishes. Has critical theory given itself a task too burdensome to bear?

Although rational self-clarity and collective autonomy are the primary values of critical theory, Fay thinks that happiness is worthy of inclusion in his triad. By happiness Fay simply means that state of feeling pleased with our lives as a whole. He links happiness to the felt dissatisfactions of a group of people, the lever point of any critical theory. "One might say," Fay avers, "that the thrust of critical social science is provided by the unhappiness of its audience. It follows from this that, though the principal aim of critical social science is the emancipation of its audience from conditions of domination, it is interested in only those conditions which manifest themselves in the felt experiences of discontent on the part of those dominated" (p. 81). This is a sticky matter: one of the most troublesome features of advanced capitalist consumer society is the extent to which people feel, almost at an instinctual level, happy because they possess commodities. This concern is explored by Marcuse in numerous works (see *One-Dimensional Man*, [1964], *An Essay on Liberation,* [1969], *Counter-Revolution and Revolt,* [1972]).

Fay insists that the "existence of feelings of unhappiness" of a particular audience prevents critical theory from becoming a form of domination itself. Critical theory must not impose a substantive notion of genuine need upon its audience. Its task, rather, is more limited: to enter into respectful dialogue with its audience regarding the possible ways our life choices are constrained and distorted. "Critical social science," concludes Fay, "arises out of and speaks to, situations of social unhappiness, a situation which it interprets as the result both of the ignorance of those experiencing these feelings and of their domination by others. It is this experience of unhappiness which is the wedge critical theory uses to justify its entrance into the lives of those it seeks to enlighten and emancipate" (pp. 82–83). Anyone can question Fay about his exclusion of certain values from his framework—bodily pleasure, play, love, aesthetic self-expression. Indeed, postmodernist thinkers often affirm these values against reason. But unless the core values of rational self-clarity, collective autonomy, and social happiness are in place in the everyday lived experience of human beings, cultural-expressive values will have little chance of undistorted unfolding.

2

Transformation Theory of Adult Learning

Jack Mezirow

This chapter presents a current summary and elaboration of an evolving transformation theory of adult learning (Mezirow, 1990, 1991). The theory involves an analysis of the psycho-cultural process of making meaning, the nature of meaning structures and how they are transformed through reflection, rational discourse, and emancipatory action. The education of adults is understood as organized activity facilitative of this process. The ideal conditions for reflection, critical reasoning, and discourse in adult learning suggest the vision of a reflective learning society and provide the foundation for a philosophy of adult education.

THE PSYCHO-CULTURAL PROCESS
OF MAKING MEANING

Learning becomes possible because we interpret the meaning of each new sensory experience by imaginatively projecting images and value-laden symbolic models upon our sensory experience and, by metaphorical inference, construe meaning. The symbols (a swastika, a national anthem, a flag, or the Statue of Liberty) become emblematic of such values as the good, fair, decent, brave, beautiful, patriotic, compassionate, normal, and so forth, or their opposites. Each such projection calls for an imaginative interpretation, using the symbol and its attendant values as a template. Learning involves processes of scanning, construal, imaginative insight, and interpretation, directed by a line of intentional action and selectively preconditioned by the structures of meaning described below.

Symbols do not require language categories or words to enable one to make an interpretation. Although language is instrumental in acquiring symbols, images, and values, one does not get into a self-dialogue—using words—about the values emblemized by symbols unless it becomes necessary to explain or justify them to yourself or someone else or to pose or solve problems. Words, like all signs, are separate from their referents. The word "dog" can refers to a particular category of very different animals. One may or may not make the connection. Abstract terms can have a range of meanings. Symbols, on the other hand, embody and project the values of their referents. This may be why symbols are so powerful in making meaning without requiring words to communicate. Symbols, metaphors, and imagination are central to constructing meaning.

Creating meaning refers to the process of construal by which we attribute coherence and significance to our experience in light of what we know. Presentational, propositional, and intentional construal are different and complementary interactive ways of making meaning, of giving coherence to experience (Heron, 1988). Propositional construal refers to tacitly experiencing things learned, using language categories and words to make meaning. Presentational construal refers to apprehension, making meaning without using language. In Heron's words, "we construe the real shape and size of something from its apparent shape and size; the total temporal form of a process from its serial occurrences; a distinctive presence or entity from its unique signature of form and movement" (1988, p. 41). Presentational construal, as interpreted here, does not involve an internal dialogue.

Schon (1983, pp. 51–54) notes that Chester Bernard identified "non-logical processes" revealed only through decisions made or actions taken; Polanyi described how "tacit knowing" is involved in the way we recognize faces and use tools; Alexander pointed out how we can recognize the bad fit between a form and its context, although we usually are unable to say why, and Vickers contended that this is true of all judgments; Schutz and those he has influenced studied how the rituals of everyday behavior—in elevators, in crowds, in greeting others— are based upon tacit knowing; and Birdswhistell showed how physical movement and gesture is similarly grounded. Loder describes the imaginative act as insight resulting from intuition, "two habitually incompatible frames of reference conversing, usually with surprising suddenness, to compose a meaningful unity" (1981, p. 32).

Those who assert that categories of language are the very foundation of consciousness or being do not provide us with an explanation of how, inasmuch as we are so bound by the limitations of language and of the past as perpetuated in language, we can perceive and articulate the novel, the creative, the unexperienced, the transformative. Differentiating between presentational and propositional construal suggests a direct role for language in propositional and intentional but not in presentational construal of meaning.

Presentational construal may be understood to involve our sense of directionality, movement, entity, event punctuation (when an event begins and ends), color, style, texture, light and dark, sound, our feelings, physiological reactions, physical balance, kinesthetic awareness, recognition, empathy, and identification with others—all these extremely important dimensions of knowing are involved in making meaning without the direct and immediate use of language categories or words.

There are obviously several different functions of presentational construal including: judging immediate physical sensation, as when we learn to ski or ride a bike; inspiration, like our feelings at beholding great beauty or great virtue; aesthetic judgment, as when we perceive a flaw in design or a discrepancy between form and context; love, as joyful awareness of the essential worth of any aspect of life or life itself; acts of conscience, as when we spontaneously act upon our feelings regarding right and wrong; reality recognition, as when we recognize that we are in a play, game or dream; intuition, as when a decision about to be taken just does not feel right; non-verbal play, as when we play with a dog and a stick; solidarity, a feeling of oneness with others; and transcendence, as when we identify with a cause larger than ourselves about which we feel strongly or feel a sense of oneness with humanity or with God. Feelings in presentational construal become emotions in propositional construal. Emotions influence propositional construal by helping us to remember by giving weight to what we learn and by motivating us to take action.

Propositional and presentational construal are both tacit, outside of our intentional focus. A third type of construal is intentional, as when we are deliberately attempting to pose or solve a problem, describe or explain. This type of construal involves purposeful awareness of our use of logic, inference, analysis, reflection, evaluation, and the giving and assessing of reasons through rational discourse. We engage in intentional construal when propositional or presentational construal becomes problematic. Intentional construal involves either internal and/or external dialogues.

Our value decisions are seldom judgments involving reflection and rational discourse (even with ourselves); they are spontaneous projections of assimilated symbols with which we make meaning through presentational construal. Of course, we may acquire the values in the first place through intentional construal. Symbols are emblematic of narratives. Symbolic models can embody the values we hold most dear, including those associated with our self-concept—like our desire to lead a healthy life as an autonomous, self-directed person in a safe and humane society. We may or may not have articulated or analyzed these or other values, but we have them and we act upon them. We often convert the images in our imagination into value-laden symbols. A lion symbolizes monarchy, a pig sloth, and a swan grace and elegance. This is the way we internalize and project the cultural values of society in our construal of meaning.

The relationship between presentational construal and propositional or intentional construal involves the relationship between sensation, the feeling of something happening to me now, and perception, which involves awareness informed by knowledge of the world. Humphrey (1992) has recently proposed a theory that animals have evolved two separate ways of representing what happens at the body's surface, the feeling sensation, which characterizes consciousness, and perception which is not affect-laden. Sensation involves feelings which lead to actions designed to control those feelings and evolves into intended actions. Other theorists (Miller, 1992) hold that perception is primary. Sensations are held to be abstractions from perceptions created when we deliberately attend to those aspects of perception that arise directly at the body's surface. Consciousness from this perspective becomes a matter of managing attention rather than one of having sensations. This unresolved issue is central to the persistent mind-body dilemma posed by Descartes over three centuries ago and to the ancient and fruitless debate over the nature of consciousness.

A symbolic model may be emblematic of a *meaning perspective*, a general frame of reference, set of schemas, worldview, or personal paradigm. A meaning perspective involves a set of psychocultural assumptions, for the most part culturally assimilated but including intentionally learned theories, that serve as one of three sets of codes significantly shaping sensation and delimiting perception and cognition: sociolinguistic, (e.g., social norms, cultural and language codes, ideologies, theories), psychological (e.g., repressed parental prohibitions which continue to block ways of feeling and acting, personality traits) and epistemic (e.g., learning, cognitive and intelligence styles, sensory learning preferences, focus on wholes or parts).

Meaning perspectives are not simply categories for understanding; they also significantly influence and delimit the horizons of our expectations. These abstract, paradigmatic meaning perspectives become articulated in a *meaning scheme*—the specific set of beliefs, knowledge, judgment, attitude, and feeling which shape a particular interpretation, as when we think of an Irishman, a cathedral, a grandmother, or a conservative or when we express a point of view, an ideal or a way of acting. Meaning schemes are specific belief systems.

Meaning perspectives and meaning schemes are the structures of meaning. Both operate propositionally, presentationally and intentionally to provide the frame of reference within which we engage in intentional learning. Meaning schemes and perspectives selectively shape and delimit expectation, perception and cognition by predisposing our intentions and purposes, that is, setting our line of action. We have a strong tendency to reject ideas which fail to fit our preconceptions by labeling them aberrations, nonsense, weird, or mistaken. If what we learn is so influenced by meaning perspectives and schemes, where do these perspectives come from in the first place? We interpret a speech act, along with other human actions, in two dimensions. One is its literal, pragmatic meaning which is a product of its specific context. Another is its "subtext," or learning's "hidden curriculum." Examples are such socially invariant structures or properties of language as its syntax or semantics. We learn these "rules" of language without their being taught or intentionally learned. An implication of this kind cultural assimilation is that intersubjectivity precedes subjectivity so that self-understanding is derivative of understanding others (Semin, 1990).

This kind of intercontextual learning involves generalizations. Both presentational and propositional construal involve the identification of instances of their categories. Words are also categories. Words and sentences mean all of the things which can be designated by them. To fully understand their meaning, we must understand all the situations in which they are true. We are each aware of different situations in which they pertain and hence understand the meaning of a word or sentence somewhat differently, but we have enough common understanding to permit us to communicate with each other. We learn new ways to use the language to give meaning to the unfamiliar by discovering how others use words or sentences differently than we do. This property of language to generalize over specific instances and the experience of different persons in different times and places is referred to as intersubjectivity.

When we want to transmit knowledge to another person, we have to generalize, to ascribe it to a known category, class type or group. The statement, "I cut my finger," implies that the person to whom you speak can tell the difference between fingers, toes, and teddy bears, also between cut, break, or crush. In this sense, the words finger and cut are generalizations or categories of things. Vygotski writes that "social interaction necessarily presupposes generalization as the development of word meaning, i.e., generalization becomes possible with the development of social interaction" (1956, p. 51).

Meaning perspectives and schemes are learned as generalized subtexts which we have assimilated from our narrative interaction with our culture and our parents. They are symbol systems which are projected on our sense perceptions as habits of expectation rather than being "stored" information to be retrieved through memory. Culture itself can be understood as a set of meaning perspectives which, together with idiosyncratic perspectives of our parents or primary care givers, constitute the universe of meaning perspectives to which we are exposed and from which we learn our perspectives through assimilation.

TRANSFORMING THE STRUCTURES OF MEANING

While we assimilate and are guided by meaning perspectives and schemes, changing events in our lives can make us feel that old meaning perspectives have become dysfunctional, that no matter how much harder we try, things do not seem to fit old ways of seeing any longer. It is this kind of problem that leads many persons to psychotherapy. It is what happened to many thousands of women in recent years through consciousness raising in the context of the women's movement. The age-old perspective limiting women to careers of wives, mothers, housekeepers, and good neighbors was found too constricting and was replaced by a perspective which added a wide range of career options and new ways of redefining old relationships and oneself. The process of transformation is the same as that which Paulo Freire has called "conscientization." It is a generic process of adult learning.

Intentional construal is required to transform our meaning schemes and perspectives. We do this through *reflection*, understood here as an apperceptive assessment of the justification for our beliefs, ideas, or feelings. Ordinary reflection involves intentional assessment of the nature and consequences of these learnings. The kind of reflection which includes and relates the circumstances of their origin with their nature and consequence can be understood as *critical reflection*. It should be apparent how this natural mode of adult thought has been overlooked by the behaviorists, whose positivist-instrumentalist mode of analysis traditionally limits inquiry to the nature and consequences of an activity. This is the reason why the behaviorist mode of inquiry has served us poorly as an approach for understanding how adults learn.

When we assess or reassess reflectively the content or process of problem solving, we often transform our meaning schemes. If the problem is to assess whether George is bad, *content reflection* might cause us to reassess those bad things George has done. *Process reflection* might ask whether we have generalized about George's bad behavior from too limited a number of observations or perhaps we have overlooked his redeeming acts and have judged too hastily. Process reflection can include an assessment of strategies, tactics and theory, one's feelings for a situation or one's role as actor within a specific situation. Process reflection does not have to be in words. Schon points out that jazz musicians improvise through a "feel for the music," a recognition of the scheme of the music which suggests complementary melodies, and baseball pitchers find their groove though a "feel for the ball" in the same way (1983, pp. 55–56). Reflecting on content or process is the way we always change our minds about any experience to improve performance and may result in a transformation of our meaning scheme. *Premise reflection*, on the other hand, might cause us to ask why we have to judge George bad or good in the first place. What is it about the way we see other people that compels us to make such a polarized, summary, value judgment? When we critically reflect on the premise or presupposition of the problem we are often able to transform a meaning perspective. Critical reflection is the process by which we engage in premise reflection.

Thus, there are two different types of transformation which may be effected by reflection, everyday transformation of a meaning scheme, through reflection on content or process and, less commonly, more profound transformation of a meaning perspective through critical reflection on premise. All reflection is potentially transformative of our meaning structures. When critical reflection of premises involves self-reflection, major personal transformations can occur.

It is necessary to differentiate between operational and structural critique in understanding reflection. Operational critique involves reflecting upon how to solve a problem within a given structure, for example, an economic system; structural critique is reflecting critically on the structure itself. If a group of corporate managers in a workshop become critical of and reject a command and control managerial approach in favor of facilitating employee group decision-making, this reorientation can constitute a operational transformation. If they reflect upon and reject the validity of the premise of labor being paid to produce a product to be sold by an employer for profit, this would constitute a structural critique. If they reflect upon and reject the validity of their own habitual beliefs about management or about the system, this critical self-reflection is likely to lead to a significant personal perspective transformation. Operational critique is more likely to involve reflective reframing of content or process. Structural critique is more likely to involve premise reflection. A progressive series of process reflections can also lead incrementally to challenging the premise of one's belief and thus effect a transformation in meaning perspective. Self-reflection may be included in either operational or structural critique.

Whenever we consciously think through, describe, explain, or critically analyze a situation or belief, we intentionally use language categories as our means of doing so. Intentional efforts to think or learn usually involve describing, explaining, problem posing (identifying the problem), and problem solving; intentional construal is the way we engage in reflective thought and reasoning. Reflection, as it is used here, is a process by which we attempt to justify our beliefs, either by rationally examining assumptions, often in response to intuitively becoming aware that something is wrong with the result of our thought, or challenging its validity through discourse with others of differing viewpoint and arriving at a best informed judgment. The result is a transformation in meaning structures. Reflection is the apperceptive process by which we change our minds, literally and figuratively. It is the process of turning our attention to the justification for what we know, feel, believe, and act upon. We reflect by critically reassessing the assumptions we have taken-for-granted which prop up the way we think and feel. We sometimes identify these assumptions and look critically at how we acquired them and their consequences in action or in our feelings.

In earlier writing, I have made a potentially misleading distinction between the kind of "retroactive" reflection just described and "reflection in action"(Mezirow, 1991). By the latter, I referred to the momentary pause in the course of action in which one draws upon past experience so as to recognize that an anticipated move would be a wrong one. But, of course, all reflection is retroactive; reflection can take a second or a decade. Reflection-in-action is of the momentary kind and is immediately used to guide next action steps. For example, in playing a game or a sport, reflection-in-action involves a brief moment of recognizing from past experience that a potential move on our part will be likely to evoke an anticipated response on the part of a competitor so that we modify our actions accordingly.

Figure 1 shows the structures of meaning and how they become transformed. We use intentional construal, for posing and solving problems, making explanations or for describing what happened. Reflection—"attending to the grounds of our beliefs"—is the means of effecting change in our meaning structures, but responding to feelings, intuitions and dreams are the ways in which we make meaning through presentational construal. These ways of knowing can make meaning by serving as cues to help us assess the decisions we make. The process of making an interpretation in a new situation involves an activity sequence something like this: a sense perception → scanning → imagining →← intuiting → projecting a meaning perspective →← sometimes reflecting on its appropriateness → interpreting →← intuiting → acting →← sometimes reflecting → acting upon reflection (praxis). Intuition guides our imaginative formulation of what we experience and serves as a check on our final interpretation. A major complement to rational thought and learning is the process of presentational awareness, or what Jungians Boyd and Myers (1988) identify as "discernment."

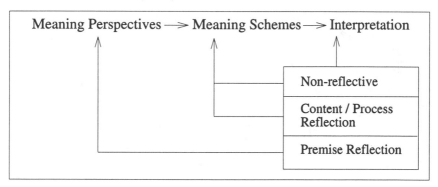

Figure 1. The Transformation Process

Art, music and dance can evoke presentational construal. They are the "language" forms of presentational construal. It does not make sense to allocate arbitrarily understanding of presentational and propositional construal to psychologists and psychiatrists and understanding intentional construal to adult educators. Rationality and discernment are two highly interactive and mutually dependent dimensions of learning. Rationality tells us the meaning of presentational construal; discernment tells us whether the conclusions of propositional construal are aligned with what we know through presentational construal.

Transformation theory is not simply a theory of rationality, although a theory of rationality is central to it. This position recognizes that repressed and neurotic feelings which affect meaning perspectives are crucially important perceptual and cognitive codes. Imagination is seen as the central process by which we attempt to make sense of our experience, by creatively projecting symbolic models to interpret, primarily through metaphorical analogy, what we experience. Intuitions, feelings, and dreams are posited as the principal links which allow us to be influenced in our rational thought through presentational construal. Transformative learning, which may involve a reassessment of one's self-concept, as is often the case in perspective transformation, is threatening, emotionally charged, and extremely difficult. It is not enough that such transformations effect a cognitive insight; they require a conative and emotional commitment to act upon a new perspective as well. Transformative learning involves movement from alienation to agency, and "centering," movement from a lack of authenticity, being true to one's self, to authenticity (Loughlin, 1990).

Memory involves this same process of imaginative construal, guided by previous interpretations, especially (1) those interpretations which we have made frequently before, and (2) those which have been associated with strong feelings. We forget when an event is no longer recognizable, its context has changed or our frames of reference and resulting habits of expectation have been transformed. We remember by recognizing an object or event that has had meaning for us in the past and has either reinforced or transformed an existing meaning scheme or perspective. We forget what we do not structure (Bruner, 1990, p. 58). Bartlett (cited in Loughlin) holds that to remember, we first associate affect—pleasure, anger, pain, and so on. Memory is seen as under control of an affective attitude. Recall is a reconstruction which, in effect, justifies the affect. Adults have a greater breadth of biographical and historical perspectives. We are more able to place specific actions in a developmental perspective, and our memories tend to be less contextually limited, hence less "magical" than children's memories.

Learning, in this sense, may be defined as the process of using a prior interpretation to construe a new or a revised interpretation of the meaning of one's experience in order to guide future action. Action may include making a decision, revising a point of view, posing a problem, reframing a structure of meaning or changing behavior. There are two domains in which learning has fundamentally different purposes, logics and processes. Each requires a very different educational intervention. Instrumental learning involves learning which pertains to controlling or manipulating the environment or other people. It involves predictions about observable events which can be proven correct, determining cause-effect relationships and task-oriented problems solving. The logic of instrumental learning is hypothetical-deductive. It is prescriptive and amenable to empirical tests of truth (that something is as it is asserted to be). Communicative learning, on the other hand, involves understanding what somebody means or the process by which others understand what you mean. It involves understanding values, ideals, feelings and normative concepts like freedom, autonomy, love, justice, goodness, responsibility, wisdom, and beauty. We communicate orally and through the written word as well as through the arts. Communicative learning is designative rather than prescriptive. It identifies and clarifies the unknown through a process whereby each step suggests the next (abductive logic). Metaphoric analogies are also used to fit the unknown to the familiar. Prior learning—articulated beliefs, feelings, and judgments, including meaning schemes and perspectives—are validated (justified) in communicative learning through a process of rational consensus. "Communicative competence" refers to our ability to negotiate purposes and meanings for ourselves. Most learning involves both instrumental and communicative learning. Learning about oneself, for example, involves learning what one is capable of doing—instrumental learning—while construing the meaning of our performance involves normative assessment and rational discourse—communicative learning.

Within the domains of instrumental and communicative learning, we can differentiate four kinds of learning, two of which are transformative. One is learning within meaning schemes—learning to add, further differentiate or integrate ideas within a pre-existing scheme. A second is learning a set of beliefs, feelings, judgments, attitudes, and knowledge which constitute a new meaning scheme. A third is learning that through critical reflection on the content or process of problem solving, rational discourse and action transforms a meaning scheme. A fourth is learning which transforms a meaning perspective.

There are several interacting contexts which influence learning: the situation encountered; the line of action in which learning occurs (directed by the learner's intention and purpose); the learner's meaning schemes and perspectives; the conditions of communication (language mastery, language codes delimiting categories, constructs and labels, ways of validating problematic assertions); and the self-image of the learner. All these dimensions should be taken into account to understand how, what, and why adults learn.

Perspective transformation is much less commonplace than transforming meaning schemes. It can happen either through an accretion of transformations in related meaning schemes or through an epochal transformation triggered by a life crisis or major transition. Perspective transformation appears to follow the following movement of creating meaning, although not always in this exact sequence: (1) a disorienting dilemma, (2) self-examination with feelings of guilt or shame, sometimes turning to religion for support, (3) a critical assessment of assumptions, (4) recognition that one's discontent and the process of transformation are shared and others have negotiated a similar change, (5) exploration of options for new roles, relationships, and actions, (6) planning a course of action, (7) acquiring knowledge and skills for implementing one's plans, (8) provisionally trying out new roles, (9) renegotiating relationships and negotiating new relationships (10) building competence and self-confidence in new roles and relationships and (11) a reintegration into one's life on the basis of conditions dictated by one's new perspective (Mezirow, 1991, pp. 168–69).

Older adults often move to a more mature level of cognitive differentiation involving enhanced awareness of social context, psychological factors, individual and collective goals, and premises. Older adults become more autonomous, socially oriented, and dialectical (Labouvie-Vief and Blanchard-Fields, 1982, pp. 204–6). They are more likely to integrate logic and feelings. They may become increasingly critically reflective of assumptions if this is the mode of their earlier development.

Neurologists and psychologists distinguish between episodic, semantic, and implicit memory. Episodic refers to remembering personal episodes, semantic to recalling impersonal facts, and implicit to remembering skills that are automatically exercised, like ice skating. The skills of remembering appear to be related to language acquisition and to early learning how to shape events into story form. Older adults appear to use semantic memory for distant memories and rely upon a less reliable episodic memory to remember recent events. There is no evidence of decline in semantic and implicit memory with age. Decline in episodic memory in the 70s appears due to lack of active use of mental facilities (for example, due to retirement) rather than aging (Tulvig, 1989; Goleman, 1990).

Brandtstadter notes the current interest among developmental psychologists concerned with the lifespan in an emerging "actional perspective" with roots in Aristotle's theory of action and the *Geisteswissenschaftlicke Psychologie* of Dilthey and Spranger in Germany (1990, pp. 86–88). This paradigm places a central emphasis on the recognition that individuals are the co-producers (with their cultures and the idiosyncratic influences of primary care givers) of their development. Gould (1987) identifies the search for hidden false assumptions of earlier developmental stages and overcoming their influence as the liberating transformative tasks of development.

According to Labouvie-Vief (1984), a crucial difference between preadolescents and adults is that preadolescents decode biological and encode cultural "automatisms," and adults critically assess the assumptions behind these culturally assimilated ways of knowing, believing, and feeling. Adults validate these and competing assumptions through rational discourse to acquire more developmentally advanced structures of meaning. There is a significant difference between the formative function of learning in childhood and the transformative function of learning in adulthood. Meaning structures—both perspectives and schemes—may be considered more "developmentally advanced" when they are more inclusive, discriminating, permeable, integrative of experience and are validated through rational discourse. Development, especially in adulthood, centrally involves movement toward more developmentally advanced meaning structures. Changes range from viewing the educator as authority from whom truth is accepted and then presented back in evaluation to an ultimate adult understanding that beliefs are justified through informed rational discourse. Kitchener and King (1990) have charted a significant seven-stage sequence of development of this movement toward critical judgment reflecting differences in age and education. However, transformation theory holds with Sloan (1986) that developmental stages or phases in adulthood are best understood as "sequential moments of meaning becoming clarified." Perhaps Loder's (1981) concept of orthogenesis—living organisms, personality, society, or symbol system tend to individuate in a given direction regardless of environmental constraints—pertains to our persistent movement toward making meaning through more developmentally advanced meaning schemes and perspectives as well as our extreme inability to tolerate areas of meaningless.

Many life span developmental psychologists characterize postformal reasoning as a step beyond Piaget's formal operational reasoning (Commons, Richards, and Armon, 1884; Kramer, 1983; Kramer and Bopp, 1989; Sinnott, 1989). Sinnott (1989, 1991) has formulated a theory of relativistic postformal operations predicated upon the concept of "self-reference." Because adults become aware—critically reflective— of the fact that we are never free from the limitations of our system of knowing—our meaning schemes and perspectives—they can take into account that all knowledge is to a degree subjective and incomplete. To be able to act, we make a critically reflective choice among competing systems of logic and truth to select one to impose on the data, depending upon the context. There is a parallel, interactive, self-referential coordination of perspectives on the emotional level as one develops as well. These concepts of adult development are highly compatible with a transformation theory of adult learning.

Transformation theory understands knowledge as a set of shared, subjective, often taken-for-granted meanings and assumptions which are socially and historically constructed (Gergen, 1982). Our interpretations of the external world must be differentiated from the world itself. We interpret from past experience, and past experience varies among interpreters. The process by which we attempt to communicate our interpretations, to comprehend those of others and to find common ground is a process of intersubjective negotiation which significantly shapes our understanding of existence. This is the learning process.

THE ASSUMPTIONS AND CONDITIONS OF DISCOURSE

When we communicate or have doubts about the truth or authenticity of the assertion, the truthfulness of the speaker, or the appropriateness of what is asserted in light of relevant norms, we often seek the best judgment of the most informed, objective, and rational persons we can find. We engage them in a special form of dialogue which Habermas refers to as "discourse." Discourse involves an effort to set aside bias, prejudice, and personal concerns and to do our best to be open and objective in presenting and assessing reasons and reviewing the evidence and arguments for and against the problematic assertion to arrive at a consensus. When we critically reflect on assumptions in communicative learning and arrive at a newly transformed way of knowing, believing, or feeling, we need to validate the assertions we make based upon these transformative insights through this process of discourse.

The resulting consensus is our best test of the justification of the problematic assertion only until new perspectives or evidence are introduced which require further discourse. And all consensus is subject to review by other groups more inclusive in their composition, just as the acts justified by the Nazi consensus concerning genocide of Jews in Germany was ultimately judged as criminal by the international community. In this sense, consensual refers to a universal consensus. As I have indicated elsewhere, it is also universal in the sense of the consensus arrived at by a jury in which the assumption is that one juror may be substituted for another without changing a collective verdict based upon a rational examination of the arguments and evidence. In effect, this form of institutionalizing rational discourse is an imperfect but long established method of establishing the justification of problematic assertions of what is true. Discourse is most often conducted on a one-to-one basis—a series of interactions with one person at a time rather than a group determination, although we often seek discourse through various types of support groups and formal educational formats. Discourse, for example, is institutionalized in university seminars.

Discourse has been sometimes misunderstood and discounted as a patently unattainable ideal in a real world in which individuals of different races, sexes, classes, and degrees of power are historically so unequally benefited educationally, economically, politically, and socially. The impact of these realities obviously so distort communications and the process of rational discourse as to make the ideal seem an unrealistic assumption because it is never encountered in real life. But we never encounter most of our ideals in real life. What is important is that ideals be understood as indispensable to enable us to set standards against which to judge performance and to provide us with goals and a heuristic sense of direction. Acquiring critical judgment, involving rational discourse, appears to be related to education and aging (Kitchener and King, 1990).

The assumptions of rational discourse are: (1) that beliefs should contain no logical contradictions, (2) that reasons for believing them can be advanced and assessed, (3) that concepts will become more intelligible when analyzed and (4) that we have criteria with which to know when the belief is justified or not. Even the most extreme postmodernist writers who argue that universal concepts of rationality and discourse are impossible (Sleeper, 1992; Rosen, 1992), implicitly accept these universal "rules" in advancing their viewpoint.

Discourse requires what Lenore Langsdorf (1992) calls an "interpretative stance" necessary to approach written or oral texts critically. Everyday dialogue involves content and a "communicative event," that is, the personality of the participants and the circumstances of the conversation. To become critical, we must shift our focus from the event to the content. The criteria by which a viewpoint or belief is justified through discourse include the degree to which it is inclusive, differentiating, permeable (open to other viewpoints), and integrative of experience. Under ideal conditions of discourse, implicit in the nature of human communication, participants will: (1) have accurate and complete information, (2) be free from coercion and distorting self-deception, (3) be able to weigh evidence and assess arguments objectively, (4) be open to alternative points of view, that is, to care about the way others think and feel, (5) be able to become critically reflective upon assumptions and presuppositions and their consequences, (6) have equal opportunity to participate in the various roles of discourse, and (7) be willing to accept an informed, objective, and rational consensus as a legitimate test of validity until new perspectives, evidence, or arguments are encountered and are subsequently established through discourse as yielding better judgments.

There is much justifiable skepticism about such a statement of ideals, especially in light of postmodernist rejection of absolutes—any single rationality, morality, or theoretical framework—and the perceived saturation of all social and political discourse with power or dominance and the celebration of difference. It is when these concerns become a presumption of incommensurability—that we cannot hope to understand each other across race, class, and gender differences—and a denial of the possibility of intersubjective understanding through discourse that some postmodernists fall into the egregious error of throwing out the baby with the bath water.

There is no question of the claim that dialogue is often made impossible in a society structured by power and inequality and that creating a forum in which participants have the right to speak is inadequate. It is not just fear of retribution which keeps individuals from marginalized groups from participating. People are silenced by being demoralized, unable to believe that what they have to say will be valued, having been previously silenced, frustrated, or made insecure by contesting ideas. Assertive challenges of beliefs or evidence can impede further dialogue. Awareness of being less articulate than others can be an impediment to full participation. Participants may be silenced by the belief that discourse cannot make a difference in resolving a problem. One upsmanship, personal competitiveness, bias and prejudice, and past experiences with oppression and domination can suffocate communication. Dialogue can be aborted by deep differences in language, culture, and meaning perspective. However, Burbules and Rice note: "There is no reason to assume that dialogue across differences involves either eliminating those differences or imposing one group's views on others; dialogue that leads to understanding, cooperation, and accommodation can sustain differences within a broader compact of toleration and respect" (1991, p. 403).

Despite the diverse ways that power and influence distort dialogue, transformation theory holds that dialogue and discourse can proceed in a critically self-reflective manner that aims toward more sensitive, respectful, non-dominating, and non-distorting communication. Facilitating the kind of learning which views difference an opportunity, a challenge to our abilities to communicate, understand, and learn, is precisely what adult education is about. Dialogue may result in agreement and consensus. Even when dialogue partners fail to agree, it is possible for them to deepen respect across irreconcilable and incommensurable difference (p. 409).

The success of dialogue across differences depends upon external, institutional factors and the meaning perspectives and schemes participants bring with them. It also depends upon what Burbules and Rice call "communicative virtues," and Siegel (1992) calls "the critical spirit," which help make dialogue possible and sustainable over time. Burbules and Rice write:

These virtues include tolerance, patience, respect for differences, a willingness to listen, the inclination to admit that one may be mistaken, the ability to reinterpret or translate one's own concerns in a way that makes them comprehensive to others, the self-imposition of restraint in order that others may have a turn to speak, and the disposition to express oneself honestly and sincerely. The possession of these virtues influences one's capacities both to express one's own beliefs, values and feelings accurately, and to listen to and hear those of others. (p. 411)

Burbules and Rice suggest that these communicative virtues are learned through association with others who are disposed towards tolerance, patience, and respect for others, and they are improved by practice and may be nurtured. Adult educators will see fostering the ideal conditions of discourse and the communicative virtues as cardinal goals.

Postmodernists reject the idea of a theory which speaks in universals; they would instead focus exclusively on situated learning and "local" analyses (Husper, 1991; Nicholson, 1990). Habermas' concept of dialogic consensus of validity claims has been also challenged by adult educators (Usher, 1991; Clark and Wilson, 1991) and philosophers like Richard Rorty (1985). Rorty contends that the normative concept of "valid arguments" should be replaced with the concept of "arguments held to be true for us at this time." Habermas, in response, agrees that reason is inescapably situated in history, political culture, body, and language. Still, he holds that this does not warrant equating reason with what is acceptable at a given time or place. He sees this relativistic position as grounded in an "objectivist fallacy" (1985, pp. 194–95):

We could not even understand the meaning of what we describe from a third-person perspective as argumentative conduct if we had not already learned . . . what it means from the perspective of the first person to raise a validity claim that points beyond the provincial agreements of the specific local context. Only this capacity gives our opinions the character of convictions . . . the question of which beliefs are justified is a question of which beliefs are based on good reasons; it is not a function of life-habits that enjoy social currency in some places and not in others.

For Habermas, "the presuppositions of the rationality of processes of reaching understanding " may be presumed to be universal because they are unavoidable" (1985, p. 198).

The ideal conditions of discourse and the communicative virtues are also the ideal conditions and requisite virtues of collaborative adult learning. They constitute the goals of an adult education which places a major emphasis on collaborative learning. These ideal conditions and communicative virtues also imply a set of social values and preconditions which must pertain if adults are to be permitted to explore fully the meaning of their experience. The implicit values include participatory democracy, tolerance, freedom, education, equality of opportunity. Preconditions would include a good formal education, and at least adequate safety, health, shelter, and economic security to assure equal opportunity to participate, think, and reason with others.

In contemporary western society change is omnipresent, old structures of authority have become attenuated and the power of the monetary system, bureaucracy, and depersonalization create and perpetuate devastating inequalities of class, gender, and race. Pitted against these forces is the heroic promise of adult education, that through critically reflective discourse, sensitive and responsive to differences, we human beings can, as Matthias Finger as puts it, "learn our way out."

Jürgen Habermas (1987b) differentiates the process of rational discourse in which knowledge claims are validated through consensus (in the lifeworld) from opposing systemic forces, such as the monetary system and bureaucracy, which create constraints on free and full participation in rational discourse. Adult education and social movements may be understood as collective efforts to resist the hegemony of the system. The social goal toward which adult education strives is one in which all members of society may engage freely and fully in rational discourse and action without this process being subverted by the system. Such subversion occurs in everyday life when communication becomes distorted by unequal distributions of power and influence. Transformation theory holds that adult education's intervention is to redress this distortion or "violence" by creating protective learning environments with norms which assure everyone more free and full participation in emancipatory discourse. Adult educators' attraction to the field of group dynamics—with all its limitations—is directly predicated upon the conviction that individuals can become more critically self-reflective of their own and other members' roles in groups, including those depending upon influence and power, and through this reflective awareness, modify these roles.

THE ROLE OF THE ADULT EDUCATOR
IN FOSTERING COMMUNICATIVE LEARNING

Adult educators have often misinterpreted instrumental learning as coterminous with all adult learning. Learners are encouraged to set objectives in terms of anticipated learning outcomes and measurable behavior change. These are determined by an analysis of the "skills" or "competencies" required by a specific task and by an assessment of those already acquired by the learner. The skills for which the learner is found deficit are taught. Through explanation, demonstration, trial, and critique, the learner is assisted, moving from the concrete to the abstract, to acquire the relevant skills to do the task.

This simplistic formula may have relevance for learning some manual skills and certainly gives itself to establishing "accountability" to funding sources. It does not, however, address most significant adult learning which occurs in the communicative learning domain. Communicative learning involves identifying problematic ideas, values, beliefs, and feelings, critically examining the assumptions upon which they are based, testing their justification through rational discourse and making decisions predicated upon the resulting consensus. This is the central activity fostered by adult educators. The essential "skills" for this kind of learning have to do with those necessary for a greater degree of full participation in critical reflection, discourse, and action. In communicative learning, the educator cannot assess the learner's "needs" before he or she arrives at an educational venue except in the most superficial sense. The learners cannot know their "real" needs because they can not know what they would need if they could see things from a more developmentally advanced perspective (one more inclusive, differentiating, permeable, and integrative of experience). The subject matter of transformative adult education is the learner's experience and the learning process ought to foster the learner's understanding of the origins, nature, and consequences of his or her beliefs. This is precisely what Eduard Lindeman's pioneering group of adult education scholars, known as "The Inquiry," was about in the 1920s and 1930s (Schemel, 1992). Transformation theory has expanded this conception to attempt to explain how all reflective learning, that this, learning involving a change of mind, is potentially transformative in nature.

Action is an indispensable phase of the process of adult learning. But action can mean making a decision, being critically reflective or transforming a meaning structure as well as a change in behavior. Critical reflection often results in the learner deciding to take collective social action to effect changes in the system, in institutions, or in social practices. The work of Paulo Freire in adult literacy in Latin America and of Myles Horton through the Highlander Research and Educational Center in Tennessee have become major influences in adult education. Consequently, many adult educators are deeply involved in social action education. This common concern of adult educators has also become a professional area of specialization in the field, albeit a neglected one.

Praxis, taking reflective action, often requires instrumental learning of tactics: how to collaborate, discourse, plan, anticipate resistance, "read" the implicit signs, inventory approaches, select an activity, and to dialogue and act collectively. However, the central function of adult educators (especially in literacy) is to facilitate and precipitate critical reflection by the individual learner and free full participation in discourse as well as praxis. The only anticipated learning outcome here is a more rational and objective assessment of assumptions. The adult educator cannot set the specific result of this assessment in advance. To set the educational process up as one requiring the learner to share the convictions of the educator's own view of social reality would be tantamount to indoctrination. Once learners have gained reflective insight and have resolved to take action to effect social change, the adult educator who has the skills and understandings necessary may join a partisan battle by helping learners learn how to take collective social action. This is fundamentally different from setting education up as a device of conversion.

Criteria for assessment of learner gains would include context awareness, reflectivity, and more effective participation in discourse and interpretations which are more inclusive, differentiating, permeable, and integrative of experience. Such assessment could be made by independent raters and differences resolved through rational discourse. Kohlberg's form of assessment involving hypothetical case studies is particularly relevant. The criteria suggested here could be used by independent raters to assess changes in interpreting such hypothetical situations or case studies before and after an educational program. Educators need training in assessing development of critical reflection, participation in rational discourse, and reflective action. Portfolio assessment is another promising mode of evaluation of learning gains. Learners and teachers rate the evidence of this development over the educational experience through learner assignments, essays, notes written to the instructor, learning projects, case studies, participation in role play and discussion groups, educator's anecdotes, observation check-lists, educator-designed tests, and so on. When more than one teacher rates learner progress and inter-rater correlations are determined, reliability of assessment is enhanced.

Adult education is indispensable because of the distorted communication created by unequal power and influence. A major function of adult education is to develop protective environments with enforced social norms which assure that all may fully and freely participate in discourse. Learners can be assisted to become more aware of frames of references—their own and others'—identify assumptions and presuppositions, assess evidence, weigh arguments, become more open-minded, and improve the quality of their participation in discourse. Adult educators are social environmentalists and empathic provocateurs. They want active involvement in discourse rather than reverence for great books, historical consciousness and self-reflection rather than timeless values, and continual expansion of our cultural canon to foster fuller and freer participation in critical reasoning and action. Adult education, far more than any other field of education, has, from its inception, perceived its mission as that of creating conditions in which adult dialogue across differences is a *sine qua non*. It has defined itself as a form of education designed to overcome just the kinds of intrusions in learning of power, influence and inequality which has led some postmodernists or antimodernists to condemn reflection, dialogue, and education as illusionary goals (Ellsworth, 1989).

In her survey of adult education professors in North America, Suanmali (1981) found unanimous consensus on such objectives as:

1. Progressively decrease the learner's dependency on the educator.

2. Assist the learner to assume increasing responsibility for defining learning objectives, planning his/her own learning program and evaluating progress.

3. Foster a self-corrective, reflexive approach to learning—to typifying and labeling, to perspective taking and choosing, and to habits of earning and learning relationships.

4. Reinforce the self-concept of the learner as a learner and doer by providing for progressive mastery and for a supportive climate with feed-

back to encourage provisional efforts to change and to take risks; by
avoiding competitive judgment of performance; and by appropriate
use of mutual support groups.

These goals resonate with those of Eduard Lindeman who defined the
aim of adult education as "a cooperative venture in non-authoritarian,
informal learning . . . quest of the mind which digs down to the roots of
the preconceptions which formulate our conduct. . . . The teacher
moves from acting as an authority figure to become . . . the guide,
pointer-out, who also participates in learning in proportion to the vitality and relevance of his facts and experiences" (Brookfield, 1987, p. 4).

In *The Theory of Communicative Action* (1987b), Habermas dis-
cusses the difficult dialectic between the "system"—the socio-economic system which provides employment and security in exchange for
loyalty—and the "lifeworld," which is characterized by reflective discourse, consensual validation of beliefs, human rights and responsibilities, and interpersonal relationships. We all have to live in some kind of
system with implicit tensions in its relationship to our individual and
collective lives. From my point of view, what is important is that educators identify specific systemic influences which are inimical to adult
reflective discourse and action, and hence to adult learning, in the lifeworld [see chapter 5 for a full explication of this theme—Ed.].

One's capacity to make meaning of one's experience through equal
opportunity to participate democratically in discourse, requires conditions which are not threatening, exclusionary, prejudicial, exploitive, or
dependency-producing. Each participant must be capable of being open
to new perspectives, analyzing arguments and evidence, making appropriate inferences, and being critically reflective of assumptions. This
clearly implies prior learning and a basic education in how to think critically. The fundamental human right to understand the meaning of one's
experience through discourse implies, not only a basic education to
develop cognitive skills, but also physical security, health, employment,
and shelter. Ignorant, frightened, ill, hungry, homeless people can not
realize their fundamental human right to understand their experience by
participating as equals in discourse. This is why social change is essential. Transformation theory suggests that human rights to freedom, justice, tolerance, equality of opportunity, and democracy may be similarly
grounded in our foundational human right to understand the meaning of
our experience through discourse.

When deconstructionist writers emphasize the importance of critical reflection of beliefs and their assumptions, respect for diversity, and suspicion of universal truths, they are speaking in a transformative voice. While some contemporary critics of the project of modernity may to identify these interests as constituting a new historical period of "postmodernism," my version of transformation theory is more inclined toward a social historical interpretation like that of the German sociologist Ulrich Beck. Beck (1993) has developed a persuasive rendering of the direction of modernity which provides a plausible cultural context for transformative theory's understanding of the development of adult learning in contemporary society. His theory challenges the currently fashionable postmodernist stance which sees the concept of modernity itself as passé. Beck identifies a new set of problems which tranforms the priorities of industrial modernization into a phase of " reflexive modernization," one now involving greater emphasis on individual autonomy and reflectivity.

The priorities of traditional modernity were dominated by the value of economic growth and resulting problems of unequal production and distribution of social wealth. In place of industrial modernity, Beck posits an evolving "risk society" in which the emphasis on economic growth and problems of inequality are subsumed and redefined in a new context of social and individual survival problems. These new dilemmas have been created by the uncontrolled and unpredictable influences of ecological disturbances and pollution, population growth, scientific innovations, including nuclear and biogenetic developments, and new technologies, including those in communications, such as computerization and television. All of these developments generate unprecedented new risks and redefine inequality as transcendent of traditional class, sex, or age distinctions. Moreover, with the attenuation of traditional sources of authority and solidarity—the family, church, community— we have experienced a significant expansion of individual freedom of choice and decision making. While this has resulted in a new critically self-reflective individualization, self-reflectivity is no guarantee of autonomy or emancipation. A major intervening variable is the possibility of a greater dependency on influences of economic and political institutions and procedures which pose several threats (Jansen and Van der Veen, 1992).

One threat involves avoiding the rationalization of personal choice by simply defying convention by embracing a looser lifestyle, expressing one's preferences in ways of dressing, use of leisure, home furnishings, use of language, types of relationships, and opinions about work and careers. This often results, however, in dependency on trends and fashions which soon become commercially exploited. Lifestyle can denote a pattern of conspicuous consumption which substitute material values for traditional religious and political values. A second threat is that reflective individualization may lead to the assumption of responsibility for situations for which a person may be ill-prepared or beyond one's ability to influence—situational, psychological, and knowledge constraints on action. A third threat is that giving meaning to life and one's purposes, yearnings, and values becomes a private matter. When one encounters the dilemmas associated with major life transitions, there are fewer prescribed solutions, so these periods assume crisis proportion and become more difficult to negotiate. A final threat is the evolution of new forms of social inequality. Unemployment and poverty is no longer the collective, joint fate of a particular social class, but has become an individual fate crossing class lines.

Jansen and Van der Veen (1992) propose that adult education take on a new orientation to respond to the needs of reflexive modernity and the risk society. They propose that adult education in the risk society must foster both critical reflection of social conditions and of personal motives, needs, wants, and actions. One at the expense of the other will be dysfunctional. Adult education neither should be neutral nor should it take sides with a specific deprived group. Adult education should be understood as a cultural rather than a social policy. So many different groups of actors are involved in creating, sustaining, and overcoming the problems of deprived groups or political movements that these problems are not solvable by the effected groups or grassroots movements alone. Adult education should not just work with victims and advocacy groups. It should also work with employers, officials, community agencies, and other stakeholders wherever education can contribute to a solution. Adult education in a risk society needs to act as a broker to bring together the network of those involved in collaborative problem solving. Jansen and Van der Veen recognize new dilemmas inherent in making this prescription: "On which values should this be based? What types of contracts between educators and their clients are feasible? Do we need a code that describes the professional autonomy, which doctors and advocates have, when adult educators work with social movements as well as with employers?" (p. 282).

Transformation theory would ground the answers to these questions in the nature of adult learning. The values upon which the role of adult education should be based are those implicit in a professional commitment to foster individual transformations toward more inclusive, differentiating, permeable, and integrative meaning perspectives and schemes. The adult education commitment fosters social change to make possible more ideal conditions of critical reasoning and adult learning for enhanced emancipatory participation in democratic decision making. Adult educators may work with any learners who subscribe to these values. This set of values clearly imply a professional code defining the role of the adult educators.

The risk society calls for an adult "education of hope" which does not dwell on impending disaster but instead helps individuals and groups answer the question of what they can do in their local situation and functions as a go-between for social movements and political and economic institutions. Adult education should also strive to counter a trend toward the deterioration of traditional communities by supporting new forms of community which embrace fewer aspects of life, have less impact on their members, and are less hierarchical and more dynamic. Community organizations can serve as the vehicles for critical cultural debate and social action. They constitute a "civic society" which can serve as opposition to the power of economic and political systems. Community adult education is needed to support networking on broader issues, training new leadership, and helping participants to learn conflict resolution and to develop their own identity and competency.

For Jensen and Van der Veen, adult education for critical self-reflection should address survival problems, such as those of the environment, science and technology, existential problems, such as personal growth and giving meaning to life, as well as the new forms of social inequality. In a high-risk society adult education will extend its traditional identification with deprived people to the needs of all working-class and middle-class people. It will stay closer to learner's daily hopes ands worries and be more prepared to foster critical reflection and rational discourse between those of conflicting experiences, interests, and beliefs. From this vantage point, "adult education is not propaganda for certain ideals and solutions, but a place for critical discussion of social developments and their impact for personal and social life. Its intellectual and spiritual inspiration could be better derived from general values, like 'the defense of human rights' and 'democratic control of society' and from an 'ecological rationality' than from partisanship with specific groups or ideologies" (p. 268).

TOWARD A PARTICIPATORY
DEMOCRATIC LEARNING SOCIETY

From its early beginnings in the Workers' Education Association in England and in the folk schools of Scandinavia, before its establishment as a field of study and practice in the United States, throughout the period of progressivism in education to the present in both the United States (Muller, 1991) and Europe (Finger, 1989), adult education has been cleaved with an unresolved fundamental issue. This is the division between those who argue that adult education must have has its primary objective changing the social order and those who place primary emphasis on personal development, often as a means of effecting social change.

Kenneth Lawson (1991) traces the emergence of adult education in the evolving context of rational empiricism, a line of philosophical thought descending from Locke and Kant to such contemporary philosophers as Nozick and Rawls. In its beginnings, rational empiricism was a position challenging the absolute authority of monarchy. A good state has limited functions, and individuals are free to decide for themselves what is good. This orientation emerged as "individualistic, libertarian, egalitarian, and democratic." Central values include freedom, justice, equality, rationality, rights, and duties. As individuals are autonomous centers of consciousness, they can become moral agents. In this view, self-development and freedom are inherent in becoming a mature human being and rationality is the highest moral virtue.

In the rational empirical view, echoed in transformation theory, the individual's ability to make judgments is central, so education has to do with the development of rationality. Adult education, in this tradition, holds that the individual's beliefs become knowledge claims which are tested against the experience of others. Lawson writes: "In principle, every knowledge claim is testable. Moreover in a liberal democracy, equal access to the resources for producing knowledge is also regarded as a right. Individual rather than societal aspirations are paramount" (p. 294). Finger (1989) reports that, while new age movements have rejected the abstract ideals of the Enlightenment, they believe that their social goals must be achieved through individual development of the awareness and insights essential for critical reflection and praxis, a position coming full circle.

Mainstream adult education in the United States, with its individualistic and often self-serving emphasis, has been strongly challenged by those who maintain that learning occurs in social and existential contexts in which power and oppression are ubiquitous and their learning needs are socially and politically constituted and understood. It has become a cliché to note that education is never value-free. Adult education must be dedicated to effecting social change, to modifying oppressive practices, norms, institutions, and socio-economic structures to allow everyone to participate more freely and fully in discourse to understand his or her experience, to learn, and to help others learn. As we have seen, this implies making society more humane, educated, equal, tolerant, free, and democratic.

John Dewey's project (1916, 1927, 1939) was to establish a philosophical system that would provide a rationale for people to control the institutions that affected their lives. The society toward which we must move involves participatory democracy in families, schools, workplaces, communities, and the state. Participation was understood as essential to self-realization. The only political order appropriate to human dignity was one in which people participated directly in the decision-making process. Education was the means for engaging individuals in learning to serve this socio-economic and political objective. The proper task of education is to nurture our ability to reflect on our experience and to contribute to the common good. Individual development, productivity, and creativity were seen as the means to the social goal. Decentralization of authority, democratization of the workplace, redistribution of wealth, strengthening of civil liberties, and the representative institutions essential to dissent and the diffusion of power were essential elements in Dewey's vision of a "learning society."

Transformation theory advances the argument that the nature of adult learning itself mandates participatory democracy as both the means and social goal. Following Habermas, this view identifies critical reflection, rational discourse, and praxis as central to significant adult learning and the *sine qua non* of emancipatory participation. Reflection involves a critique of the justification for one's beliefs and understandings. Rational critical discourse is the means by which one participates thoughtfully and insightfully in participatory democracy. Indeed, one learns democracy by practicing it, and we all do this when we engage in rational discourse—to the extent we can freely and fully participate in the process of examining the evidence, hearing the arguments, engaging in critical reflection of assumptions, and arriving at a most informed consensual judgment—a contingent judgment open to new evidence, ideas, and points of view. Politics in any democracy must increasingly become a matter of rational persuasion. While force is sometimes necessary, it must rest upon a base of rational discussion.

Transformation theory argues that, because so many of our beliefs or knowledge claims involve assumptions about the coherence, truth, authenticity, or normative appropriateness of the claim or the truthfulness of the individual making the claim, we must rely primarily upon consensual validation to resolve these issues. This means discourse in which participants must advance and argue about reasons and evidence and become critically reflective of assumptions behind knowledge claims and intentions. Discourse, as a deconstruction of beliefs by a critical examination of assumptions, means that the achievement of insight and understanding is a task for human beings in community. Individual transformations are often precipitated, facilitated, and validated through social transformation. Progress in vision becomes a function of implementing the transformation in our own lives and in society.

Throughout this chapter I have argued that the justification of our beliefs and ideas is dependent upon consensus, freedom from coercion, access to full information, equality in the roles involved in discourse. It also involves helping others to explain their views and feelings, and to acquire mutual respect and openness to new perspectives as well as a concern for justice. All of these factors are involved in arriving at a collective judgment. These components of significant adult learning are the elements of a democratic society: they are predicated upon emancipatory participation.

This position fully recognizes the crucial importance of power and influence of the dominant structures in a bureaucratic and capitalistic society in defining learning needs and opportunities and structuring upward mobility. It seems painfully obvious that existing institutions cannot be easily reconciled with true participatory democracy. They must be adapted to the needs of a learning society. In a democratic society, the task is to educate the population to understand the need for continuing revision of existing economic and bureaucratic systems to foster critical reflection, rational discourse, and collective decision-making and action. This calls for creating open communities of discourse within existing institutions to foster internal pressure for change while pushing for systemic change for greater democratic decision-making through discourse on the inequities of society and collective political action.

Transformation theory grounds its argument for an emancipatory participative democracy in the very nature of adult learning in a modern society. In late modernity, old structures of authority have become eroded and the necessity for adults to cope with change has accelerated as never before. To decide the issues which confront us, our only option to reverting to tradition, authority, or brute force is critical reflection, rational discourse, and collective participatory action. Freedom, community, and democracy are not mere disembodied political ideals of the Enlightenment. They are essential conditions for human beings to understand their experiences. They are requirements for both individual development and social progress.

Adult education is the handmaiden of adult learning, a social process. Adult education attempts to redress distortions in communication and learning caused by unequal power and influence by creating "free space" in protected learning environments in which the practice of freedom, democratic participation, tolerance, equality, justice, and the "communicative virtues" are norms for rational discourse. Discourse involves critical reflection of assumptions, including social assumptions. Reflection on the origins, nature, and consequences of such presuppositions behind social practices and norms leads to informed social action to effect needed changes in society. Social action is not always dependent upon prior reflection on social assumptions, but this is the only kind of praxis with which adult educators, as educators, may be appropriately associated.

Transformation theory asserts that the dichotomy between individual and social development is a spurious one for educators. Educators are dedicated to fostering social change to achieve a society in which all may participate more freely and fully in critical discourse and reflective action, that is, in a democratic learning community. As citizens of a democracy, we are obligated to engage in political solutions to assure greater freedom, equality, and democratic participation in decision-making. As citizens, we must resort to politics because not all issues are amenable to resolution through rational discourse. As adult educators, we can foster critical reflection, rational discourse, and action in the conviction that informed rational adults will determine the need to take collective social action to overcome social practices inimical to their development. We can also hope that they will restructure institutions or social systems to make them more responsive to the needs of those they serve.

Praxis, taking reflective action, often requires instrumental learning of tactics: how to collaborate, discourse, plan, anticipate resistance, "read" the implicit signs, inventory approaches, select an activity, and dialogue and act collectively. Taking action can also require that a learner be helped over emotional hurdles deterring reflective action. Facilitating such learning is a specialty area within adult education—social action education—although all adult educators should be prepared to provide such assistance.

To set the educational process up as one requiring the learner to share the convictions of the educator's view of social reality (e.g., society cast as a simple dichotomy of oppressor vs. oppressed) is indoctrination. Such framing of reality delimits inquiry just as effectively as do unexamined cultural canons. When adults in modern democracies come to understand their acquired but unexamined beliefs, how they were created, by whom, and their consequences, they will determine the need for action and will act accordingly. It is important to note that learners need to become critical of assumptions underlying both the social structures themselves as well as operational practices conducted within existing structures.

In conclusion, emancipatory democratic participation refers to free full participation in democratic decision-making based upon critical reflection and rational discourse. It requires communicative competence. Emancipatory participation in critical discourse and reflective action is both the means and the goal of adult education, of adult development, and of social action in a democratic society. No person can become a fully functional adult in a democratic society without coming to see the need for social action and resolving to act. Activists who have not engaged in critical reflection on the issues calling for social action are as benighted as their protagonists. Emancipatory participation in democracy is the means and the end of both personal and social development. There is no short cut to emancipatory participation in democracy. The assumed values of adult education are those involved in an organized effort to assist individuals to learn to take action guided by a perspective which is more inclusive, discriminating, permeable, and integrative of experience. This emancipatory action may be achieved only through critical discourse. Transformation theory is an expression of democratic culture: it demands that we become aware of how we come to our knowledge and about the values that lead us to our meaning perspectives. As individuals, we are accountable for what we know and how we have come to know it. Effective learners in an emancipatory, participative, democratic society—a learning society—become a community of cultural critics and social activists. Our goal is a viable pluralism supported by openness to new perspectives, critical reflection, rational discourse, a willingness to negotiate differences, and action based upon these conditions.

3

Critical Commentaries on the Role of the Adult Educator: From Self-Directed Learning to Postmodernist Sensibilities

Michael Collins

TOWARD THE YEAR 2000 AND IMMEDIATE PROSPECTS FOR ADULT EDUCATION

By early 1993 even the most artful politician had difficulty denying the existence of a worldwide recession. Though its effects on different classes of people and from one region to another vary significantly, the economic indicators on the recession are starkly apparent. In advanced Western economies, governments are intent on persuading the people that national budget deficits must be cut (with dire consequences for publicly funded services such as education, health, and welfare support), and that the harsh realities of survival in an increasingly competitive global marketplace need to be confronted. These imperatives are accompanied by free-trade initiatives establishing the ground rules according to which global competition on a grand scale is to be played out. It is almost certain that the rules will work to the disadvantage of most developing, or underdeveloped, political economies with deleterious consequences for the vast majority of their populations. And it is far from clear that the vast majority of ordinary men and women in the advanced economies will benefit from the "New World Order." (The enlargement of free trade and global competition, along with a remarkable increase in nationalistic barbaric warfare, are among key developments which have signalled to us what "New World Order" rhetoric really means. It will be recalled that former President Bush's triumphal announcement about a "New World Order" followed the Western Alliance's immense deployment of military force in the Gulf War.) In any event, ready access to cheap labor enhances the bargaining power of international business interests at the expense of ordinary working people, who are encouraged to view their counterparts in other countries as competitors.

The tendencies broadly identified in these opening paragraphs are reported on, with varying degrees of sophistication, in the news media and popular journals, as well as receiving more substantive analysis in academic and political commentaries. Yet concern for critical global developments, and the localized effects to which they give rise, is significantly absent from the conventional discourse of modern adult education practice. (In this chapter "discourse" refers to written commentaries and everyday goal-oriented activities which are in line with, and contribute toward, the definition of a distinctive field of practice.)

At the outset of this final decade of the century, even the more thoughtful newspapers had joined forces with the popular media in parroting "end of history" rhetoric. And adult education, along with many other intellectual collectivities, has been surely remiss in not posing questions about the extent to which this messianic declaration is being embraced. The "end of history" rhetoric is a manifestation of the accelerating series of events associated with the Soviet Union's disintegration. Future prospects for humanity, according to "end of history" assertions, are now very much tied to the developmental tendencies already staked out under prevailing forms of corporate capitalism. Thus, "end of history" celebrates the triumph of capitalism, in the forms it has taken within Western democracies, over state capitalism (or bureaucratic communism) exemplified in the former USSR and its Eastern bloc satellites. At a strictly ideological level, "end of history" means the demise of the socialist project.

In this regard, it is worth noting that Pope John Paul II, a relatively conservative occupant of a traditionally conservative office, recently declared that "Europe's worst problems stem as much from the extreme manifestations of capitalism as they do from communism's legacy" (*Manchester Guardian Weekly*, 1993). He insisted that "the legitimate fight against the unjust, totalitarian system which defined itself as socialist should not mean throwing out those seeds of truth in socialism." And in what seems to be a turn about on his views about liberation theology, the Pope expressed solidarity with the Third World's struggle for freedom. Even more surprising was his suggestion that in some ways ordinary men and women who, until recently, lived under the hegemony of Moscow and dictatorial communist parties may have been better off then than they are now:

> The proponents of capitalism in its extreme forms tend to overlook the
> good things achieved by communism: the efforts to overcome unem-
> ployment, the concern for the poor. . . . In communism there was a
> concern for the community, whereas capitalism is rather individualis-
> tic. (*Manchester Guardian Weekly*, 1993, p. 1)

While there are yet no substantial indications of restored confidence
in the socialist project (quite the contrary, in fact), triumphalist media
reports and academic accounts about capitalism's durability are already
items of historical interest. President Bush's "New World Order" was
the year before last or thereabouts. Persistent high levels of unemployment and increasing poverty, along with desperate social problems
which accompany these trends, are major features of most advanced
Western economies. Prospects for the alleviation of large-scale deprivation and suffering in other regions of the world have become increasingly difficult to envisage.

This generalized introductory "gloom and doom" account of the
way things are in the world is not intended to press on adult educators a
sense of hopelessness about the 1990s. Nor should it be interpreted as
an invitation for adult educators to pass on their fears, however realistically based, to other adults. Rather, the intent here is to stress that for
the modern practice of adult education to realize any level of relevance
in today's society it must incorporate a critical engagement with issues
and tendencies outlined in the opening paragraphs of this chapter. If
modern adult education practice is to sustain itself as a distinctive field
of practice and research, it should embrace forms of teaching and learning, curriculum design and program planning, in which pressing global
circumstances are *deliberately* taken into account.

These normative assertions may seem overly polemic. Yet they
point to a problem of relevance at the heart of modern adult education
practice, a practice which during the past four or five decades has been
steered along a narrow-gauge professionalizing discourse. This discourse has tended to focus attention, in both theory and practice, onto
the characteristics of the individualized learner. Thoughtful engagement with critical global issues, and their local manifestations, has been
until recently either completely absent from the conventional discourse
of modern adult education practice or dealt with at the margins of the
field. In this regard, the way Paulo Freire's concern with consciousness
raising, empowerment, and the politics of education (Freire, 1973,

1974, 1978, 1985) has been brought in from the margins of modern adult education and homogenized to conform with conventional individualizing pedagogical formats, is instructive. There are good reasons, then, to be emphatic about the need for a reconstruction of modern adult education practice if it is to survive as an identifiable influence in our institutions and our community settings. The task of reconstruction requires a level of analysis and the kind of legitimation which is appropriately provided, though not exclusively, through university-based studies on adult education theory and practice. Accordingly, an immediate challenge presents itself to those responsible for the preparation of adult educators: how to keep alive the study of adult education in the contemporary academic milieu.

Given the relentless cut-backs to publicly funded education and the on-going erosion of gains made in earlier decades, it is not surprising that relevant critical discourse in education is pervaded by a seige mentality (Aronowitz and Giroux, 1985, 1993; Cultural Studies Group 11, 1992). This preoccupation is informed by a sensible understanding of what is at stake for education under the prevailing political ideology around publicly funded services. It makes sense to focus even attenuated energies in protecting the fort once defenders are convinced that the terrain defined by its boundaries is worth preserving against the odds. If the seige is prolonged, and there is evidence that this will be the case for education, occasional carefully planned forays into the terrain of the philistines should be embarked upon even though the gains to be made are slight. The heartening image of "pedagogue as warrior" (Regnier, in press) may be stretching the military metaphor somewhat too far, but these images of defense represent a call for a renewed emphasis on the agency of adult educators. At a very basic level, the immediate task for adult educators of the critical persuasion entails learning how to sustain a field of practice in which critical perspectives can emerge despite on-going roll-backs in publicly funded education.

A vocational imperative for a reconstruction of modern adult education practice, while defending the institutional and community-based locations in which it is currently enacted means more work for overworked adult educators. The fact of the matter is that most adult educators who are fortunate enough to hold full-time positions have too much to do and too few resources to get things done. However, while a majority of adult educators are scrambling to fulfill the increasing bureaucratic requirements of holding down a job in an educational institution, others are not yet engaged to anywhere near what their capacities can bear.

As adult educators we are being shaped by the conditions identified in our critical theorizing. We cannot pretend to be above and beyond the fray while objectifying our practice around some reified notion of an individualized adult learner. There is a need for us to attend to our own education, especially as it pertains to pedagogical practices. In this regard we can focus more assiduously on which strategies we bring to bear in teaching our adult classes and planning our educational programs in the face of powerful interests (Forester, 1989) antithetical to what we are about. Even as "progressive" adult educators, our everyday discourses—the adumbrated forms through which we communicate with each other and our strategic actions—have to be viewed as exemplifications of an increasingly overmanaged society and of the fractured communities depicted in the critical theorizing we invoke. There is a pressing need in these times for us, as adult educators, to reflect on our role as moral and political agents and on how we are critically situated in carrying out this role. It is from this apprehension of our roles that we shall *re-present* a craft of teaching adults that does not objectify our students, ourselves, and our ways of knowing.

ANDRAGOGY AND THE PROFESSIONALIZATION TENDENCY IN THE MODERN PRACTICE OF ADULT EDUCATION

Introducing "a new label and a new approach," the publication of "Andragogy, not Pedagogy!" (Knowles, 1968) in the April 1968 issue of *Adult Leadership* marked out a clear-cut initiative to distinguish adult education from conventional schooling. The article is the script of an address given by Malcolm Knowles at an annual banquet to commemorate Delbert Clark. (Clark had been vice-president of the Fund for Adult Education provided by the Ford Foundation.) Knowles commenced: "Adult education is, I believe, on the threshold of a technological break-through" (p. 350). In highlighting the growing significance of adult education he had this to say: "Adult education is now big business. Enormous sums are being spent by the government, by educational institutions, by business and industry, and by voluntary agencies for adult education. Adult education is no longer suffering from marginality" (p. 350). At the same time, Knowles observed, adult education was "developing a new technology—methods, techniques, and characteristics of adults as learners" (p. 351). The new adult education technology, to distinguish it from the technology of pedagogy, was presented by Knowles as "andragogy." Besides serving to characterize an emerging technology, the term was elevated to a high moral plain: "Andragogy is based upon the deep insight that the deepest need an adult has is to be treated as an adult, to be treated as a self-directing person, to be treated with respect (p. 351).

Subsequently, andragogy has become the touchstone for those eager to professionalize adult education practice. While it offers important common sense advice on the need for adult educators to respect the adult status of adult learners, andragogy (the spelling changes from "androgogy" between 1968 and 1970) also provides a useful category to which the trappings of a tendency towards professionalization can be attached. In his influential text *The Modern Practice of Adult Education: Andragogy versus Pedagogy,* Malcolm Knowles (1970) explained that "some European educators have already been using the coined term 'andragogy' to describe the new technology of adult education" (p. 305). This information about the source of "andragogy," presented in an appendix, is of interest. But more significant, in terms of a quest to professionalize the field, is the connection made between andragogy and a "new technology of adult education."

Malcolm Knowles has since qualified the abrupt dichotomy established in opposing his notion of andragogy with a conventional view of pedagogy. Knowles now acknowledges that the kind of activities characterized as andragogy are, or should be, carried on within our schools. Moreover, he realizes that it would not be difficult to identify in adult education settings organized activities which could be described as pedagogical according to his 1968 article. Knowles (1975) dealt with this difficulty in a later publication:

> These definitions do not imply that children should be taught pedagogically and adults should be taught andragogically. Rather, the two terms simply differentiate between two sets of assumptions about learners, and the teacher who makes one set of assumptions will teach pedagogically whether he or she is teaching children or adults, whereas the teacher who makes the other set of assumptions will teach andragogically whether the learners are children or adults. (p. 19)

It is noteworthy that in the second edition of *The Modern Practice of Adult Education* (Knowles, 1980), the second part of the title was altered to read "From Pedagogy to Andragogy" in place of the original, "Andragogy versus Pedagogy." There is clearly something at stake in retaining andragogy as a category for defining adult education practice. Paulo Freire, who makes the actual experience of learners central to his educational project, has no difficulties in using the term 'pedagogy' to describe adult education activities. In his best known work, *Pedagogy of the Oppressed* (1974), as with his other major books (Freire, 1973, 1978, 1985), Freire calls for careful commitment on the part of the educator which eschews any prospect for a professionalizing agenda. Under andragogy, however, the individual learner as client becomes the object of an emerging field of professionalized practice.

The tendency towards professionalization, and away from the conception of adult education as a social movement exemplified in the works of Moses Coady (1939, 1971), Eduard Lindeman (1961), and Richard Tawney (1964), was already discernible by the 1950s within mainstream discourse on adult education in the United States. In particular, the work of prominent American adult education professors Cyril Houle (1956) and Coolie Verner (1964) evinced a determined effort to mark out adult education as a professionalized discipline for university study. A Canadian professor of adult education, whose published account on learner directed education (Tough, 1966) preceded that of Knowles, acknowledged the pre-eminence of Houle's contribution in the early efforts to define a distinctive discipline around the predisposition of adults to learn on their own initiative: "It was Professor C.O. Houle of the University of Chicago who first focused attention on men and women conspicuously engaged in learning. The inquiry was then taken up and developed in a variety of studies by younger colleagues (Tough, 1981, p. iv).

The case for professionalization in adult education is readily understood. It is usually argued from a standpoint that professionalization provides assurance to adult learners (increasingly referred to as "clients") about the competence of those from whom they rely on for pedagogical guidance. At the same time it is anticipated that professionalization will bring with it greater job security and a more dependable income for practitioners. The references to efficiency, expertise, and systematic organization which accompany the aspirations to professionalize evoke the conventional discourse of established professions. In this evocation, adult education professor Ronald Cervero discerns a clear-cut and irresistible trend towards professionalization which adult educators ought to accept. A somewhat more critical perspective on the issue (Collins, 1992) raises questions along moral and political lines, adding that, in any case, the professionalizing tendency has failed to provide jobs, job security, and dependable incomes for adult educators. Further, it is argued from this critical perspective that a misguided pre-occupation with professionalization has diverted adult educators from other forms of organization that could be more empowering for themselves and for their students.

A prevalent argument in favor of professionalization initiatives centers around the need for practitioners, both the professional clients adult educators serve under the rubric of continuing professional education and adult educators themselves, to keep abreast of new developments in their field. Adult educator Stanley Grabowski (1981) addresses this concern in the following terms: "The basic need for continuing education results from the danger of two kinds of obsolescence: rustiness resulting from the lack of proper use of professional knowledge and failure to keep up with new developments" (p. 85). And leading Canadian professors of adult education, Gordon Selman and Jindra Kulich (1980), are decisive in laying out what they mean by professionalization in the field: "By professionalization of the field is meant those elements which have placed emphasis on providing adult education with a sound theoretical base, have emphasized research and the application of scientific standards to methods, materials and the organization of the field and have promoted the need for professional training and staffing" (p. 109).

In light of Michael Welton's analysis in this book of system and lifeworld [see chapter 5—Ed.], drawing on the work of Jurgen Habermas, the article by Selman and Kulich ("Between Social Movement and Profession—A Historical Perspective on Canadian Adult Education") becomes particularly instructive. The authors juxtapose "professionalization" as scientific with "social movement" which, implicitly, is viewed as non-scientific. Their historical commentary on adult education practice is pervaded by a taken-for-granted acceptance of a technocratic ideology in which system imperatives must inevitably engulf lifeworld interests. Significantly absent from the non-critical perspective on professionalization taken by Selman and Kulich are prospects for *informed* resistance to a significant de-skilling of work, the undermining of competent performance (Collins, 1987), that is occuring in lifeworld contexts. Accordingly, a professionalized modern practice of adult education abandons its connections to social movements and lends its weight to the world of specialization—the system.

Although it is not entirely expressed in theoretical terms, much of the literature which critiques professionalization tendencies in adult education stems from a concern about the cult of efficiency (technical rationality) embodied in system discourse. This critical discourse reveals how an eagerness to serve the conventional professions, through the provision of continuing professional education, shapes modern adult education practice. In particular, the work of adult education critic, John Ohliger, is instructive in showing the way an obsession with technique, combined with the drive to professionalize, leads adult educators to endorse *mandatory continuing education*. The sharply crafted polemical essays, "Must We All Go Back to School?" (Lisman and Ohliger, 1978) and "Is Lifelong Education a Guarantee of Permanent Inadequacy?" (Ohliger, 1974) illuminate the stark contradictions confronting adult educators who espouse principles around the notion of independent learning while embracing the ideology of professionalization. Andragogy, shaped by system imperatives from the outset and steered by a dubious need to professionalize, leads us all back, as Ohliger (1974) demonstrates, along tracks forged by system imperatives. Accordingly, it has become all the more difficult for adult educators who do not buy into the ethos of professionalization to foster alternative discourses among institutionalized routines, the effects of which Ivan Illich (1970) has brilliantly illuminated with his schooling metaphor. In this regard, Illich's (1977) commentaries on the *Disabling Professions* and *The Expropriation of Health* are also particularly enlightening.

If the lifeworld/system differentiation Jürgen Habermas (1987b) makes is taken seriously by adult educators, it is clear that the preservation of what is vital in our everyday life, especially the capacities for self-direction, depends upon the will to defend its autonomy against further encroachments by disabling system imperatives. Such a commitment could well be supported by appropriate initiatives for the reclamation of valuable community-oriented aspects of everyday life. In this regard, the work of some environmentalist groups can be instructive to adult educators seeking to check the further erosion of what Illich (1983) defines as the "commons." Illich's apt metaphor corresponds closely to the lifeworld concept of Jürgen Habermas. The commons draws attention to those constantly threatened, yet still non-commodified, customs, practical activities, and generative locations in our every-day lives which are so essential to our well-being.

A standpoint on adult education practice that distances itself from the quest to professionalize, entails a willingness to acknowledge that emancipatory learning requires on-going struggle within institutional-ized settings and communities at large. The nature of this struggle can be partly defined in resistance to a technocratic ethos, charged by sys-tem imperatives, which is not mitigated by lifeworld interests. Occa-sions for resistance and pro-active positioning arise continuously and on a day-to-day basis. Clearly, careful strategies have to be thought through, and later assessed, about what issues to address, how and when they should be addressed, and when it is judicious to refrain from engagement.

An unwillingness to recognize the steering effects of entrepreneur-ial activity serves to mask the contradictions between what is espoused on behalf of independent learning and what is actually embraced in the name of professionalization. The professionalization tendency in adult education, with its identification of the individualized learner as object (client) for professionalized practice, glosses over the failure to deal actively with those circumstances which frustrate genuine "self-directed learning." (After all, in a genuinely democratic society could there be any other kind?)

SELF-DIRECTED LEARNING:
ANDRAGOGY'S LINCH-PIN

Self-directed learning has attached itself to the masthead of modern adult education practice. Modern adult education practice, in this con-text, is characterized by the largely professionalizing discourse that draws much of its legitimation from university-based graduate pro-grams in adult and continuing education. Though modern adult educa-tion remains under-resourced and experiences unrelenting cut-backs in funds, adult educators mislead themselves when they buy into the notion that their field is still a marginalized activity. Malcolm Knowles (1968) is right on the mark in this regard. Adult education is now typi-cally viewed by policy makers as having a part to play in economic development. In recent decades adult education has been increasingly associated with social control policies such as training and welfare reform initiatives, and correctional education. Business and professional interests often invoke adult education as a means to increase efficiency and profitability, while many community groups look to adult education's potential as a vehicle for social reform. Decked with slogans such as "lifelong learning," "continuing education," "competency-based instruction," and "human resource development," modern adult education has sailed in from the margins and rides uneasily on a shifting anchor.

Still out on the horizon is an alternative discourse on adult education which is driven by marginalized moral and political commitments. These commitments, exemplified in the works of Paulo Freire (1973, 1974, 1978, 1985), aspire to *re-make* adult education as part of the social change process itself. Accordingly, they cannot be realistically incorporated within a conformist professionalizing discourse. The progressive tack modern adult education practice occasionally takes from its conventional moorings steers it well clear of risky pedagogical currents which challenge status quo arrangements. Unhappily, these arrangements serve interests which may or may not be bothered to keep the ship afloat when the going gets rough. The level of support for adult education envisaged by Knowles (1968) has not materialized, and during the early years of the 1990s the situation is becoming rougher even for an enterprise that is not overly venturesome.

Functioning as andragogy's primary methodological device to distinguish adult education from conventional schooling, self-directed learning holds together a notion that has been studiously developed into a complex structure. The methodological basis of the distinction between andragogy and conventional schooling practices resides in the fact that with self-directed learning the needs and activities of the learner assume greater significance, and are subject to closer scrutiny, than those of the teacher. The teacher becomes a mere *facilitator* of the learning process. There is no mystery, then, to self-directed learning. At a common-sense level, it is an acknowledgment that adults can learn (of course), and that they can learn, or learn better, without undue pressure from directive pedagogues. In this regard, self-directed learning refers to educational contexts where the experience of adult learners, their relevant ways of knowing (cognitive styles) and their interest in undertaking relevant learning projects on their own initiative are taken into account. Many elementary and secondary school teachers, even a few with classroom management-disciplinary control-forever on their minds, would no doubt be pleased to learn that an approach they endeavor to incorporate into their classroom is the sterling feature of modern adult education practice. By the same token, they could well be puzzled at the high degree of importance that has been attributed to self-directed learning in its function as a method which distinguishes modern adult education practice from conventional schooling.

Undoubtedly, self-directed learning lends credence to educational practices which are less prescriptive than those still experienced in many school classrooms and some adult education settings. Among the many influential commentators on self-directed learning, Bill Draves (1980) expresses his high regard for the concept in the following terms: "Self-directed learning begins with the learner. It sees the learner as the primary impetus for and the initiator of the learning process. Teachers, classes, and other educational features are put in a secondary light, as aids to the learning process rather than its central elements" (p. 191).

In recent years self-directed learning has exerted its influence on a wide range of adult education settings within modern adult education practice. As an authoritative pedagogical technique it provides legitimation for adult basic education, continuing professional education, the preparation of nurses and medical doctors, and even Ph.D. students. Usually, the approach adopted entails the negotiation of a formalized learning contract whereby a student (client) identifies a learning project and specifies learning objectives, learning resources, and evidence of accomplishment (Knowles, 1980, 1986). In determining criteria for formal evaluation, the student as client is often invited to negotiate, well in advance, the level of grade to be assigned in return for work accomplished. Under these circumstances, the adult educator assumes a professional role in mediating institutional interests with a student client's expectations of what the institution will provide. The educational experience is nicely commodified. There is even an instrument on the market—a learning readiness scale—that will measure to what extent an adult is ready for self-directed learning (Guglielmino, 1982). It is not difficult to understand how, within the discourse on andragogy, the role of the adult educator has been transformed from that of teacher to *facilitator* or *broker*. In *facilitating* the pedagogical process through contractual terms, adult educator as facilitator or broker treats the student, albeit with respect, as the consumer. The felt (consumer) needs of learner as client (customer) are systematically addressed and, with the nature of the exchange relationship thus defined, commodification of the educational encounter is substantially achieved.

Within the self-directed learning motif, adult learners experience the same kind of freedom they enjoy in shopping malls. This market-place analogy is indicative of how self-directed learning appeals to business management interests, professional organizations, and large-scale institutions. Individuals are viewed as attending to their own choices via formal learning contracts within an overall context determined by institutional interests. As well as being prospective customers for educational services, adult learners are designated as *human resources*. This objectifying move from one of *relating to* human beings to *dealing with* human resources is revealing. While holding together a scenario of adult men and women autonomously shaping their own educational experiences, self-directed learning effectively delivers their learning to experts who serve predominantly institutionalized interests.

Ironically, these experts of modern adult education practice (human resource developers), despite aspirations towards professionalization, become increasingly de-skilled as they surrender their agency as teacher for the less pro-active role as broker of commodified educational services. At the same time, the privatizing effects of self-directed learning on individual learners, and the instrumental rationality on which it is forged, have set a course for the further development of pre-packaged learning formats. The growing tendency towards standardizing pre-packaged curriculum development for adults draws legitimacy from the andragogical consensus and, thus reinforced, adopts the popular labels of the self-directed learning discourse—"individualized," "learner-centered," and "self-paced."

CORPORATE PEDAGOGY: COMPETENCY-BASED EDUCATION AND HUMAN RESOURCE DEVELOPMENT

While self-directed learning has been viewed as the guiding "conceptual and methodological orientation" of andragogy (Brookfield, 1986), the capacities for technocratic and individualizing curriculum development it contains are exemplified in competency-based adult education (CBAE). The competency-based education (CBE) model is virtually paradigmatic of contemporary functionalist approaches to curriculum design and educational policy implementation.

The widespread adaptation of CBE from its origins in U.S. public school system to the modern practice of adult education would seem to belie the distinction which many adult educators have sought to establish between their work and that of school teachers. A critical account of CBE's modularized and narrowly prescriptive approach to curriculum design and program development in adult education has been undertaken elsewhere (Collins, 1987). From a critical perspective, the highly reductionistic intent of CBAE curriculum formats serves to de-skill the role of the adult educator while focusing on the guided responses of the individual adult learner. Competency-based packaging lends itself very effectively to computer programming, a circumstance which escalates the demotion of the teacher's role to that of facilitator or learning resource manager.

The CBE model is a fairly recent manifestation of the behaviorist influence on curriculum design and evaluation. Instead of behavioral objectives, CBE pundits now refer to competency statements as the basic measurable component of their curriculum format. The epistemological assumption here is that a correct reiteration of the behavior in each component confirms acquisition of the necessary degree of competence. Dr. Spady, a leading exponent of the CBE model a few years ago, is now leading the charge on the latest development in the behaviorist agenda for curriculum design—outcomes-based education (OBE). From either a technical or educational standpoint OBE is scarcely a variation on CBE, but OBE has been harnessed to a discourse on what the educational system must be to prevent the nation failing to keep up in an increasingly competitive global marketplace. Tough times for teachers worldwide, while the gurus of standardized curriculum packaging have a ball promoting their wares on an international scale. Meanwhile, after the two decades or more since it was first introduced to publicly funded school systems and adult education in the United States, CBE has yet to match claims of its proponents that their curriculum model is *causally* connected to the actual achievement of competent performance. CBE has been deployed within many adult education settings including professional education (for example, the health services field), university undergraduate and graduate programs, and technical-vocational education. The CBE approach is altogether pervasive and has been adopted in a number of countries—mainly, though, in the United States, Canada, the United Kingdom, and Australia.

CBE curriculum has a certain appeal because it keeps the learner busily engaged responding to multiple-choice questions and other "fill-in-the-blank" formats. In this regard, CBE diverts learners away from careful reflection on their work. They are immersed, instead, in a busyness syndrome (Collins, 1987, p. 3) which saps energy while allowing for pedestrian, frequently achieved, minor satisfactions. The widespread deployment of CBE attests to the enduring influence of Taylorism on educational curriculum and program development. Following a behavioristic rationale, educational policy-makers and administrators during the 1920s were attracted to Frederick Taylor's formulations for breaking down work in factories and offices into standardized, measurable units. Taylor's notion of task analysis, reducing work on the factory floor and in offices to a series of repetitive mechanical operations, was promoted within the context of a growing preoccupation with efficiency. This cult of efficiency, epitomized by the shop-floor production-line and invoking Taylor's notion of scientific management, provided impetus to the aspirations of experts in education who were seeking to rationalize curriculum and the day-to-day administration of schools. Competency-based education and, even more recently, outcomes-based education, belongs to a continuing legacy of technocratic deployments within the sphere of public education.

Technical rationality, exemplified in the jargon of scientific management and legitimized in the discourse on CBE, also provides a justification for impoverishing the work of educators (Jackson, 1989). CBE curriculum effects a restructuring of the educational process, reducing it to a series of simplistic tasks virtually denuded of any creative impulse. Through the medium of the curriculum, and according to the logic of Taylorism, the educator is progressively de-skilled, becoming more readily replaceable. At the same time, the learner is imbued with narrow expectations about education, and about the world of work, which stem from the ideology of technique underlying CBE. Thus CBEs technocratic curriculum designs play a significant role in the construction of social control mechanisms (adult education tied to welfare initiatives, for example). The CBE approach lends itself to the development of a flexible surplus labor force with reduced expectations about the quality of work available to it. In this regard, the research project of Harry Braverman (1974) on de-skilling, and its consequences for ordinary men and women, remains an important source of analysis in making the connection between curriculum design and the world of work.

From a critical perspective informed by an understanding of how system world imperatives determine priorities in a modern political economy, it is hardly surprising that the CBE model can withstand any epistemological analysis of its shortcomings. An exposition of the excessive reductionism inherent in CBE, the prescriptive strategies entailed in its deployment, and its failure to establish a proven connection with the actual achievement of competent performance, has not been sufficient to check its impetus.

Where implementation of the model has been dictated through educational policy initiatives, CBE demonstrates its effectiveness in marginalizing, or rejecting, educators who want to contest its presuppositions. After all, it is difficult to argue against the prescriptive techniques of curriculum experts who have attached their model to the notion of competence. And the approach does lend itself readily to self-directed learning. CBE is individualized and allows for self-pacing. Yet the self-directedness is confined within very restricted, and *restricting*, parameters. Via CBE—and variations on the theme—andragogy has returned the adult educator and the adult learner to the conventional schoolhouse—to the most pedestrian forms of authoritarian pedagogical practice. In response to the question posed by Lisman and Ohliger (1978), "Must We All Go Back to School?," critical commentators might well respond, in the same vein, "Are we ever allowed to leave?" There is a discernible tendency in curriculum formats such as CBE, and pedagogical strategies along the lines of self-directed learning, which effectively induce self-discipline and self-surveillance in accordance with institutionalized (vested) interests. Who is determining what constitutes competence on behalf of ordinary men and women? What interests shape the modern practice of adult education?

While competency-based adult education conceptualizes learning needs in line with what its designers perceive to be the interests of business and industry, this Taylorist curriculum model is still largely, though not entirely, associated with publicly funded educational institutions. Within business and industry, and organizational settings other than education, education and training is being constituted under the bailiwick of human resource development. HRD can include any number of curriculum strategies, including CBE. As a relatively new category HRD incorporates both education and training, and personnel management. Though more all-encompassing than the CBE model, HRD is guided by the same ideology of technique, combined with an emphasis on individualisic and individualizing behavior, which shapes CBE. Where HRD is deployed to support popular notions emerging from business and industry—notions such as "team management," "partnerships," and "quality circles"—its primary purpose is consensus formation around agendas clearly understood by the chief executive officers (CEOs). Consequently, strategies that emerge from the process tend to confirm predetermined institutional interests. HRD is a workplace pedagogy in the service of the CEOs.

In describing how HRD has evolved from training and development Leonard Nadler (1980), a prominent professor of adult education in the United States, aligned the concept with modern adult education practice in a chapter entitled "What is Human Resource Development?": "HRD is concerned with providing learning experiences for people" (p. 2). And in his essay on "The Field of Human Resource Development," Nadler added this definition: "Human resource development is the career within an organization that focuses on changing and improving the capacities of human beings to contribute to the success of the organization" (p. 1). Nadler is unequivocal in describing HRD as "a management tool." Subsequent accounts of HRD by academic adult educators offer a somewhat broader definition (Watkins, 1990) than Nadler. However, it remains clear that the discourse of HRD within adult education is advanced from employer and management orientations. When HRD is taken up in trade unions, it is bureaucratic interests which define worker education. In arguing for an alternative perspective to that offered by HRD, Mechthild Hart (1992 [see chapter 4 below—Ed.]) reveals how important the workplace still is for an adult education practice committed to the interests of working men and women rather than to those of the CEOs. Her critical analysis around the distinction between commodity and subsistence production, the difference between careers and jobs, the internationalization of labor, and the exploitation of women's work envisages prospects for adult education to reconnect more relevantly with the world of work in general as well as with the conventional industrial workplaces.

In the meantime, with the alignment of HRD and the corporate ethos and modern adult education practice, adult education abandons all confidence in the collective capacity of ordinary men and women *to organize* industrial production, distribution, and the delivery of services. It fails to engage with the moral-political problem of what gets in the way of ordinary men and women realizing the potential which resides in the collective *competence which they already possess*. Hence the anomaly, within modern adult education, of *directed* self-directed learning.

If these claims appear overly-determined, it should be borne in mind that the adoption of prescriptive, industry-driven curriculum such as HRD, and the HRD phenomenon itself, have not reduced employers' complaints about the inadequate education of the work force. More to the point, the curriculum initiatives and corporate ideology with which modern adult education practice now identifies have emerged alongside reduction in profits, de-skilling of labor, and the loss of jobs on a massive scale. At the same time, the enthusiastic adoption of a business corporate ethos and aspirations toward professionalization have not yielded secure job prospects for adult educators themselves. There may now be nothing to lose for adult education in repositioning itself within the workplace along interests which differ from those of the CEO. Andragogy notwithstanding, and in the light of HRD, ordinary men and women are still being educated on behalf of their rulers.

MEANING IN CONTEXT AND THE CRITICAL TURN

In recent years discernible, though far from decisive, concerns about the shortcomings of its functionalist orientation have been emerging within modern adult education. These concerns have manifested themselves at a theoretical level in the form of interpretive studies (phenomenological investigations and hermeneutics) and critical theory. In particular, feminist writing has served to highlight the extent to which modern adult education practice helps sustain prevailing hegemonic social arrangements. At the very least, the slight move away from technocratic approaches to adult education research and practice has cleared the way for more thoughtful reflection on the meaning of adult education. In this regard the following observations by Stephen Brookfield (1985), a leading commentator on adult learning from within the andragogical paradigm, are instructive:

> The task of the educator becomes that of encouraging adults to perceive the relative, contextual nature of previously unquestioned givens. Additionally, the educator should assist the adult to reflect on the manner in which values, beliefs and behaviors previously deemed unchallengeable can be critically analyzed. Through presenting alternative ways of interpreting and creating a world to adults, the educator fosters a willingness to consider alternative ways of living. (p. 284)

The adult educator is, in effect, being asked to put aside the certainties of functionalist curriculum and programmatic blue-prints. The alternative, however, is far more demanding. It calls for the creation of learning strategies which are *contextually relevant* (Collins, 1987). There is transformative potential for the individual adult learner and a significant mediating role for the educator in the renewed emphasis on critical reflection which Brookfield's work evokes.

The slight turn to critical social theory and postmodernist thought in modern adult education practice, together with feminist discourses which draw pragmatically on numerous theoretical perspectives, have been helpful in illuminating how prevalent social structures, vested interests, and hegemonic practices impede the most adept facilitator of adult learning. In terms of the sharper perspective on practice defined by the critical turn it becomes incumbent on adult educators, as "reflective practitioners," to address these systematic impediments to transformative learning. This vocational obligation entails, at the very least, a frank acknowledgment of the contradictions between what is espoused and what is actually put into practice. Yet critical adult education, even as it has emerged within the andragogical consensus, implies that ethical and political choices have to be made by adult educators about whose interests they should serve. As the choices are made, the contradictions become even more apparent and have to be addressed. Herein lies an important difference between critical thinking informed by an individualistic humanistic psychology (Rogers, 1969) and educational practice which draws on critical theory. From a critical theory perspective, the "freedom to learn" Carl Rogers so treasured can only be realized for ordinary men and women through counter-hegemonic pedagogical strategies.

The critical turn in modern adult education practice is largely inspired by Frankfurt School critical theory. In particular, the research project of Jürgen Habermas, the Frankfurt School's leading contemporary exponent, featured prominently in the development of critical adult education [see chapter 1 for a detailed explication of this theme—Ed.]. The critical insights of the Frankfurt School's founding figures, Max Horkheimer and Theodor Adorno, led them to give up on any prospect that an autonomous collective emancipatory force (that is, the working class) could emerge to transform industrialized society. Though they subsequently supported their assessment with empirical studies and careful theoretical work (Adorno et al., 1950), the founding figures of the Frankfurt School are viewed from a classical Marxist standpoint, as having failed to understand the nature and transformative potential of working-class interests and of giving in to bourgeois intellectual despair. Nevertheless, the theoretical work of early Frankfurt School critical theory has demonstrated that denial of reason lies at the core of technical rationality (Horkheimer, 1947). Critical theory in this vein provides important insights into the way conditions under modern capitalism—that is, under both corporate capitalism and the state bureaucratic capitalist formations under socialism as it has already been experienced—distort learning processes (human experience) in all aspects of everyday life.

Without rejecting the relevance of work in psychology—Eric Fromm and Herbert Marcuse were both important figures in the Frankfurt School tradition and *The Authoritarian Personality* (Adorno et al., 1950) is a major psychological study—Frankfurt School critical theory makes it eminently clear that more attention should be paid to political, economic, cultural, historical, and social factors which combine to shape the contexts in which adult educators practice their vocation. It is to the work of Jürgen Habermas largely contained in the two volumes describing his theory of communicative action (1984, 1987b), that adult educators can look for the basis of a substantive learning theory. In his theory of communicative action, Habermas provides an emancipatory transformative potential by positing the capacity for speech communication as the ontological distinguishing characteristic of what it is to be human. Thus, the reasons and potentiality for genuinely democratic decision-making and, hence, an emancipatory pedagogy are to be found within speech communication. Giving ontological priority to spoken communication sets Habermas off on a different tack from Marx. Hence, while retrieving for critical theory a concern for establishing rationality as the basis for explaining and guiding human action, Habermas, like his Frankfurt School predecessors, is able to relegate the significance of class analysis.

It is around a theory of communicative action, then, that Habermas' work informs the emerging critical discourse within the modern practice of adult education. The explanatory force of Habermas' research project is impressive. And it can be comforting for a socialism of the academe since an expression of solidarity with working-class struggle need not be invoked. Rather, from the Habermasian project can be derived an explanation of how coercive aspects of modern life prevent people from coming to *reasonably* agreed upon "understandings in common" of what is at stake in making decisions about how we should be and act in the world. Hence modern life is viewed as being largely shaped by the imperatives of strategic action stemming from a technical rational which runs counter to the practical and emancipatory interests of ordinary men and women. Further, the work of Jürgen Habermas reinforces that of his Frankfurt School predecessors in showing how acquiescence to the deployment of manipulative, coercive strategies is obtained at the expense of an enlargement in emancipatory potential and genuinely transformative learning.

Yet the notion that the human capacity for speech signifies an innate potentiality for making practical decisions around reasonably presented arguments, free of coercion, provides a hopeful scenario for an emancipatory practice of adult education. There are, undoubtedly, limits to the usefulness for adult education practice in the abstract formulations constructed around an "ideal speech situation" and "communicative competence." Nevertheless, in holding out the possibility that initiatives to realize non-distorted communication within the learning processes foster emancipatory interests, Habermasian critical theory adds credence to counter-hegemonic discourse.

As already noted, the recent critical turn in modern adult education practice has not been entirely driven by Frankfurt School, or Habermasian critical theory. Some impetus comes from postmodernist thought which has been effectively incorporated into feminist critique of the way patriarchal arrangements structure the discipline of modern adult education practice and determine its content. From this critical purview, andragogy is far from being *androgynous*. The brilliant insights of Michael Foucault, in particular, can be instructive in revealing how pedagogical strategies such as CBE, HRD, and self-directed learning sustain existing relationships of power and systems of surveillance (Collins, 1988b). Although any reference to its roots or founding sources is hardly in accord with a *deconstructionist* tendency, contemporary postmodern discourse can be traced to the philosophy of Friedrich Nietzsche. Hence, an emphasis on power relationships, and on the will to power as a primary motivating force within both the individual and society.

Following the example of postmodernist trends in literary criticism which challenge the authority of canonical texts and conventional rules as a basis for critical assessment, this tendency in education deploys deconstructionist analysis to unsettle all allegedly authoritative criteria for guiding how we should understand, and act in, the world. Simply stated, postmodernist sensibilities in adult education signify the potential force that resides in many points of view and many different views. Hence, within the critical discourse of modern adult education practice, postmodernist thought has been drawn on to support the empowerment of "other voices"—of the relatively silent minorities and the under-represented—in their struggle to be heard. The strategic intent (though a postmodernist sensibility would be evasive about intent) is to destabilize the dominant discourse of status quo interests, creating possibilities for disempowered groups and individuals in society to assert themselves.

It should be understood that the postmodernist tendency differs from any critical theory which still holds to the view that human beings have the capacities to identify rational criteria for how we should be and should act in the world. For critical theory it still makes sense to engage in discourse about marking out directions for future development. Postmodernist sensibilities scorn the quest to identify the *rational grounds* from which "the just society" can be conceived and constructed. Such a quest is viewed as a *totalizing* project, an expression of a dubious yearning for certainty and authority.

Nevertheless, there are some interesting academically oriented initiatives under way to effect a rapprochement between critical theory and postmodernist thought. Significant developments along these lines for adult educators can be discerned in the "Birmingham School" genre of cultural studies. Cultural studies at Birmingham is traceable to the founding work of British adult educators, Richard Hoggart and Raymond Williams. In recent years cultural studies inspired by the "Birmingham School" has been influenced by a combination of postmodernist thought and the Marxism of Antonio Gramsci (Johnson, 1983). For critical adult education, perhaps the juncture between postmodernist thought and critical theory is most usefully effected around a concern for both ethical and political commitments, leaving aside any preoccupation with resolving ontological differences.

ROLE OF THE ADULT EDUCATOR IN TODAY'S SOCIETY

In May 1968 the student uprising in Paris almost toppled the government of General De Gaulle. And it was in "the Prague Spring of 1968" that peaceful demonstrations for a more democratic way of life in Czechoslovakia coalesced, bringing to a head the popular resistance movement that was to be ruthlessly suppressed by the Russian army. These events marked the high tide in an era of popular movements and organized protest when large groups of people, and not only from the younger generation, had a strong sense that they could change the way things are. And for the better. The year 1968 also marked the emergence of andragogy as a "new label and a new approach" for adult education practice. It would be wrong to suggest that a concern for vital social issues of the time disappeared from the discourse of mainstream adult education with the arrival of andragogy. By 1968 the notion of adult education as a major social movement was already significantly absent from mainstream literature. (It had little to say about the war in Vietnam, the movement for civil rights, and student unrest.) Since that time the professionalizing discourse of modern adult education practice, while acknowledging the persistence of progressive and radical alternatives, has tended to avoid engagement with major political issues of the time. In his thought-provoking essay, "'Vivisecting the Nightingale': Reflections on Adult Education as an Object of Study," Michael Welton (1987) graphically describes how the professionalizing tendency "neglects social, cultural and political dimensions of adult education" (p. 54). With the emergence of a more critical discourse, the question is whether modern adult education practice can make up, in these times, for the flawed professionalization agenda and capture a sense of relevance that resides in the notion of adult education as a social movement with an emancipatory intent.

A quarter of a century after Malcolm Knowles' introductory essay on "Andragogy, not Pedagogy," Stephen Brookfield (1993) has published an article remaking the case for self-directed learning and linking it to the critical practice of adult education. Brookfield's arguments are carefully presented. They convey a thorough grasp of the extensive body of work written about self-directed learning and a keen appreciation for the critical commentaries which question the esconcement of this pedagogical notion within mainstream adult education practice. Briefly stated, Brookfield argues for the reconceptualization of self-directed learning in a way that takes into account political considerations and the relevance of social contexts. While recognizing the validity of their analytical insights, Brookfield suggests that critical theorists within adult education (Collins, 1985, 1988b, 1991; Griffin, 1983, 1987; Little, 1991) are remiss in failing to recognize the empowering potentiality of self-directed learning. He offers some interesting examples of how a pedagogical discourse, ostensibly empowering for the individual learner, can be mustered around the notion of self-directed learning. The examples highlight a far more reflective practice, incorporating a greater awareness of social contexts and political contingencies, than is evident in the typical texts on self-directed learning.

The problem for the critical practice of adult education is not with the notion of self-directed learning (from a critical perspective, should there be any other kind?), which is relevant to the development of children as well as adults. Rather, the critique stems from the way self-directed learning is reified in support of professionalizing aspirations within modern adult education practice. Careful reflection on relevant political issues within the context of modern adult education practice can occur without making self-directed learning into a commodity. It is the commodification of adult education (Briton and Plumb, 1993), and the part played by the discourse on self-directed learning, that is of concern to a critical practice of adult education.

There is much more of consequence for critical adult education in Brookfield's essay that must be addressed more fully elsewhere. For example, the suggestion that a sensible rapprochement can exist between critical theory and American pragmatism without the former relinquishing its essential critical edge merits further examination. Undoubtedly, a way back to looking at learning again from a critical perspective that eschews both the functionalism and individualizing tendencies of the self-directed learning construct can be made via the work of such outstanding pragmatist philosophers of education as John Dewey and William James. To an extent, it is this way back to looking at learning again that the on-going research project of Jack Mezirow (1991) has held open for an adult education practice still preoccupied with methodizing its mediation in adult learning processes.

Given the immediate challenges confronting adult education and the critical shortcomings of the andragogical model, there is a pressing need to refocus on the role of the adult educator prior to looking at learning again. This re-emphasis does not, of course, imply any neglect for adult learners' interests, which can be relevantly conceived from a critical perspective more along the lines described in the work of Sullivan (1990), Lave and Wenger (1993), and Vygotski (1978). Rather, a relevant shift in emphasis calls for more careful attention to the commitments and activities of the adult educator. With the unravelling of the andragogical consensus and its pedagogical trappings, such as self-directed learning, a primary task within the modern practice is for adult educators to educate ourselves.

A renewed emphasis on the agency of the adult educator also calls for the *courage to teach* (Palmer, 1991). To what extent this commitment to teaching has been undermined in the wake of the self-directed learning phenomenon is open to question. However, the role of the teacher, and by the same token that of adult educator, carries with it a moral force and a sense of engagement lacking in the concept of "facilitator." The term "facilitator," which emerged under andragogy alongside self-directed learning, belongs more to the argot of management than to a discourse on education. In quoting Myles Horton verbatim, Brookfield (1993) makes it clear that for the celebrated founder of Highlander Folk School "facilitator" is, at best, a weasel definition: "There's no such thing as just being a coordinator or facilitator, as if you don't know anything. What the hell are you around for, if you don't know anything. Just get out of the way and let somebody have the space that knows something, believes something" (p. 233). Yet a primary aim of the Highlander Research and Educational Center has always been to enhance the decision-making capacities of adult students. The commitment to emancipatory educational practice at Highlander has thrived without recourse to the andragogical model, the method of self-directed learning, and the relegation of adult educator as teacher of adults to a diminished role implicit in the notion of a "facilitator."

While a renewed and sharper focus on the role of the adult educator cannot be sensibly achieved at the expense of a continuing concern for adult learning, it is around the agency of the adult educator that a case for adult education as a distinctive field of practice can be advanced. In this regard, the preparation of adult educators becomes relevant. From the perspective of a critical pedagogy, the task can be viewed as one of identifying contexts appropriate for the development of adult educators as teachers and intellectuals. Any notion that the preparation of adult educators should be confined to one institutional context is undoubtedly antithetical to what critical adult education is about. At the same time, and from a critical perspective, it can be argued that it is still important to preserve a place within the academy for the preparation of adult educators in conjunction with studies in the theory and practice of adult education. Where it does not succumb completely to a professionalizing ethos, the preservation of adult education as a distinctive area of study in a university setting almost inevitably entails on-going struggle for survival. It is in the context of this struggle, in the creation of sites for careful reflection and collective (non-idiosyncratic) action, that a clearer understanding of the educator's role in today's society can be realized.

Given the individualizing culture of academia, and its careless tolerance for idiosyncratic behavior which undermines prospects for collective work, it would be a mistake for an emerging critical theory and practice of adult education to stake all on establishing a vantage point within the university setting. The fostering of a critical practice within such a milieu depends upon the development of a capacity for solidarity around relevantly determined issues. There are good reasons for making sensible efforts to identify a legitimate location for a critical practice of adult education within the university. Apart from providing access to an important source of knowledge production and legitimation, academic adult education programs constitute a meeting place for interdisciplinary discourse. In adult education academics and students from various conventional disciplines encounter an intellectual environment where they can give freer rein to the expression of their ideas and commitments. The extent to which engagement in cross-disciplinary discourse contributes to the development of adult educators in the academy has yet to be explored, but the tendency is undoubtedly significant in creating a forum for the emergence of a theory and practice of adult education.

The prestige of the university and that of academics is declining. Yet, despite the loss in status and the deleterious effects of relentless financial cut-backs on academic standards, access to universities is still an important concern especially in regard to the interests of people from social backgrounds where university education is a rare experience. Adult education operating within the academy is strategically well placed to advocate improved access for such people. In times of severe budget restrictions which too often translate into claw-backs of progressive gains made in the past, advocacy around the issue of wider access is far from inconsequential.

Adult education in the academy is undoubtedly a most likely source from which to begin looking at learning again from a critical perspective, along with careful reflection on the role of the adult educator in today's society. In this regard, it is significant that in a recent review essay, "From Freire to Feminism: The North American Experience with Critical Pedagogy" (Cunningham, 1992) which appeared in the leading academic journal *Adult Education Quarterly*, the selections were written, for the most part, by academics. However, from a critical perspective, which distances itself from the agenda of professionalizing discourses within universities, locations beyond the academy assume considerable significance in the preparation of adult educators and in marking out relevant directions for future development. This circumstance in itself highlights prospects for critical adult education to effect a conjunction of knowledge production in the academy with popular education and progressive community-based initiatives. Thus, university-based adult education is in a position to play a role in diminishing the universities' monopoly on certain forms of knowledge, directing some of this knowledge away from conventional corporate, and bureaucratically sanctioned destinations. Such a role, however, runs counter to the professionalizing aspirations of modern adult education practice. From a critical perspective, herein lies the moral and political dilemma for graduate programs in adult education.

The recent critical turn, which poses a significant challenge to foundational ideas about the theory and practice of modern adult education (Welton, 1991c), has been largely initiated within an academic milieu. It is to critical adult education in the academy, then, that the immediate challenge concerning the agency of adult educators presents itself:

Now that we know, what must we do?

The question is not a demand for immediate solutions (we have been that route before), but it cannot be sensibly evaded.

4

Motherwork: A Radical Proposal to Rethink Work and Education

Mechthild Hart

During the last decade we have heard a great deal about sweeping changes, revolutionary transformations, and fundamental restructurings in the world of work, and in the way we organize or think about work. Writers from different fields have addressed many different aspects of this issue, ranging from a discussion of changes in the nature of work or people's attitudes toward work in a "postindustrial" service society, descriptions and prognoses of demographic changes in the labor force, to analyses of how new technology requires fundamentally new or different kinds of work-related knowledge and skills. Within the field of adult education, two main responses to this situation have emerged. One, following a more optimistic line of reasoning, sees many new possibilities for combining work and learning as coming out of these changes, with technology playing an important catalytic role (Welton, 1991a, and to some extent Marsick, 1987, and Watkins and Marsick, 1993). The other approach focuses on the (current and projected) demographic changes of the labor force, particularly with respect to sex, race, ethnicity, and nationality, and how these changes pose a problem for employers as they represent a "startling demographic reality" (Carnevale et al., 1988, p. ii). A "widening skills gap" is deplored as "emerging between the relatively low education and skills of workers entering the labor force, many of whom are disadvantaged, and the advancing skill requirements of the new economy" (Chynoweth, 1989, p. 2).

In line with the overall preponderance of the "learning for earning" (Cunningham, 1992) approach to work-related issues, it is this aspect which seems to dominate the popular, practice-oriented discourse in adult education. This is not surprising since it fully accords with the predominant ideology of what constitutes the norm of economic progress and development: reconstructing a diminishing competitiveness in the world market. We are also dealing with a context of rising temporary and part-time forms of employment as well as unemployment, with issues of environmental degradation and destruction (see recent debates concerning NAFTA), and of an increase in scope as well as social acceptability of different forms of violence—all of which are pushing themselves into the horizon of public awareness. Seen within this deteriorating material and cultural context, to speak of training adults to acquire skills for jobs that either give them a wage (no matter how small), that help them to move up in the ladder of economic mobility, and that introduce them to ways of dealing with diversity, a more participatory form of management, and forms of work entirely dependent on new technology—all these suggestions seem to receive a special legitimacy from the general "learning for earning" vision.

As the examples given above show, a new language and new concerns are evolving in both general and adult education approaches to work-related issues. These ideas make the following questions seem rather appropriate. Has not the old Taylorist approach to work finally been replaced by a more democratic, cooperative form of management (never mind the tremendous loss of middle management positions)? Are not managers (and workers) now really trying to deal effectively with a multicultural, diverse work force (never mind the constant major layoffs and a generally high job instability)? Have not obsolete work-related skills that got workers in touch with the dust, grime, and sweat of the tangible underside of production been replaced by the wonderful sterility of gleaming computers (never mind that there are still dirty diapers to change)? When one moves within the realm of such a hopeful, if not progressive way of dealing with current problems and crises, a radical critique of underlying assumptions appears unrealistic, to say the least. And any fundamental criticism of not only the human capital approach to work and education but also of the generally accepted notions and definitions of work is inevitably stigmatized as too polemic or radical. This criticism is put in the box filled with the ideas of other marginal thinkers and practitioners who are clearly indebted to leftist, feminist, anti-racist, anti-imperialist, and ecological thoughts and actions (for an excellent critique of the co-optation of "liberal" adult education ideas by the New Right, see Dykstra, 1993). However, people placed in this ideological box are engaged in a vital discussion about truly alternative forms of life, work, and, by implication, education.

It is the hierarchy of values underlying the dominant concept of work I have been analyzing elsewhere (1992, 1993), an analysis which I want to continue in this chapter. I want to select the aspect of motherwork for my critique of some of the main problems with a (still predominantly) Western, Eurocentric, and masculinist framework which is rooted in fundamental conceptual dualisms. Such a binary frame opposes "family" and "work," "the private" and "the public," "productive" and "reproductive" labor (among many other things). My critique expands the foundation of an alternative concept of work, where the involvement in body and mind, in nature and culture, is seen as creating and nourishing life. From this perspective, work is a basic issue, not only in terms of survival but also in terms of representing a particularly dense web of cultural notions of competence, ability, skills, knowledge, and ways of knowing or coming to know, all of which are essential concepts within education. It is a web that can be unravelled into all its many strands of oppression, division, exploitation, degradation and destruction, *and* into a however muted alternative economic, cultural, and ecological orientation.

My analysis will move through several steps. I will first highlight the ideological assumptions underlying a predominant notion of work-related knowledge and skills, especially how they affect women's work (as wage earners or caretakers of children). I will then try to develop an alternative concept of work, and end by pointing to issues relevant for expanding our critical perspectives on adult education.

THE DOMINANT DISCOURSE ON WORK:
SILENCES AND ABSENCES

The debate centering on the changing composition of the work force has two main, mutually dependent features. First, in human capital discourse, numbers and figures abound, growing like cacti in an analytically bleak landscape. This is true particularly in its watered-down, abbreviated versions which we find sprinkled throughout various adult education and training publications, where a lack of analysis is made up for by the evocative power of a formula that seems to have become commonplace: the future of the American work force is in jeopardy because of the large influx of "women, minorities, and immigrants." This demographic change seems to leave no room for optimism—the second main feature of this debate. A "new majority" of workers is seen as ushering in a severe "human capital crisis" and even "looming disasters," all part of the overall BIG crisis of America losing its number one place in the war of international economic competition (see, for instance, Carnevale et al., 1988; Dole, 1989; Lee, 1988; Perelman, 1984). There is a certain seductive ease with which such a strong link is established between a new majority of "women, minorities, and immigrants" and looming human capital disasters. Such ease is part of an argument that seems to glide happily down the well-worn tracks of ideological assumptions about these groups, greased by the many real fears and worries people have about their jobs in a general climate of insecurity, instability, unemployment, and poverty.

The argument is usually laid out by citing statistics about widespread functional illiteracy. These statistics vary according to definitions, and the numbers become larger the more literacy is defined in reference to specific jobs or job skill requirements (Chynoweth, 1989; for a critique of conventional approaches to the problem of illiteracy, see references in Kazemak's 1990 essay; see also Merrifield and Bingman, 1993; Quigley and Holsinger, 1993; Ziegahn, 1992). Frequently, numbers about illiteracy are directly juxtaposed to prognoses about future higher skill requirements due to the introduction of new technology into many, if not most, workplaces (for a more detailed discussion of this idea, see Hart, 1992, 1993; Watkins, 1986). Such argumentation is flawed because "the labor force" remains a mythical construct if not accompanied by an analysis of its profoundly segregated nature. It is not as if a large number of illiterate workers simply confront a large number of jobs with skill demands beyond their ability. We have an elaborate system of cultural assumptions about who is fit to do what kind of work. These assumptions are often only indirectly related to actual skills. However, it is values attached to age, skin color, sex, national origin, and so on. It is those ideas which influence whose work and skills are deemed more valuable. Cunningham (1993) summarizes well the problem underlying this view: "Race, gender, ethnicity, and class are not visualized in places of privilege in the social structure that has systematically discriminated against this new work force but rather the 'new workers' are seen as being in deficit needing specialized training if they are to form the modern competitive production team" (p. 14).

How could we otherwise explain that female college graduates on the average earn less than male high-school dropouts? Or that black college men earn only a few dollars more than white men with a high school degree ? Or that the most recent census figures show a racial salary gap? (Ammott and Matthaei, 1991; U.S. Census, 1993; *Occupa-*

tional Segregation, 1988; Polakow, 1993)? How do we explain that occupational segregation functions irrespective of existing skills? As Hacker (1992) remarks, refering to African-Americans:

> It is frequently remarked that many black men and women lack the kinds of skills that modern employment requires. However, these charges are hardly new. They were also common in the past, when blacks were shunted to the end of the line even for laboring jobs. And today, whites who barely make it through high school continue to get the first openings in the building trades. Moreover, blacks who do stay in school soon learn there is no assured payoff. Those who finish college have a jobless rate 2.24 times that for whites with diplomas, an even greater gap than separating black and white high school graduates. (pp. 103–4)

Thus, while "diversity" now allegedly signals a more open, democratic attitude towards the new "multicultural" work force. However, on-the-job experiences with diversity training exposes the deeply entrenched masculinist Eurocentric views and power structures regulating workplaces in many different ways (see Williams, 1993; Murray, 1993).

Work itself is highly divided in terms of skills, where unskilled work is often deliberately created as a way to keep labor cheap and expendable (aka "flexible"), and, above all, controlled. This process is similar to the way Frederick Taylor extracted the knowledge from the skilled crafts workers, made it available to management, and left the workers with the execution of only mindless tasks (Braverman, 1974; Zuboff, 1988). As Cunningham (1993, p. 14) points out, even where Taylorism and the idea of "the lazy pig iron worker" is left behind and everyone, whether worker or manager, is wearing the same white coat, the knowledge of the worker can become high-tech material for the robot, and ultimately nothing has changed. But aside from glorifying the participative management of the "new" workplace (for a critique of the importance of the underlying need for management control, see Lamphere et al., 1993, pp. 277–82), the corporate wisdom of having to deal with the lazy pig iron worker lives on in many if not most other workplaces. When McDonald's uses a cash register that has pictures in place of numbers, most of the knowledge is contained in the technology itself. However, as Garson (1989) reports, managers do not allow their workers to learn more than absolutely necessary. Hence the managers control even the small surplus of knowledge not entirely absorbed by the machine. We cannot simply interpret this as a response to the (presumed) illiteracy of the workers at McDonald's. We must see it as a systematic utilization as well as creation of illiteracy as a means of greater worker control.

At the same time, any discussion of skill deficits needs to take into consideration the regional differences, and resulting problems, of where the new jobs are going. Such a dispersed job growth not only leaves a vast group of racial and ethnic members of society not only without paid work, but even without a means for transportation, adding to the spreading conventional (although unspoken) wisdom that most of the inner-city poor constitute a superfluous population. At the same time, the move to the sunbelt region "has been based largely on low-wage, labor-intensive enterprises that use large numbers of underpaid minority workers" (Zinn, 1992, p. 81). Regional differences in losses of jobs and growth of new jobs show the inevitable link between corporate needs to find cheap and non-unionized workers and the issue of skills.

Undoubtedly, the question of literacy and skills is an important one. Both are vital for access to information and, at least potentially, to a decent job (for the most recent government data, see Celis 3d, 1993). However, the connection between skills and meaningful work, just like the one between skills and wages, is anything but direct. If such a link is nevertheless unequivocally stated in the debate under scrutiny here, it fulfills an important ideological function. The entire unequal structure of choices (the unequal distribution of jobs and joblessness, wages, access to information and knowledge, training and education, etc.) disappears entirely. In turn, such a screening out of issues related to discrimination, and to built-in, well-entrenched structures of inequality precisely allows for the ideological construction of an alleged link between skills and jobs, skills and wages, and, consequently, between the projected "new majority" of workers and a threatening human capital crisis. To portray these groups as categorically deficient human capital relies on sexist, racist, and nationalist constructions of inferiority. These portrayals have traditionally served, *and continue to serve*, the special exploitation of these groups. If we in adult education revel in diversity and participative management instead of engaging in the painful effort of trying to understand the entrenched mechanisms of oppression and exploitation, "we unabashedly side with management to develop human capital and to make workers responsible for production from which the managerial class profits first and foremost" (Cunningham, 1993, p. 24).

This is the second important ideological and economic function served by the argument of decline: the portrayal of women, minorities, and immigrants in the gloomy terms of deficiency not only relies on but also affirms once more their devalued status in society. In its frantic search for cheap labor, corporations are more than ever dependent on ideological constructs which legitimize special forms of exploitation, and they have to safeguard against trends that would erode these beliefs. A majority of women (irrespective of their color), minorities, and immigrants may make demands to be treated like the norm of human capital, which businesses could ill afford. As discussed elsewhere (Hart, 1992), all human labor, including that of white adult males, is today devalued or "cheapened," as indicated, among other things, by the continuous decline in wages (see, for instance, DeParle, 1992), and by the equally continuous rise in poverty (Funiciello, 1990, 1993; Hacker, 1992; Katz, 1989; Polakow, 1993; Reed, 1992; *Vanishing Dreams: The Economic Plight of America's Young Families*, 1992).

In many ways, therefore, the dominant discourse on "good workers" also relies on a notion of culture which is ultimately racist/ethnocentrist and sexist, and therefore not different from the dominant discourse on poverty (Katz, 1989). An education that focuses on the production of the good worker, and that looks at racial, ethnic, and sexual difference as inseparable from deficits good adult education practice could help to alleviate, likewise fails to name and investigate how the bottom line is directly dependent on a harsh form of exploitation which relies on however adjusted racial and sexual prejudices.

Since they are mentioned in the same breath as minorities and immigrants, how do "women," as a separate category (since women are also minorities and immigrants), enter into this issue? What allows women to be separated out while simultaneously being counted as one of the three main categories of low-grade human capital? Above all, there is a commonality of prejudice which constructs women as a group similarly inferior as minorities and immigrants. All three groups are, by long-standing social consensus, *categorized* as low-grade human capital, which in economic terms translates into cheap labor. To put it simply, they are low-grade because they deviate from the norm: they are "non-male" and/or "non-white" (Ehrlich, 1988). However, regardless of the particular focus of analyis, gender is a "*specific* analytical category," and "gender ideologies" even underlie such issues as "cultural explanations of racial inferiority" (Zinn, 1992, p. 85). Therefore, the issue of gender, or sexual difference, intertwining in complex ways with class, race, ethnicity, or nationality, is itself irreducible to any one of these categories. Sexual difference has determined not only access to training, education, degree of occupational segregation, definitions of what counts as skills and what is simply "naturally feminine," and wage levels (to name only a few issues): it also has determined what is considered "work" and "non-work." It is the latter which is, and remains, the central entry point for making gender the focus for understanding typical notions of work, and for trying to arrive at alternative notions. Any attempt to understand the ideological and economic mechanisms of sexual divisions and socially accepted definitions of work has to burst through the confines of a Western, masculinist framework by refusing to continue the concealment of essential forms of capitalist and patriarchal exploitation of women of all races. This is true for educational discourses as well which have, like other dominant discourses, played "a vital role in eclipsing patterns of abuse" (Thorne and Yalom, 1992, p. 11), not only the abuse of children, but also of women, no matter what color or age. Such a focus therefore also refuses to continue the "professional" division of labor that allows a few of our female colleagues to analyze how "women" have rarely appeared as a special category in adult education literature, an investigation that still does not move to the logical next step of engaging in a feminist rather than simply gender-based analysis (for a critique of this approach see, for instance, Sissel, 1993).

By making gender a primary analytical category, and by being critical of established binary frames of thinking about work and education, the analysis will show the fundamental underlying connections between apparently oppositional concepts, especially "family" and "work," but other related dichotomies as well. In other words, it will contribute to a better understanding of the complexity of a part of reality that is most intimately connected to basic issues of survival, issues that equally fundamentally influence theories and practices of education.

THE IDEOLOGY OF THE MONOLITHIC FAMILY

If one starts one's analysis of work and education with the realization that current fundamental restructurings of work are not only the result of an increasingly competitive international capitalism, but also of a capitalism that is inseparable from patriarchal ideas, many of the hidden assumptions behind the skill-deficit model of work and education become visible. Looking at type and income of women's paid labor alone, one is confronted with the workings of a sexist prejudice which weaves in and out of racist or nationalist prejudice but nevertheless has very separate ingredients as well. For instance, by simply looking at definitions and valuations of skill, these biases appear as social con- structions which rely on the notion that women are overall less capable than men. This mirrors the idea that it is more naturally feminine to be more easily exploitable. Clearly, only part of this view is attributed to an alleged absence of skills, or to a greater degree of illiteracy in women than men. In fact, sexist prejudice relies on *sex-stereotyped* notions of skill, which include the idea that feminine-type skills are of lesser value than masculine-type skills. As the "comparable worth" movement has revealed, we are here not talking simply about a lower level of skills in women, but a social construction and ideological perception of "women's skills," or sex-typed "feminine" skills as lower *by definition* (Blum, 1991; Cockburn, 1991; Evans and Nelson, 1989; Phillips and Taylor, 1986).[1]

The ultimate reasons for a varied hierarchy between feminine and masculine skills (with variations due to racial and ethnic differences) is the extremely strong association of all women with their family. Again, types of association vary depending, among many other things, on the class or ethnicity of the women under question. But they all pivot around the ability (or "handicap") of women to bear and raise children. As Felice Schwartz, the original proponent of a separate "mommy track" for women managers with children, so aptly put it in an interview with the *Chicago Tribune* (3 May 1992, sect. 6, p. 3): "I think men think of women, and as soon as they think 'women' they think 'babies,' and as soon as they think babies, they think of lack of commitment." Thus, women bring a realm of experience into the "world of work" which threatens to disrupt the entire masculinist construction of work and jobs, cemented by a rigid social division between work and family. In Cockburn's words, "with women trundle along the principles of reproduction, domesticity and care," "infesting" not only "the public sphere," and "upsetting the fundamental tenets of male political and civil life" but also threatening to upset "the masculinity of the hierarchy" at work (1991, pp. 220, 216).

The association of women with babies has different connotations depending on the class and race/ethnicity of employed women (Polakow, 1993). But the dominating definition of a true family and, correspondingly, of the good mother, relies on an ideology that has reinforced the economic exploitation of all women (Thorne and Yalom, 1992, p. 7). "It is this ideology which continues to see women as citizen mothers, not citizen workers, thereby perpetuating low-wage temporary employment, low-status pink-collar jobs, and the unavailability of public child care and maternity leave provisions" (Polakow, 1993, pp. 51–52). The operation of sexist prejudice in the work force, and the mechanisms which make women a cheap, devalued labor force, have above all relied on the idea that women are more attached to their families than to their jobs. Aside from different meanings associated with this "attachment," differences which are inseparable from racism and ethnocentrism, there is nevertheless an equity among women resulting "largely from the fact that few women of either race rise far in the earning hierarchy" (Hacker, 1992, p. 96). Although Hacker correctly states that achieving "equality is easier within an underpaid cohort," this phenomenon of female underpayment is inseparable from the fact that children, that is "the family," are a women's issue (p. 96). Thus, despite all the historical shifts and changes in what counts as family, "our 'metanarratives' persist to unusually strong degrees in maintaining stable enduring images of the natural order of things" (Polakow, 1993, p. 22). Polakow continues by saying that "while families have changed in profound ways, particular myths of *the family* and consequently of motherhood have endured, myths that have placed mother in a specific domestic and social space in relation to husband, children, and the state" (p. 23). It is this "Eurocentric family legacy" (Polakow, 1993, p. 23), the "ideology of the monolithic family" (Thorne and Yalom, 1992, p. 6) which remains a strong and distorting image, and it is behind the particular "cheapness" of female labor.

Although "contemporary U.S. family arrangements are diverse, fluid, and unresolved," and "'the' postmodern family lurches forward and backward into an uncertain future" (Stacey, 1992, p. 94), it remains a "woman-tended domain." It leaves the unpaid work of mothering in the hands of women, and it remains an allegedly legitimate reason for super-exploiting women (p. 107). In other words, even under fluid, "postmodern" conditions, women's automatic association with responsibility for children is either sentimentalized into "traditional" family structures by a resurgent conservatism (Zinn, 1992, p. 74), or it is used to keep intact sex-specific forms of economic exploitation. Thus women are distinguished from other forms of deficient capital.[2] Even in otherwise critical studies the conservative ideal of true women with children being married is alive and well. As Katz (1989) shows, many writers emphasize that in the inner cities the "menacing underclass" is frequently identified with unmarried black women. Lamphere and co-workers (1993) focused on "working mothers" in the sunbelt region and came to a similar conclusion about "the importance of marital status" which is "shaping women's lives," and it is their lives within the household or (paid) workplaces (p. 13). Workers without a husband are cheap labor for capital (Polakow, 1993, p. 48) and they can seldom achieve a family wage. Even when married, most husbands leave the responsibility for housework to women. As Hochschild (1989) showed, aside from the wage gap between men and women there is a "leisure gap" inside the household as well.

By being identified with motherhood or a greater family orientation, women are defined as inferior workers. This is true regardless whether they are mothers or not, whereas men are not afflicted with this orientation whether they are fathers or not (Chilman, 1993; Reed, 1992; Vogel, 1993). The cultural norm of a homogeneous family unity is asserting more control than ever during a time when the possibility of having a male head of the family is rapidly disappearing. This is also a time when the growing involvement of women in the paid labor market is identified with greater women's autonomy (regardless of the conditions and pay of these jobs). This flies in the face of the old patriarchal family autonomy which has traditionally stood against women's independence from a male breadwinner (Stacey, 1992, p. 278). It is not surprising, therefore, that Americans are currently witnessing an upsurge of conservative ideologies about "the family," a logical response to the fact that our current "family crisis" is, when seen from a conservative perspective, primarily a "male family crisis" (Thorne and Yalom, 1992, p. 17).

We need to keep in mind that the family wage has traditionally been a white male domain (Polakow, 1993, p. 51). Its existence is therefore central to the "women as supplemental income earner" idea which has been a reality primarily for white, European-American women. With black men's employment opportunities severely restricted and clustering at the bottom of the job hierarchy, black women have had consistently high labor-force participation rates, and their contributions to their families have been anything but "supplemental" (Jones, 1986; Ammott and Matthaei, 1991; Hacker, 1992). Black women have not been rewarded with a family wage. They have been maligned as "matriarchs" threatening their men's masculinity which white male society has traditionally seen as anchored in the decidedly patriarchal role of main provider and head of household.

Obviously, the rise in white women's involvement in paid work "seems to generate profound ambivalence about the eroding breadwinner ethic" (Stacey, 1992, p. 101). At the same time, this is an ethic which in the past placed greater financial responsibility on men for their families. Perhaps it is especially the rising unemployment of black men which has contributed to a "men's liberation," where young fathers are "able to point to a child they have sired . . . seen as tangible evidence of manhood, an important laurel for men unable to achieve recognition in other areas" (Hacker, 1992, p. 77). But the fundamental changes in family structures have also resulted in a general inability or unwillingness of fathers (no matter what their color) to provide financial support for the children they "sired."

Thus, while women's (alleged or real) family orientation is considered a blemish on female human capital, society as a whole has not let up on expecting "real" women to be wives and mothers, and to define their femininity in those terms. Again, this is and has been true primarily for European-American women. Women of African descent, on the other hand, have had to shape or preserve their family orientation in the face of massive social, legal, political, and economic proscriptions against doing so (Jones, 1982). As many of the contributors to *Double Stitch* (Bell-Scott et al., 1993) make clear, in the context of black women's history the definition and experience of a "family" places them into a collective, communal rather than into the individualistic, solitary context of a white middle-class nuclear family (see especially Collins' essay in the Bell-Scott collection; see also Naples, 1992).

The same society which today praises upper-middle-class (white) women for giving up promising careers and returning to full-time motherhood, "suggesting that home is where she truly belongs" (Abramovitz, 1991, p. 381), stigmatizes poor African-American women who stay home with their children as "welfare mothers." They are characterized as having babies at the government's expense, and their families are portrayed as "pathological" or "dysfunctional" because they do not fulfill the "modern" norms of heterosexual, married coupledom (Abramovitz, 1991; Burnham et al., 1989; Hacker, 1992; Katz, 1989; Lamphere et al., 1993; Polakow, 1993; Stacey, 1992; Zinn, 1992). As Stacey (1992) writes: "Families without a married male head, such as single-parent or grandparent-headed families are, in the common usage, broken, deformed, or incomplete families, and thus do not qualify for . . . assumptions regarding family unity" (p. 271). At the same time, it is especially the low appeal of women's jobs which make the value and rewards of women's work at home with their children look far more attractive. Especially for African-American women, "the decision to be a wife and mother first in a world which defined African-American women in so many other ways, the decision to make her family the most important priority was an act of resistance to a system which would define her place for her in terms of its own economic and racist needs" (Brown, 1993, p. 81). Moreover, as the history of employment of African-American men and women shows, economic and racist needs have not only prevented most women from living up to the middle-class nuclear-family ideal. But, they are also behind the above-mentioned government and state regulations that are trying to force "welfare mothers" to leave their small children and find work, even if the wages from these jobs fall way below the official poverty line.[3]

In addition, employment signifies a rising demand in time spent at one's job, regardless of whether the worker is responsible for raising children or not. As Schor (1991) documents, instead of the work week continuously shrinking, as generally assumed, Americans are actually working longer and longer hours, putting in about 164 extra hours of paid work per year. This is largely due to corporate cost-cutting measures, with fewer employees expected to work more, and businesses saving on wages as well as training and fringe benefit costs. American workers put up with this situation because they know that others are already in line waiting for their jobs and the protective influence of unions has eroded over the past decades.[4] In addition, the mushrooming of part-time and temporary work, two-thirds of which are covered by women (Cobble, 1993; Kahn, 1993), is adding to the pressures on single mothers who cannot afford part-time wages.

At the same time, flex-time policies are "not helpful for workers with heavy child care responsibilities" since they do not signify any changes in the full family and work load (Chilman, 1993, p. 452). But this is true for regular full-time employment as well, as it does the opposite of reducing the "maternal overload of both full-time family and out-side jobs" (ibid.). As Kahn (1993) reports,

> job flexibility as conceived by business is often actually antagonistic to women's interest. In practice, it means employing women in part-time jobs with low wages and no benefits, granting or denying mater-nity benefits on the basis of a corporation's need to attract qualified labor while containing labor costs and favoring low-cost 'family-friendly' policies like 'flex-time' and day-care referral services over day-care centers. (p. 27)

In general, "flexibility" is one of the euphemisms describing longer hours of work for less pay, a particular form of stress for women with children.

This situation, therefore, also cuts into one of the prime resources for the work with children: time. But time is not the only resource lack-ing. The fact that women and their children comprise the largest part of the poor is probably the most appalling indicator that material support is not given to the work of raising children. The main cause for this pov-erty is employed women's low wages (Blum, 1991; Chilman, 1993; Cobble, 1993; Gelpi et al., 1986; also Kessler-Harris, 1990; Tomask-ovic-Devey, 1993; and Vogel, 1993). This touches upon the issue of sin-gle motherhood, most dramatically associated with poverty (Polakow, 1993), and that of racially motivated income gaps. Hacker (1992), for instance, describes that "if black families had the same mixture of single parents and married couples as white households do," only about half of the income gap between whites and blacks would by closed (p. 95).

There has been a rapid increase in maternal employment. The rise in the cost of living, frozen or declining wages, the increase in mother-only families, and the shift from a manufacturing to a service economy (where most jobs are typified as "feminine") are some of the compelling reasons (Chilman, 1993, p. 451). As mentioned above, it has been these economic reorganizations and the corporate need for cheap labor ("non-white" and/or "non-male") which have been working against the old capitalist-patriarchal full-time motherhood ideal primarily on a material level. In other words, neither public nor private sector policies show any indication of supporting the unpaid work with children. This lack of support also affects middle- and upper-middle-class women. As data from studies on women and men in professional careers show (presum-ably those which require the highest degree of commitment to work), the more "successful" the women, the less likely they are going to be married or have children (Hensel, 1991).

It is highly questionable whether "working mothers" "threaten" to bring about a fall in productivity. For instance, Milagros Reyes, who earns $12,000 a year as a clerk, was threatened with dismissal after two absences because she had to tend to her sick son. Milagros, like many other women, now goes to work even when her child is sick (Dugger, 1992). In this case, lack of resources and desperation force a "solution" which gives primacy to employers' needs, in the process harming both mother and child. On the other end of the spectrum, with more resources at their disposal, married women with children, in higher paying jobs, go to great lengths and display considerable willingness to self-sacrifice in order to reconcile the demands of family and jobs or careers. By so doing, they let down neither their employers nor their husbands (Hochschild, 1989). Similarly, Hensel (1991) cites studies on women in academe which show no significant difference in the productivity of female professors with and without children. The women with children simply gave up whatever leisure time they had left (p. 36). She quotes another study which found "that marriage acted as a depressant for women's productivity but as a stimulant for men's" (p. 36). Clearly, women and men "have" families in quite different ways. This is also indicated by the way the term "working father" has not taken a hold in our everyday discourse on work. Have we ever heard demands for creating a "daddy track" (Stacey, 1992, p. 108)?[5]

THE FEMINIZATION AND INFANTALIZATION OF POVERTY

Because of the enduring myths of "normalized motherhood" against which "deviant" mothers are measured (Polakow, 1993, p. 23), these myths cannot be separated from an equally strong metanarrative of "normalized workers." This still powerful notion of the normalized worker, who is definitely not "non-white" or "non-male," must also be seen in connection with the pressure on poor women with children to switch from victimizing the welfare system to becoming "normalized single mother workers." In other words, they must do work which pays them less than welfare (Chilman, 1993; Funiciello, 1990; Polakow, 1993). It also means leaving full-time child-rearing responsibilities in the hands of poorly paid child-care workers (for the latter, see Chilman, 1993; and Noble, 1993b), or, more likely than not, in the hands of kin (Bell-Scott et al., 1993; Lamphere et al., 1993). Further, the gendered nature of welfare is relying on the predominant social attitude toward caring work: "When done for pay, it is usually devalued; when unpaid, it is often taken for granted" (Lamphere et al., 1993, p. 19). At the same time, affluent women become more like "fathers" by "appropriating the labor of other women to do the daily work of child care and even to physically bear children" (Thorne and Yalom, 1992, p. 17). We cannot ignore the importance of class and race/ethnicity differences that make such a female appropriation of female labor possible (see also Collins, 1985; and Romero, 1992, for a description of how class, racism, and ethnocentrism regulate the labor relations among women).

Poverty is afflicting a growing number of people in America (Pear, 1993). This means that we also cannot look at major economic trends as if they were gender *or* race/ethnicity neutral. Likewise, any debate on work and education cannot ignore poverty as an inevitable result of "our economy." Since we are dealing with a "feminization" as well as (growing) "infantilization of poverty" (Polakow, 1993, p. 59), it is necessary to give poverty a specific focus. This focus brings together all the issues of a gendered labor market, welfare system, underclass, and non-market work in a particularly pronounced form. The reality of poverty in the old centers of capitalist progress and development also sheds light on the importance of looking at regional differences in the current reordering of all work, and to highlight simultaneously any underlying consistencies in individual household and market workplaces. Undoubtedly, to understand the gendered nature of poverty is likewise essential for developing an educational theory and practice that does not silence the life circumstances of millions of Americans. A critical adult education theory must understand that the life circumstances of the poorest members of our society reveals best what this society, in its local and global repercussions, is all about.

By looking at cities, the old centers of capitalist modernity, in the light of the current reorganizations of the capitalist world market, one sees where poverty is growing fastest (Katz, 1989).[6] The change from a primarily industrial manufacturing to a growing service economy has been accompanied by "shifts in the geographical location of jobs from central cities to the suburbs and from the traditional manufacturing cities (the rustbelt) to the sunbelt and to other countries" (Zinn, 1992, p.

79). With rising unemployment in the inner cities they not only become centers of poverty, they also show that poverty is a predominantly black and Hispanic phenomenon.[7] As Zinn (1992) demonstrates, the expansion of the sunbelt region "has been based largely on low-wage, labor-intensive enterprises that use large numbers of underpaid minority workers; and a decline in the northern industrial sector continues to leave large numbers of Blacks and Hispanics without work" (p. 81). Clearly, despite the differences of poverty rates among Hispanics, a look at the effect of macroeconomic shifts in the world economy and labor markets shows that, structurally speaking, poverty is inseparably associated with minority status. At the same time, while this "structural model" investigates how a decline of economic opportunities rather than a deficient culture is behind the rising poverty of Hispanics and blacks in inner cities, "structural approaches have failed to articulate gender as an analytical category even though the conditions uncovered in contemporary research on the urban underclass are closely intertwined with gender. In fact, the problems of male joblessness and female-headed households form themselves around gender" (Zinn, 1992, p. 86).

When looking at the racialization *and* feminization of poverty one is bound to see, for instance, that "the disenfranchisement of large numbers of Black men . . . affects the meanings and definitions of masculinity for Black men, and it reinforces the public patriarchy that controls Black women through their increased dependence on welfare" (Zinn, 1992, p. 87). As mentioned above, the ideal of a "traditional" heterosexual married couple, where men and women occupy their respective places, stigmatizes "welfare mothers" as dysfunctional or incomplete, *and* expects them to find work instead of caring full-time for their children, even if they are only above three, or in some states, above one year old. In other words, as long as mothers are not tied to an income earning husband, the cult of true womanhood or full-time motherhood immediately loses its meaning. And where live patriarchal control is missing, state and government regulations need to take over.

Economically speaking, women's primary orientation towards the family has provided a number of justifications for making the exploitation of all women easier, a justification which has become even more important by relying on women as a naturally cheap labor force. In more positive accounts of current restructurings of the work force, "feminine" qualities are now allegedly more accepted or even sought after.

Typical of analyses that deal with positive dimensions, the qualifications of women in management or similar supervisory or leadership are investigated (see, for instance, Noble, 1993a). These discussions talk about the potentially superior management or leadership abilities of women. Feminine qualities are described as being useful for new approaches to management, where workers' feelings are now taken into consideration as well, and where women's special training in tact, empathy, and emotional expressiveness can be harnessed for successful management. The claim is made that an interactive leadership style is now more effective, as we move from a manufacturing to an information-service economy, and the leadership style of men which is heavy on the command and control side is no longer suitable (*Ways Men and Women Lead*, 1991).

This may, perhaps, be true on a certain level of management. But what is the ultimate function of these new sensitive, interactive managers? "Feminine qualities," such as nurturing, empathizing, working in cooperation rather than competition, and so on have ethical implications which directly clash with the amoral, competitive foundation of our economic arrangements. As long as the bottom-line remains the ultimate grounds for rational and ethical decision-making, women's special qualities will be once more exploited, this time directly and explicitly. This fosters the old delusion of progress emanating from corporate citadels, a delusion increasingly difficult to uphold in an increasingly ruthless world. In this climate of fierce economic competition, "masculine" not "feminine" qualities are called upon to make cold-blooded decisions affecting many people's lives.[8] *Business Week* (Walsh, 1991) reports that American corporations are now "hunting" for "a much more dispassionate view on their business," where managers "can bring a more detached and clear-eyed approach to a company." In come the new "tough bosses for tough times," the "new, cold-eyed breed of CEOs," the "blood-and-guts," "laser-sharp," or "steely cost-cutters," who "slash" payrolls, and "squeeze" concessions from workers. A time for celebrating feminine qualities?

If women's special ways of leading are to become the model of future managers working within the framework of "new paradigms," these "special" qualities will be drawn into an overall context of exploitation which remains not only fully intact but which is given additional legitimacy. We can also speculate to what extent these abilities, shaped outside of the male-defined world of work, will now become eroded or distorted when tethered to the strategic context of bottom-line thinking, which fosters callousness and greed, and places naked self-interest—be it on an individual or on a national level—above anything else. If some of my students, steeped in the corporate culture, defend corporate practices after watching a film about farm workers' children who have been mutilated by the pesticides their parents are exposed to at their work, I take this as a measure for the overall corruption of moral thinking. Are women's special qualities, when utilized in a corporate context otherwise unchanged, to reinject some morality into economic decision-making?

Clearly, typically feminine emotional abilities have always been used in the work place. Women have never been a neutral "labor force," as their femininity has always been part and parcel of their exploitation. They have always been confronted with (and expected to meet) expectations that prove their "femininity," ranging from cushioning conflicts at work to giving emotional or sexual attention to male colleagues. A "gender ideology" may be more explicitly employed as a way to soften particularly harsh forms of exploitation. Hossfeld (1990) quotes a manager from a large firm in Silicon Valley (employing mostly minority women in the most hazardous, minimally paid jobs), that "gender tactics . . . are designed to 'boost' morale by reminding the gals that even though they do unfeminine work, they really are still women." In the same firm, the color-coding of smocks also stresses the worker's "femininity": "While the men's smocks are color-coded according to occupation, the women's are color-coded by sex, regardless of occupation" (p. 160). It is small wonder that so many men (and some women, too) simply "don't get it" when women workers complain about sexual harassment. Women workers are perceived as *sexual* beings first and workers second. This perception is deeply entrenched in our culture (for an analysis of sexual harassment within an adult education context, see Stalker, 1993).

When one leaves behind the narrow and silencing perspective on women in leadership positions, one cannot avoid expecting any proof that feminine qualities have attained greater social acceptability in concrete, material governmental and corporate support for families, and for combining employment with the work of raising children. In Chilman's (1993) words: "Perhaps public policies should make it possible for at least one parent to stay home with her or his young children rather than working full-time, if that seems to be the wisest choice for the family" (p. 455). Perhaps it is time for reintroducing a "family wage," allowing all those who have to take care of children to do so with the necessary material and temporal support. At the same time, any governmental or corporate support for employed mothers needs to look at the needs of those who have none or very little market resources and consider the policy of income replacement (Kahn, 1993, p. 26).

LIBERATING WORK AND EDUCATION
FROM THE BOTTOM LINE

Only large-scale material, structural support for the work of raising children would cease to make a "family orientation" into the infectious disease which now afflicts all women workers. After all, it is this orientation which has given rise to and is the source of feminine qualities. In other words, the "socially necessary" work of giving birth to and raising children is the primary (although not the only) arena for developing the abilities of caring, nurturing, and empathizing within a context that is profoundly productive (where productivity is defined as producing and enhancing life itself rather than the bottom line).

Employed women (and a few men as well) who seem to hold on tenaciously to their "family orientation" are the bearers of experiences and knowledge, and of an overall orientation to work and production that needs to be acknowledged, understood, and made available. The work of raising children requires an orientation that aims to sustain and preserve life. This orientation clashes directly with the rationality of "our economy" with its built-in imperative to exploit or disregard all living things.

The sexual division of labor still gives an almost exclusive responsibility for the raising of children to women because this work is devalued. And, women are devalued by their association with giving birth to and raising children. The fact that we have to be born and nurtured into independence continues to remind us of our dependence on nature. This is why "superiority has been accorded in humanity not to the sex that brings forth but to that which kills" (DeBeauvoir, cited in Hartsock, 1985, p. 244)—killing, or taking physical life, is the ultimate act of dominance over nature. The sexual division of labor is therefore inseparable from our overall cultural attitude to the body, to sexuality, and to nature. Likewise, it is inextricably woven into the cultural glorification of science and technology. Within this context, new and future reproductive technologies take on a special meaning: they can be seen as attempts to seize hold of this part of nature, and to break the female monopoly over the uterus.

If today a revolution is in the making (or can be envisioned), calling for a fundamental restructuring of work, this revolution does not come from the introduction of new technology. I would not call it revolutionary to divest work from its last vestiges of physical or bodily involvement in production and glorify the symbolic manipulation of a distilled reality into the ultimate form of progress. Rather, I would call it the culmination of century-old trends in Western culture: to control nature by banning it from our reality as much as possible. By engaging in a large-scale social and cultural denial of our inescapable bond with nature, we have in the process destroyed nature. Acknowledging that we have bodies and are an integral part of nature would be truly revolutionary, calling for a radical rethinking of our cultural heritage and value hierarchies. The experience of working with children (and other experiences of "subsistence work," see Hart, 1992) should therefore cease to be considered "a special need," or a problem to business. Children should also cease to be considered "a woman's issue" but an issue of general concern. Why should it be a woman's issue (regardless of the woman's color) to raise the next generation of workers and citizens?

If we were to move "feminine qualities" up the ladder of social values, we would also begin to dismantle the unhappy dichotomy between "feminine" and "masculine" qualities, as men as well as women would be associated with this productive task. Above anything else, however, we would demythologize the concept of "the family," and of a corresponding "family orientation" by reframing it *as living and working with children.* As such, it would be the work of mothering, or motherwork, which would become an issue for all workers and where the very term "worker" would include this reality. By making the issue of living and working with children a central one, we would give "fatherhood" a new meaning, and change it from a biological claim, or an abstract "provider role" to an achieved status. In such a way, "fatherhood" would become more like "motherhood," and the term "parenting" would for the first time be correct, no longer silencing an unequal distribution of work and responsibilities between "mothers" and "fathers" (see Polatnik, 1984).

We would also begin to uncouple the idea of the family from its heterosexist, nuclear connotations. This would create room for the many different kinds of families that are not as yet acknowledged by social, legal, political, or economic structures. It would greatly help those millions of children whose family situations now deviate from the norm, and who are under constant pressure to "explain" or legitimize their difference. Mother-only households would cease to be stigmatized as pathological versions of the norm, as would households with gay parents (single or in pairs). In other words, our whole ideological structure of normality and pathology would crumble, creating space for much needed social recognition and support.

By looking at motherwork as a central focus for any educational thoughts and actions concerning work, we are dealing with several fundamental consequences for rethinking work and education. Above all, we cannot avoid making connections that are usually *not* made by educators, and develop a framework for thinking and acting that overcomes the conventional discourse of concealment and silencing, which, in the last analysis, is a discourse on power. We have to base educational efforts aimed at work on a thorough understanding of the political and economic dimensions of our economy; we have to see the inevitable connections between such a fundamental understanding of the politics of work with the politics of education, and we have to develop pedagogies that likewise do not fall victim to any of the material and immaterial realities of oppression. This also means that the issue of education and work cannot be reduced to the right kind of training for the right kind of skills, competencies, and attitudes—where the definition of "right" is inseparable from bottom-line thinking. And it is bottom-line thinking which always regards workers as factors of production, regardless of an allegedly progressive talk about participatory management and the importance of workers' feelings.

As I tried to show in this chapter, while race/ethnicity and nationality are an integral part of the particular forms of oppression characterizing our society and economy, gender plays a specific and essential part. If we focus on the politics of the economy, the issue of gender points above all to the concealment of the importance of non-market work. Without women's essential work of raising and caring for the next generation, we would have no future, and not even cheap laborers for the capitalist owners of production. Concealing the *economic* importance of the work done mostly by women also feeds into the predominant Western masculinist dichotomies, whether they are Marxist or mainstream. These are the binary oppositions between "family" and "work," between "private" and "public," and between the "reproductive" and the "productive." And, as the discussion of the ideology of the monolithic family has shown, the family is considered the arena of private domesticity, engulfed by reproductive issues like "chores"—where even feminists consider child care a form of "chore" the fathers hesitate to perform (see, for instance, Bergmann, 1986; Lamphere et al., 1993). Likewise, the privacy of the family is inseparable from the norm of female dependence on men—and if women are not dependent, they had better find a job no matter how young their children are. The "feminization and infantilization" of poverty, and the existence of a gendered welfare system and labor market, with diverging and converging differences and similarities according to race or nationality of the women and children involved directly, requires that we understand the primacy of gender and poverty (see, for instance, Sheared, 1993).

Seen within this context, a concern for good education is inseparable from the need for social change. Again, by placing motherwork at the center of attention, we are confronted with the need to de-privatize this kind of work, and to recognize its economic, social, and political dimensions which directly speak against individual self-sufficiency and independence—some of the prime insignia of professionally defined good adult education. There are many different interpretations and realities of social action or social movements (see, for instance, Finger, 1989; Welton, 1993b). But if one considers the vitality of motherwork, one also faces the task of developing a notion of social change that is intertwined with work and education, and that does not continue the separation of "work" and "family." As Valentine and Darkenwald (1990) write: "By its very nature, American adult education separates individuals from their families; this can create problems for all learners, but most especially for parents of young children" (p. 40).

Aside from the authors' important recommendations to build several different child-care options into adult education programs, there is a more vital aspect once "parenting" is considered a form of work. For instance, we can learn from existing struggles and abilities, especially in the African-American population, where the family and the work of mothering have always relied on a communal and social action dimension (Bell-Scott, 1993; Naples, 1992). This would also make us look more closely at the overwhelming emphasis on individualism in professional adult education, an individualism which may come in the progressive guises of individual empowerment (Kulich, 1992) or personal transformation. We could also learn about different kinds of social and cultural experiences and how they have contributed and can contribute to a better understanding and improvement of the practice of mother-work, recognizing high levels of knowledge and social-emotional "lit-eracy" mothering people from all colorations have accumulated over centuries. What would social action mean if it were based on such knowledge and experiences?

NEW POSSIBILITIES FOR EDUCATIONAL PRACTICE

This brings me to the final section: what kind of pedagogies or educa-tional processes would be appropriate? Again, there are two dimensions to this question. First, examining the entire political economy of moth-erwork is helping us to break through the stifling confines of the current debate, to open up new themes, and to deepen our understanding of the many important and complicated questions contained in the experience of work. This is also helping us to discover new links between work and education and new possibilities for educational practice, and to leave the industrialized paradigm defining "workers' education" or "work-place education." Likewise, highly effective blaming-the-victim atti-tudes towards "deficient" workers would be called into question. So would the emphasis on training for the behaviors, skills, and attitudes that are either fit for low-wage jobs or for the corporate megamachine as a whole. Nor would we look at the poor (employed or non-employed) as victims in need of critical reflection. We would look at their struggles and understand their knowledge of mothering in a gendered labor mar-ket and welfare system—a knowledge that is silenced in educational institutions. Sheared (1993), for instance, shows how policies affecting African-American women have perpetuated "their marginalization in the welfare system, in the educational system, and more importantly in the workforce." And, she writes that "their needs and concerns have rarely been portrayed in terms of their own strengths" (p. 246).

Secondly, by placing motherwork into the context of a political economy, our ideas of work-related competencies, skills, and knowl-edge would be greatly expanded. If we were to consider work such as mothering a model for good, productive work, how would our concep-tions of these central educational categories change? How can we develop forms of knowledge based on non-market subsistence work?

(Hart, 1992). How could changes effecting this subsistence knowing be translated into educational programs or proposals? Among many other things, this means that neither mothering nor caring can simply serve as a psychological model for creating an educational environment whose main goal it is to empower individual learners. Such a psychological model is especially difficult to uphold when we keep our focus on the poverty of women and children. We must face the painful fact that "poor and destitute mothers have been participants in and witnesses to the discarding or destruction of their own children" (Polakow, 1993, p. 20).[9] And as Polakow rightfully points out: "When poor women and children lack access to power within a patriarchal family structure, regulatory welfare agencies can penalize them for deviant mothering practices" (p. 29).

Once we consider this context as vital ground for truths about our society, how can we define care and motherhood within education? Clearly, just as poor single mothers cannot conform to the norms of domesticity (Polakow, 1993), educators cannot continue to adhere to the "ideology of caring" that is conceptually inseparable from both the "moral philosophy of domesticity," and race-specific feminization and infantilization of poverty. Polakow (1993) writes about "the increasing placelessness of women in the public sphere," and she points out that this is a placelessness which is "now scientifically rationalized in the language of a psychology of mothering" (p. 29). There is a growing literature on the ideology of care (Noddings, 1992; Thorne and Yalom, 1992): study of this literature aids in developing alternative theories and practices in adult education. At the same time, caring and mothering would have to be placed into a larger social, political, and economic context, and the origin of a caring sensitivity and epistemology in certain forms of work which are severely eroded or destroyed by our economic arrangements.

In our current discussions on work and education (or any other theme, for that matter), "gender issues" are strikingly absent. This is, of course, a reflection of the overall stigmatization of these issues as being unimportant. In other words, they are not issues of "general" concern. However, as I tried to show in this chapter, issues relating to or associated with the experiences of women contain vital questions of crucial importance to all members of society. Above all, they pose a number of critical questions concerning our definitions of work, what counts as "good" or "bad" work, what kind of work is socially acknowledged, and which remains in the shadow of social recognition, and why. These questions also force us to re-examine our abstract notions of productivity, and our fixation on science and technology as the primary, if not exclusive, sites of progress and development.

Finally, current proposals for restructuring workplaces to make them more "educative" (Welton, 1991a) would look quite different if new organizations of work would be systematically reconciled with the work of raising children. I believe that such a reconciliation would be a prime avenue for a much needed overall humanization of work. This is the promise, rather than the threat of bringing the issue of children into the "world of work": to disrupt this world of work and its logic, to "liberate" it from its deadly bottom line, its equally deadly fixation on ever faster, ever more efficient, and ever more risky technology, and to reconnect it with issues of life and survival.

NOTES

1.   The main characteristic of "feminine" jobs relying on women's sex-typed abilities is their "feminine" (a.k.a. low) wage and other "feminine" features such as insecurity or instability, health hazards, lack of autonomy, fewer or no promotional opportunities, etc.

2.   Within this context it is also important to note that "African-American and white working class women have been the genuine postmodern family pioneers" (Stacey, 1992, p. 103).

3.   The Family Support Act of 1988 provides a good example of this double standard: It "sends a clear message to AFDC mothers that even those with preschool children are expected to work if child care is available" (Hagen, 1991, p. 9). The act gives a wide latitude to individual states, making it possible to require mothers to seek employment even when their children are as young as one year old. See also Kahn, 1993; Chilman, 1993.

4.   This is an issue which deserves much space all to itself. Within the current context I only want to point out that in conjunction with the diminishing power of unions there is also a growing militancy among laborers, male and female, and Smith (1990, p. 131) correctly states that this labor militancy is "not the kind usually associated with organized labor, but a wholly new militancy that we might have trouble recognizing for what it is."

5.   Writing for the *Harvard Business Review*, Felice Schwartz (1989) forced corporate attention on the issue of women and children. However, it was

the critique of feminists, not of corporate leaders, which was at the center of the ensuing controversy over her suggestion that businesses create special (slower, less prestigious) tracks for women with children. In her own words, she offended feminists by daring "to violate the party line that women are not different from men" (Noble, 1992). Schwartz rightfully asserts that an abstract ideal of equality damages women for whom children pose a very different challenge than for men. While I agree with Schwartz in that respect, I think that she did not go far enough. Her proposal reinforces the idea that children, or women's need or wish to take care of children *and* be employed prevents them from giving all to the corporation—which therefore remains the ideal, once more cementing an essentially male-defined culture of work and structure of career and perpetuating underlying mechanisms of exploitation or oppression.

6. Nevertheless, the history of the South being the poorest region in the United States has not changed. According to the most recent data by the U.S. Census Bureau, the highest 1992 poverty rates are in Mississippi, Lousiana, West Virginia, and New Mexico (Pear, 1993). For a particularly striking example, see Applebome, 1993.

7. As Zinn (1992, p. 84) reports, 39.9 percent of the Puerto Rican population lived below the poverty level in 1986; for Mexicans the poverty rate was 28.4 percent, and for Cubans and Central and South Americans is was 18.7 percent. Overall, according to the latest U.S. Census Figures (Pear, 1993), 33.3% of African-Americans are poor, 29.3% of Hispanics, 12.3% of Asian Americans, and 11.6% of whites.

8. At the same time, it is also getting harder to believe that we are witnessing a growing social esteem of feminine qualities when violence, especially against women, but also against children, is on the increase.

9. Although it deserves a special place, the question of child abuse cannot be justly dealt with in the context of this essay. For a detailed historical and theoretical analysis, see Polakow, 1993; see also Gordon, 1992.

5

In Defense of the Lifeworld:
A Habermasian Approach to Adult Learning

Michael R. Welton

PROLOGUE: THE CONUNDRUM OF MARGINALIZATION

On Friday afternoon, 26 April 1957, at a meeting of the American Commission of Professors, Abbott Kaplan asked: "Are we all clear as to what the issue for discussion is? What is the content, the essential ingredient of adult education, that marks it off from other fields or disciplines?" (Knowles Papers, 1957). Kaplan's question, posed at a historic meeting of the Commission of Professors, echoes in our academic corridors and debates to this day. It continues to ring in our ears because we have not yet discovered fully what marks adult education "off from other fields or disciplines." It is no wonder, then, that some scholars of adult education are fascinated with the "disciplinary basis of research into adult education phenomena" (Hake, 1992) almost forty years after Kaplan's question. However, the word "fascination" could easily mislead us into thinking that theoretical concern about the generation of a comprehensive theory of adult learning is really a luxury, not at all integrally connected to the trouble we are in our battered world and the possibility of learning our way through this tumultuous time in global history. Can there be any doubt that humankind faces monumental learning challenges?

Paradoxically, the university-based study of adult learning and education has contributed little of profound insight to understanding the plight and potentiality of the late modern world. In the main, professors of adult education, sprinkled across North America in marginalized spaces within beleaguered universities, have not participated in the central debates of our time from a distinctive intellectual and moral social learning standpoint. A recent text, *Learning in Adulthood* (1991), written by two leaders of American adult education, Rosemary Cafferella and Sharan Merriam, contains no indexical references to family, work, consumerism, citizenship, politics, or social movements. This is more than a little disturbing. The late modern world lurches towards the brink of endemic malfunction, waves of violence fueled by racism and ethnic hatreds and massive economic restructuring sweep over the world, government bureaucracies are paralyzed, new social movements erupt on the terrain of civil society, and the adult education professoriate, still locked into a very narrow way of thinking about learning in adulthood, looks on in bewilderment.

In recent years, however, disenchantment with the way "adult education" has been constituted as a "field of study" (discipline) has intensified dramatically. In May 1992 at the Adult Education Research Conference (U.S.), in Saskatoon, Saskatchewan, a symposium on the publication of *Adult Education: Evolution and Achievements in a Developing Field* (1991) erupted in an angry attack on the largely white, male guardians of a particular way of seeing adult learning which had its roots in American racism, individualism, and a narrowly conceived professional discourse about the problems of teaching adults (what I have dubbed elsewhere the "andragogical consensus" [Welton, 1991c]). There are multiple reasons for the anger at the textual exclusion of repressed voices (women, minorities, alter identities) and mainstream abandonment of adult education's once vital role in fostering democratic social action (in the United States, this tradition is often associated with the work of Eduard Lindeman [Stewart, 1987; Stubblefield, 1988], Myles Horton [Jarvis, 1987; Bell, Gaventa, Peters, 1990], and workers' movements [Schied, 1991; Altenbaugh, 1990]). But the anger and frustration with the modern practice of adult education also has its roots, in part, in the way the study of adult learning (what I will call the Discipline) was conflated (or reduced) to the study of principles of effective teaching practice. The "essential ingredient" of the Discipline, that which "marked it off from other fields," was identified as "methodology." The andragogists contended that adults learned differently from children, adults were at different points along the life span; therefore they needed to have programs designed for them and teaching methods utilized which were attuned to the adult as learner. These methods are applicable to all adult learners, no matter what the particular context (Knowles, 1980; Pratt, 1993; Davenport, 1993 [see Collins, chapter 3 in this text—Ed.]. By the end of the 1980s, the andragogical consensus was almost totally transposed into the ideology of "self-directed learning," an incoherent ideology containing many contradictory impulses (Candy, 1991). Liberal humanists found their precious notion of "individual autonomy" buried there, and technicists were able to develop tools to direct self-directed learning in diverse learning sites. Candy correctly observes that confusion has reigned with this notion as adult educators gave their own twist to the concept. Autodidaxy, learner-controlled instruction, self-management, and personal autonomy were all lumped together. But this confused ideology of self-directed learning remained firmly anchored in a decontextualized understanding of intersubjective learning processes. In the context of business and industry, professional organizations, and large-scale institutions, self-directed learning advocates fostered the illusion, so argues Michael Collins, that "adult men and women [were] effectively shaping an important dimension of their everyday working lives while, in fact, the attendant methodology place[d] the direction of their learning firmly in the hands of experts who serve predominantly institutionalized interests" (1992b, p. 7). Thus, the boundary of the Discipline was drawn very narrowly around a set of professionalized practices and another "expert culture" was constituted in an historical period of an expansive welfare-state capitalism to take its place alongside so many other expert cultures (medicine, law, etc.).

During the 1950s, *American* adult education was constituted formally and systematically as an applied field, to be governed by its own logic (an adult constituency in particular settings [military, corporations, voluntary agencies] requiring particular educational services). Adult education was constructed, in Barry Hake's words, as a "culturally bounded normative theory of 'good' practice" (1992, p. 69). If one peers through the window of the Commission of Professors meetings in the 1950s, one can see how a professionalizing sensibility pulled the professors like a powerful riptide away from deep and difficult meta-theoretical questions of constructing a Discipline of adult learning towards a rather arbitrary piecing together of elements that might add up to a distinct methodology for teaching adults and not children. Once "adult education" had staked itself off as a separable territory in this manner (as a distinct field of professional practice), its relationship to particular disciplines such as sociology or history could only be instrumentalized. Adult education now looked particularly to psychology, as Coolie Verner put it, for "bits of psychological knowledge pertaining to the adult." Verner was, however, puzzled about just how much psychology he "should be responsible for": what he should teach and what he should leave to departments of psychology (Hendrickson Papers, 1959). This historical development was deeply ambivalent and problematic, however. Reference to various disciplines at least intimated that adult learning could be studied autonomously, apart from the activities of an adult educator. Adults in traditional, modern, and postmodern societies have always been learning; they have not always had their learning managed by a professional. "The field of adult education," Hake notes, "has undergone a metamorphosis during the transition from its origins in social movements and voluntary associations, through its recognition as a public service, towards its current status as a marketplace for educational products and potential consumers" (1992, p. 75).

One of the most powerful critiques of the modern practice of adult education (MPAE) has emerged precisely from those irredentist scholars who argue that the boundary of "adult education" has been arbitrarily constructed to exclude social movements, if not voluntary associations. Fred Schied (1991) and Kathleen Rockhill (1985) claim that adult education's historic roots in social movements has been repressed from the contemporary field's memory and excised from its disciplinary boundaries. In two cogently argued essays in *University Adult Education in England and the USA* (1985), Rockhill argues that adult education has been consciously constructed (during the crucial inter war years) to silence the left progressive agenda of education for critical consciousness, social reconstruction, and collective action. To accomplish this task of delegitimizing oppositional learning, the emergent professional field has had to vanquish alternative knowledge forms and learning processes and cast them outside the boundary of the field. Schied speaks specifically of the "omission of workers' education, or more accurately, defining workers' education in such a way as to reduce it to insignificance in the study of adult education" (1991, p. 1). For Schied, the exclusion of workers' education from adult education's boundaries is "only part of a much broader omission of virtually any adult education that deals with social change" (p. 2). He cites as example the post-Civil War "Freedman's School movement, probably the largest and most important adult education movement in 19th century America" (p. 2), and the modern civil rights movement of the 1950s and 1960s.

Arthur Wilson (1992) would concur generally with Kathleen Rockhill's analysis. He has studied the construction of knowledge in the field of adult education from the 1930s through the 1980s by analyzing the governing ideologies of the adult education handbooks which have been produced periodically. His epistemological analysis of the handbooks, however, provides a slightly different perspective from Rock-hill. He does not think that the MPAE has severed its roots or forsaken its vision. From the 1920s to the present (no handbook was produced in the 1920s), the American field of adult education has been internally driven to develop a body of knowledge ("common concerns") to be used for professional practice in order to gain a share of an educational service economy. In the twentieth century the only way to achieve this dubious goal was to rely on empirical-analytical knowledge to define and organize the field—the impulse to monopolize competence to control a piece of the increasingly differentiated social world. Adult educators emerged as part of the professional middle classes who, in the post-war era, had to "manage the learning processes" of the subaltern sectors. Others, like Myles Horton, who worked with labor and citizen's groups, were not even viewed as educators (Bell, Gaventa, Peters, 1990). Wilson says that the "virtual absence of any critical knowledge until the last two editions in the 1980s, along with the pervasive dominance of empirical-analytical knowledge, indicates that evidence for connecting the field of adult education to emancipatory interests has no presence in the adult education handbooks" (1992, p. 265). Revisionists like Rockhill do, indeed, turn to workers' education to retrieve an emancipatory interest in adult education. But to do so, they move outside a field, says Wilson, that has as its guiding philosophy the adjustment of individuals and groups to the status quo. This latter perspective—eschewing the "lost radical tradition" myth—strongly suggests that "adult education" in the modern world is an integral part of the instrumental-adaptive, disciplinary apparatus of the system (state and economic steering media), and that variations of critical practice will always have a difficult time being accepted as legitimate adult education practice (Torres, 1990). In a world where both symbolic and material reproductive processes are radically unstable—the lifeworld is increasingly stripped of its life-orienting potential and economic restructuring is wreaking havoc throughout all societal domains—"adult education" will always be called to serve two masters (system or lifeworld).

Disputes over adult education's boundaries indicate pointedly that the process of constructing a Discipline is political and normative. Those who succeed in establishing a particular vision of the academic study of adult learning as universal are necessarily determining what counts, or does not count, as objects of study. These disputes are also normative: Schied, Rockhill and Wilson (and many others) want to retrieve workers' (and other movement) education from its neglected place outside the boundary and place it within in order to "transcend the technical-functional approaches that dominate the professional discourse today" (Schied and Zacharakis-Jutz, 1993, p. 102). They believe that history provides "alternative models" (p. 102), and opens up possibilities to expand human knowing and freedom in the present. The moment social movements are included as objects of analysis within the Discipline's boundary the old paradigm collapses. It disintegrates because the old andragogical paradigm was grounded primarily in teaching practices, the ideology of the individual as learner and in a very unstable epistemological relationship to an asocial and ahistorical discipline like psychology. It simply bursts apart, unable to offer (perhaps even unwilling) any explanation for intersubjective learning processes in all of the domains within society. The old paradigm has lost its claims to scientific validity. It limps on in many university units of adult education; confusion and frustration are rampant in these graduate schools.

The collapse of the old andragogical paradigm comes at an inopportune historic moment. We are living in the midst of convulsive global changes, which are shaking to the foundations our ideas about learning, and most governments in the liberal democratic countries have now adopted the rhetoric of "lifelong learning" and speak of the need for massive "job training" and "citizen re-education" programs as solutions to the "problem" of the transition to a post-industrial society. Confronting this new situation, the old andragogical paradigm is simply overwhelmed. It does not have the theoretical richness and depth of understanding of historical learning challenges and social learning processes to address current upheavals and to speak to its possibilities. A thoroughly professionalized practice in the service of the "cult of efficiency" (Collins, 1991) easily capitulates to system-driven imperatives, offering to deliver the methods to externally determined goals of adapting individuals to irresistible technological changes. The old paradigm, textualized in the *Handbooks* of legitimate American adult education practice, consistently affirmed "society's goodness and the need to 'fix' and 'retool' people to serve its interests better. . . . (T)here is virtually no sense of a need to change society. It's all very ameliorative: fix people to serve society's need" (Wilson, 1991). The absence of a social learning (or educative) paradigm turns against our avowed commitment to the "neglected adult learner" with a vengeance. Systemic imperatives, by-passing any communicative ethical process, largely ignore our university programs and national organizations, and rush onward, radically changing the conditions under which adults might develop their potential to be critically reflective, autonomous actors. We are left in the lurch, speechless.

Ironically, at the nadir of the old paradigm's disintegration social theorists outside faculties of education in North America and Europe have placed social and political learning processes at the center of their analyses of (1) how modern societies are organized, how they reproduce themselves, symbolically and materially, and how they are propelled dynamically towards more (or less) democratic processes and institutional forms; and (2) how to understand what needs to be unlearned in modernity, and what *critical learning potential* lies unreleased within our complexly differentiated late modern societies. Jürgen Habermas, the social theorist who most consciously embodies this major shift within Western social theory, executes a veritable "learning turn" that supersedes the vaunted earlier "linguistic turn" (Rorty, 1967; Bernstein, 1983). And a growing number of theorists who work in dialogue with Habermas (Andrew Arato, Seyla Benhabib, Klaus Eder, Claus Offe, Jean Cohen, Stephen Leonard, John Forester, Stephen White, to name but a few) work within a social learning paradigm. And they do so, one must add, largely unaware of critical adult education thought and practice (with the exception of Paulo Freire).

But it is not just Habermasians who see society through a learning lens. In a follow-up text *The Good Society* (1991) to the widely discussed *Habits of the Heart* (1985), Robert Bellah and associates, speaking in the warm accents of contemporary communitarianism, identify the major barrier to the "good society" as the "individualistic assumptions of our [U.S.] culture" (1991, p. 19). They believe that Americans do not understand that large-scale structures have enormous formative power, that "all institutions are educative" (p. 15). The developmental learning potential of the individual cannot be uncoupled from "the institutional contexts to which that person has access." Institutions, as patterns of social activity and clusters of roles, form individuals and shape character by enabling or constraining possible courses of action, and ways of interacting with others (pp. 40–41). Throughout this text one finds references to the need to increase "our *democratic learning* capacity" (p. 17), the problem of how to "educate ourselves as citizens so that we can really 'make a difference'" (p. 19), to the challenge of thinking of the family as the "first, and in some respects the most important,

learning community" (p. 48). This kind of language, with its affinities
to the thought of Lawrence Cremin and John Dewey, breaks learning
theory free from its colonization by a narrowly defined educational paradigm. But in so doing, we drift uneasily into relatively unknown
waters. The new, or emergent social learning paradigm, would construct the boundary of the field as wide as society itself, and would
include everything that forms the outlook, character, and actions of
communicative agents in space and time. All of society is a vast school.
It will be my argument that Habermas' sociological theory (his dualistic
model of the system and lifeworld) and theory of rationalization (his
view of the historical unfolding of learning potential in modernity) provide us with the necessary boundary frame and constituent conceptual
elements for the study of social learning processes.

This social learning approach to institutions assumes that:

1. Institutions are the indispensable source from which our character and
   identity is formed and reformed, and one can differentiate institutions
   within the lifeworld: (i) institutions of socialization (family, schools);
   (ii) social integration (groups, collectives, associations); (iii) cultural
   reproduction (religion, art, science) from those within the domain of
   the system (the state and economy).

2. All institutions are formative in that they enable or constrain a learning
   process whereby individuals become increasingly reflective, autonomous actors. It is possible, therefore, to speak of an institution such as
   "work," the "family," or "the public" as educative or miseducative
   (Hart, 1993; Welton, 1991a; Leyman and Kornbluh, 1989).

3. When we speak of a particular institution as miseducative, we are
   assuming that an institution is not a *democratic learning community*. That is, there are blockages (or hindrances) to the learning process which are inherent in the structure of the institutional form and
   not within the character of the individual herself (inadequate motivation, etc.). This is not to say, however, that the everyday working of
   capitalism will not generate pathologies in the lifeworld, causing some
   persons to lack requisite competencies for role fulfillment in late modern social systems. One also assumes that some persons are not able,
   from birth or accident, to function as fully competent actors, and
   require special institutional care and support.

4. Following Habermas, when we speak of a democratic learning community, we are assuming that power relations (Hart, 1985, 1990a,

1990b) and interests distort the communication process. Power relations, or the asymmetrical distribution of dialogue chances, are the fundamental structural barrier to the communicative, dialogic learning process. Mechthild Hart thematizes three levels of systemically distorted communication: the socio-cultural level of ideologies, values, and belief systems (these may immunize norms against critique), the interpersonal level of distortions (the way inequalities such as racism or gender are coded into "normal" interactions), and the intrapersonal level (power relations penetrate the deep structure of the psyche). Habermas' theory of communicative ethics provides critical adult education with the normative basis for its pedagogical practice.

5. Speaking of all institutions as educative allows us to preserve the developmentalist perspective of the liberal-humanist tradition. Both critical social theorists and liberal humanists (like Rogers and Maslow) have affirmed that human beings have the capacity for self-reflection and communicative interaction (Fay, 1987). But only critical social theorists contend strongly that structural conditions must enable human beings to unfold and express their capacities as speakers, doers, makers, creators. One of the central challenges for the social learning paradigm is to distinguish those conditions that facilitate developmental and emancipatory learning (allow us to become more knowledgeable and competent actors within differentiated domains), and those that do not (Forester, 1989).

6. Habermas identifies four key roles (employee, consumer, client, citizen), which are anchored in the lifeworld and enter into exchange relationships with the media of money and power. Examining these roles helps us to understand how these roles are structured under the conditions of late modernity to enable men and women to achieve their learning potential as active, reflective, autonomous actors. Here I will pay particular attention to the roles of worker and citizen and argue the case for "developmental work" and "developmental citizenship" as guiding ideals for the contemporary adult education movement. But I would add that it is also necessary for critical adult educators to speak of the importance of a "developmental nurturing environment" as a lifeworld prerequisite for critical role performance. Reflexive learning within the "family domain" has been intensely painful and agonizing over the last few decades. We are no longer very certain or clear about how and where our children should be raised and what constitutes normative partnering in a society that is intensely preoccupied with self-expression and identity-assertion.

THE CONTRADICTORY LEARNING POTENTIAL
OF MODERNITY

Habermas' work is of *central importance* for critical educational theory and practice. Of all contemporary theorists, Habermas is the one person who has consistently and consciously placed individual and social learning processes at the core of his massive project. Habermas argues that the full accomplishment of human individuation requires rational structures that permit "non-distorted communication" and concrete opportunities to exercise autonomy and responsibility. One of the practical effects of emancipatory theory, Habermas says, is to advance the "interest of reason in human adulthood" (1973, p. 256). His theory of communicative action, therefore, has important implications for critical educational practice. Dialogue and communicative action oriented to reaching a consensus in an uncoerced and free exchange (study circles, tutorial classes) has always been historically pivotal to the adult education movement; the presence of dialogic moments in associational life in the lifeworld has not been adequately theorized by adult educators, however. Habermas' manner of conceptualizing social evolution opens up important ways of examining this historical process as a social learning process. Unlike some contemporary social theorists, Habermas believes that reason is partially realized in the differentiated structures of contemporary capitalism, and that emancipatory action demands the full accomplishment of modernity and not its hopeless abandonment. He has argued his case most thoroughly in his magnum opus, *The Theory of Communicative Action* (1984, 1987b), and he has engaged his postmodernist foes in *The Philosophical Discourse of Modernity* (1987a). Habermas's manner of conceptualizing the "system" and the "lifeworld" of late modern, capitalist societies provides us with the conceptual framework to understand how to think deeply and realistically about the systemic blockages to the achievement of a more fully democratic society.

Social theorists from Tönnies to Weber have made the "process of modernization" (the transition from traditional to modern societies) central to their social theory. Although Habermas' analysis englobes those of others, he works through them critically to his own position primarily in dialogue with Max Weber, that despairing liberal. Weber's importance for us lies not only in his spiritual-theoretical confrontation with our age's "passion for bureaucracy." He has also captured our age's queasy ambivalence about the benefits of modernity. Our world, says Weber, has been disenchanted, and we celebrate the "death of the gods" as the cumulative progress of learning. Science, organized learning, technology, ethics, and art have escaped from the dogmatic clutches of the church. Their validity claims are no longer made with reference to a reflexively impervious universal deity. But, paradoxically for Weber, this expansion of learning possibilities seems to have been achieved at the expense of human freedom and meaning. Many antimodernists would no doubt agree: science and technology appear to many as an autonomous force riding humankind toward the precipice, and the "rage against reason" (Bernstein, 1991) sweeps through academia and sectors of the "cultures of protest." The iron cage and not the promised land appears to have greeted us down modernity's seductive road.

Habermas largely shares Weber's views on the origins of modernity. A new way of seeing and acting in the world emerges out of the social learning processes oriented to resolving the internal contradictions unfolding within the Judeo-Christian worldview. As God recedes into the heavens (becoming more transcendent), the world becomes more profane and opened up to "human inquiry and action" (Benhabib, 1981, p. 357). This process Habermas calls the decentering of the universe. Until humankind breaks free from closed, sacred worldviews, developmental learning (about the world, others, the self) is forestalled (Habermas, 1984, pp. 43–74). Tradition as a fundamental source of meaning does not dry up; rather, it is subjected to a rationalizing process. Theology, and its ground in faith, is pressed toward reflexivity (Peukert, 1984; McCarthy, 1991). This precipitates an agonizing and confused social learning process within religious traditions as people sift through their heritages to discover what elements ought to persist in postmodernity. Needless to say, in a modernizing world all religions find it difficult to provide a "comprehensive and comprehending orientation to life" (Borgmann, 1993, p. 144), and two tendencies are particularly noticeable in our society: (1) religion is privatized and driven into the inner worlds of monadic egos, and (2) spirituality is commodified and packaged by televangelical empires to provide the soft halo around the commodified life. It is not accurate, however, to think of "tradition" as an exhausted or "archaic" category (Williams, 1977). Traditions are still reservoirs of potential resistance to capitalist possessive individualism and values.

Weber's controversial argument asserts that ascetic Protestantism had the paradoxical effect of driving humankind towards world-affirmation. Religious culture is, then, the catalyst for occidental rationalization: learning to conduct life methodically. Weber captures these developments in his perceptive observation:

> Only the vocational ethic of ascetic Protestantism produced a principled, systematic and unbroken unity of an inner-worldly vocational ethic with the assurance of religious salvation. . . . This inner-world asceticism has a number of characteristics not found in any other religion. It demanded of the believer not celibacy, as in the case of the monk, but the elimination of all erotic pleasure or desire; not poverty, but the elimination of all idle enjoyment of unearned wealth and income, and the avoidance of all feudalistic, life-loving ostentation of wealth; not the ascetic death-in-life of the cloister, but an alert, rationally controlled conduct of life and the avoidance of all surrender to the beauty of the world, to art, or to one's moods and emotions. The clear and uniform goal of this asceticism was the disciplining and methodological organization of conduct. Its typical representation was the 'man of vocation' (*berufmensch*); and its specific result was the rational, functional organization of social relations. (Cited, Habermas, 1984, p. 173)

Purposive and value rationality fused into a "single life-form with universal significance" (Pusey, 1987, p. 50).

The Judeo-Christian worldview (its radically "Other" God) permitted nature within Western cultures to be demythologized and social action to be subsumed under a moral order. This development prefigured what Weber and Habermas view as a central component of modernity: the differentiation of cognitive, moral, and aesthetic value spheres (the true, the good, and the beautiful) and cultural orders. Formerly, these spheres were intermeshed within a unitary religious worldview and were not subject to *self-reflective learning processes*. Religious, mythological, or metaphysical worldviews unify the traditional lifeworld, and modernity inevitably decomposes religious worldviews, queries hierarchical forms of domination and those institutions (like churches) which attempt to "characterize the society as a whole" (Habermas, 1992, p. 193). For Weber the rationalization of production and the bureaucratization of the state-administrative system ends up swallowing value-rational action. To recall his oft-quoted words:

> The Puritan wanted to work in a calling; we are forced to do so. For
> when asceticism was carried out of ascetic cells into everyday life,
> and began to dominate worldly morality, it did its part in building the
> tremendous cosmos of the modern economic order. This order is now
> bound to the technical and economic conditions of machine produc-
> tion which today determine the lives of all the individuals who are
> born into this mechanism, not only those directly concerned with eco-
> nomic acquisition, with irresistible force. (Weber, 1958, pp. 181–82)

Thus, purposive rationality is identified with reason *tout court*; its "irresistible force" propels us fatefully towards the iron cage of modernity;
our culture becomes irreversibly relativistic and cynical; and individuals are cast into a disenchanted and disheartening world to make their
own way and construct their own meanings from the increasingly taxed
"stock of knowledge" in the lifeworld.

Habermas reconstructs Weber's argument to retrieve the learning
potential inherent in modernity. Like Weber, he insists that culture and
ethics (the realm of moral-practical learning) are the pacemaker of social
evolution (1979). But Habermas argues that because Weber has not
understood that the evolution of society moves along two paths, he has
no way of accounting for the "social pathologies" of modernity. Weber
cannot analyze the irrational functions of the economy and the state; he
can only lament humankind's loss of freedom and meaning. Habermas
would not dispute the fact that "feelings of alienation and despair" may
follow "demythologization, mechanization of production, and bureaucratization." But he thinks that modernity's "enhancement of individual
autonomy vis-à-vis tradition" and the "emergence of new possibilities
of meaning" resulting from "modern art and the democratic ethos of communicative humanism" compensate for our loss of meaning and freedom" (Ingram, 1987, p. 51). Pusey says that Habermas calls us to look
into our future along a treadline between two paths—structures of the
bureaucratic system of public administration and the economy steered
by labor, capital, and commodity markets press in on our lives, and the
beckoning potential of open possibilities within a renewed lifeworld and
further democratized system domains (Pusey, 1987, p. 56).

Habermas' revision of Weber's theory of rationalization assumes
that the splintering of the dogmatism of traditional worldviews carries
critical human learning potential. We can deepen our knowledge of the
world of "objective" facts, the norms and values governing our common
life, and the inner world of subjectivity. This opening up process also

permits us to scrutinize traditional values, norms, and forms of life, formerly taken-for-granted, for their dominative character and anti-dialogic communicative practices. For instance, the detraditionalization of the lifeworld creates the possibility of a critique of taken-for-granted values, norms, and roles within the family. Many feminist theorists have spoken of women's subordination within non-reflexive families, and have linked women's consignment to the private world of domestic space to their diminished role as citizen (Pateman, 1989; Okin, 1987). But critical adult educators must also contend with the new learning challenges facing individuals who are challenging the taken-for-grantedness of family life in an increasingly "individualized society" in which the "individual has to . . . learn to conceive of himself [sic] as a center of actions, as a planning bureau in relation to his life, his capabilities, his partnerships, etc." (Ulrich Beck, cited in Habermas [1992], p. 195).

Albrecht Wellmer argues that Habermas posits that "systemic rationalization" and "communicative rationalization" are complementary possibilities of rationalization in the contemporary world. Habermas' idea of communicative rationalization is grounded, many commentators have observed, in the structure of human speech itself (Habermas, 1970a; 1979, pp. 1–68; Honneth and Joas, 1991). He contends that the idea of non-distorted communication, the ideal speech situation or communicative rationality, is not arbitrary. Wellmer elaborates:

> (T)he notion of communicative rationality is also meant to indicate a conception (and self-conception) of symbolic communication which does not allow for any validity claims to be exempt in principle from possible critical examination. This is a reflexive conception of human communication according to which validity claims, because they can only emerge from the sphere of communication, can also only be redeemed in the sphere of human discourse: there are no possible external sources of validity, since the sphere of validity is—conceptually is—identical with the sphere of human speech. This reflexive awareness of human speech as the reference point of all validity claims presupposes, so it seems, that the validity dimensions of objective truth, normative rightness, and subjective sincerity . . . have been clearly differentiated from each other. The notion of communicative rationality reflects the cognitive and moral condition of humans in a 'disenchanted' world. (1985, p. 53)

This is what Habermas calls the "linguistification of the sacred."

Habermas is not willing to clamp the door shut on the iron cage. He argues that "elements of communicative rationalization" have been preserved in the "universalist principles of modern constitutions, in democratic forms of political organization, in forms of scientific, political, or aesthetic discourse, or in the self-interpretations and goals of social movements which fight for the rights of individuals, the integrity of the lifeworld, or the democratic organization of collective will formation" (Wellmer, 1985, p. 56). These democratic achievements reveal that the history of modernity is contested terrain. Popular social movements (workers' and socialist movements as sites of collective learning) in the mid-to-late nineteenth and early twentieth centuries) have struggled to make the world more democratic and can claim partial victories in the achievements of liberal democracy. Habermas' idealized lifeworld (his communicative humanist vision) can be understood as the center of gravitation of any democratic and egalitarian form of economic, social, and political organization.

THE LIFEWORLD AS BESIEGED SITE
FOR EMANCIPATORY LEARNING

Habermas views the "fundamental problem of social theory" as knowing how to connect the "system" and the "lifeworld" (1987b, pp. 151–52). Indeed, his critique of Marx's "theory of value" and Parsonian "systems theory" moves toward an adequate formulation of the changing relationship of system and lifeworld through time. The structural differentiation of the lifeworld is not distinguished in Marx, and the lifeworld loses its autonomy in Parsons. The concept of lifeworld (*Lebenswelt*), drawn from phenomenological discourse, is the "key methodological term in Habermas' later work" (Pusey, 1987, p. 58; compare Dallmayr, 1984 ["Appendix: Life-world and Communicative Action," pp. 224–53]). But the idea itself informs his work from its earliest formulations. For Habermas, the lifeworld is the background consensus of our everyday lives—"the vast stock of taken-for-granted definitions and understandings of the world that give coherence and direction to our everyday actions and interactions" (Pusey, 1987, p. 58). As Habermas relates:

> The symbolic structures of the lifeworld are reproduced by way of the
> continuation of valid knowledge, stabilization of group solidarity, and

socialization of responsible actors. The process of reproduction con-
nects up new situations with the existing conditions of the lifeworld;
it does this in the semantic dimension of meanings or contents (of the
cultural tradition), as well as in the dimensions of social space (of
socially integrated groups), and historical time (of successive genera-
tions). Corresponding to these processes of cultural reproduction,
social integration, and socialization are the structural components of
the lifeworld: culture, society, person. (Habermas, 1987b, pp. 137–38)

Habermas uses the term culture for the "stock of knowledge" which communicative actors draw upon to "come to an understanding about in the
world." By society, he means the "legitimate orders through which participants regulate their memberships in social groups and thereby secure
solidarity." By personality, he means the "competences that make a subject capable of speaking and action" and enable him/her to participate
in "processes of reaching understanding" and "assert [their] own identity." Therefore, the "interactions woven into the fabric of every communicative practice constitute the medium through which culture, society, and person get reproduced. These reproduction processes cover the
symbolic structures of the lifeworld" (1987b, pp. 137–38).

All significant social events and processes are directly or indirectly
manifest in the lifeworld, and any adequate understanding of human
action must move inside the meanings people give to their actions (the
interpretive procedure). No single person is ever fully aware of the way
the "background consensus" is shaping their everyday lives. The lifeworld is, therefore, always more than the "institutions of civil society"
that we speak of in political discourse. The lifeworld is the realm of
intersubjective interaction and adult learning par excellence, and intrusions from the system can generate pathologies by violating the normative processes governing life and action in the lifeworld itself. In our
rationalized society, cultural traditions possess the linguistic structures
that contain the formal concepts that allow people to differentiate
between the objective, social, and subjective dimensions of life and permit "interpretive revision of tradition, participation in interpersonal
relations, and self-realization" (Ingram, 1987, p. 117). Thus, when Habermas speaks of the "rationalization of the lifeworld," he is referring to
two axial processes: (1) the structural differentiation of the lifeworld
(the lifeworld uncouples from the system in the evolution to modernity
and specific institutions emerge for cultural reproduction, socialization
and social integration) and (2) the "growing reflexivity of symbolic

reproduction" (Habermas, 1987b, pp. 145–46). Both processes, Habermas believes, do not lead inexorably to the modernist dystopia of "sensualists without heart" and "specialists without spirit."

Habermas' famous metaphor—the "colonization of the lifeworld"—is constructed both to capture the deformations of late capitalist societies and to identify the critical learning potential of our present moment. Within Habermas' modernization narrative, the economic system (steered by money) and the state-administrative apparatus (steered by power) turn back upon contexts of communicative action and set their own imperatives against the marginalized lifeworld. The colonization of the lifeworld "sets in when the destruction of traditional forms of life can no longer be offset by more effectively fulfilling the functions of society as a whole. The functional ties of money and power become noticeable only to the degree that elements of a private way of life and a cultural-political form of life get split off from the symbolic structures of the lifeworld through the monetary redefinition of goals, relations and services, life-spaces and life-times, and through the bureaucratization of decisions, duties and rights, responsibilities and dependencies" (1987b, p. 322). At the level of system steering media, the economic system channels its exchanges with the lifeworld through the roles of worker and consumer. It is within the "private sphere" of the modern, restricted nuclear family (separated from the sphere of production through the modernization process) that the abstract market economy, coordinated independently of communicative action, is provided with labor power in exchange for wages, and monetarily measured goods and services, purchased, prepared, and consumed. The state-administrative system conducts parallel exchanges which link the "public sphere" and the state system with citizens who form their political will and clients who exchange their allegiance and tax revenues for organizational results and system management. Pusey says that both "media coordinate and 'behaviorize' action by 'steering it' with the imperatives that have all the characteristics of what Durkheim called 'social facts'—they coordinate action 'from outside in,' with obligatory force, in a 'nature-like' way that is inaccessible to reflection through lived experience recalled and shared in ordinary social interaction" (1987, p. 107).

The colonization of the lifeworld must be understood from the perspective of its deep costs to humanity (the pathologies manifest in an increasingly disturbed and traumatized lifeworld). Critical adult education practice has as its normative mandate the preservation of the lifeworld and the extension of communicative action into systemic domains; the fate of critical education is tied to the fate of the lifeworld. In fact, the very idea of an *emancipatory practice of adult education* could not appear historically until the mediatization of the lifeworld began to turn into its colonization. If the lifeworld were to become radically instrumentalized (what some postmodernists like Jean Baudrillard call the "end of the social" [1983a]), then critical adult education would lose its grounding. One way of examining the task and potential of critical adult education is to examine the interchanges between system and lifeworld roles at the historic moment of the exhaustion of the utopian potential of welfare-state capitalism.

From his early formulation, *The Structural Transformation of the Public Sphere* (1989b [org. 1962]) through *Legitimation Crisis* (1975) to his recent systematic work (*Theory of Communicative Action* [1984, 1987b] and essays ("The Crisis of the Welfare State and the Exhaustion of Utopian Energies" [in Seidman, 1989], and "What does Socialism Mean Today? The Revolutions of Recuperation and the Need for New Thinking" [in Blackburn, 1991]), Habermas has tried to develop a theory of welfare-state capitalism with emancipatory intent. His argument can be explicated in three propositions.

1. Welfare-state capitalism emerges out of the crisis tendencies of capitalism, and leads to a realignment of the relations between the state and economy. The state-administrative system becomes increasingly involved in "crisis management" as it attempts to steer crises breaking out in the economy. We can speak of an "enhanced role of the political system in managing capitalism's development" (Leonard, 1988, p. 111): class conflict is defused into system-conforming rewards in clientage and consumption and the public sphere is neutralized (Habermas speaks of the "desiccation of the political public sphere" [1987b, p. 323]). Systemic integration expands, social integration weakens. The roles of employee and citizen are disempowered. Workers within the ascendant phase of welfare-state capitalism are expected to conform to systemic imperatives and citizens are expected to be satisfied with elite management of the system. Employees and citizens exchange autonomy and exercise of responsibility for security, comfort, and order. But they do so at a cost, which while unnoticed at first, breaks into the open at the historic watershed marking capitalism's radical restructuring of

the world economy. The cost lies primarily with the expansion of systemic integration into the lifeworld. European social and legal theorists speak of the process of juridification. By this they mean that the state-administrative apparatus reifies everyday life situations (family, education, old age, physical and mental health and well-being) in order to control their clients. The ones who do the actual work of managing clients are experts in lifeworld administration (like social workers, health care workers, adult educators, dieticians). Their professional practice is tugged between systemic and lifeworld interests. Thus, the compensations for adapting (more or less) to the pacification of social labor and the neutralization of participation in political decision-making processes (Habermas, 1987b, p. 351) become problematized themselves. The reification of the lifeworld increases client dependency on "bureaucracies, therapeutocracies, preempting their capacities to interpret their own needs, experiences and life-problems" (Fraser, 1987, p. 47). The juridification of the lifeworld also encourages people to pursue their life plans as strategic-rational, self-interested monads. Lifeworld solidarity is eroded and personalities are shaped by strategic-instrumental interests. The web of client relations blankets the core areas of the lifeworld, and prepares the way for the possibility of a rebellion against the systemically defined nature of the client role.

2. The professionalization process intensifies during the period of welfare-state capitalism, creating serious problems for a critical practice of adult education. Habermas reinterprets the Weberian "loss of meaning" theme as "cultural impoverishment." The problem of the differentiation and development of cultural value spheres does not lie in the differentiation process per se. Rather, Habermas identifies the "elitist splitting-off of expert cultures from contexts of communicative action in daily life" (1987b, p. 330) as the problem. Ironically, as the lifeworld is rationalized and opened up to *reflexive learning processes*, experts move in to take over their elaboration and management. The cognitive potential in the domains of science, technology, and art is removed from the people so to speak, and the Enlightenment dream of infusing daily life with the results of science scarcely lies intact today. Habermas argues that the "distance between expert cultures and the broader public grows greater. What accrues to a culture by virtue of specialized work and reflection does not come as a matter of course into the possession of everyday practice. Rather, cultural rationalization brings with it the danger that a lifeworld devalued in its traditional substance

will become impoverished" (1987b, p. 326). Knowledge produced by experts, who speak arcane languages to ever-more-fragmented audiences, is barricaded from the everyday lives of people. The lifeworld is both colonized and segmented from science, morality, and art. Society in the abstract grows smarter, people get dumber. Simply put, most of us have more and more difficulty making "effective use of the cognitive arsenal of cultural modernity" (Leonard, 1988, p. 117). For Habermas, the emergence of expert cultures, which replace enervating traditions, undermines the classic Marxian notion of ideology. One can no longer speak of ideology as the ideational glue that enables a ruling (or hegemonic) class to dominate subaltern classes. "False consciousness" has been replaced by "fragmented consciousness" (Eagleton, 1991, pp. 128–34). No longer do "cognitive interpretations, moral expectations, expressions, and valuations . . . interpenetrate and form a rational interconnectedness via the transfer of validity. . . . This communicative infrastructure is threatened by two interlocking, mutually reinforcing tendencies: *systemically induced reification* and *cultural impoverishment*" (Habermas, 1987b, p. 327). The consequences of the fragmented consciousness for persons are quite devastating. Our life compasses go awry and we do not know how to orient ourselves any longer, and it becomes more difficult to construct a coherent life narrative.

3. The exacerbation of the contradictions of welfare-state capitalism has occurred through the years of neo-conservative ascendancy. During this time the economic system has pried itself loose from the constraining effects of the political system, and the consumer role has been enhanced at the expense of the worker and citizen roles. The economic system has subjected the "life-forms of private households and the life conduct of consumers and employees to its imperatives, consumerism and possessive individualism, motives of performance, and competition" (Habermas, 1987b, p. 325). A commodified, utilitarian life-style increasingly prevails (and most continuing adult education caters to this tendency within late capitalism) and mass culture is replete with hedonistic siren-calls away from communicative rationality.

In our roles as consumers, we confront the "intensive commodification of private life: the growing categorization and redefinition of new areas of private life through the intrusion of exchange value. Leisure, family life, sexual relationships, and even one's sense of self and development as a human being, increasingly become targets of commodification, as we are presented with new and more extensive pre-selected packages of behavioral, psychological and sexual scripts" (Leonard, 1988, p. 115). Derek Briton and Donovan Plumb even argue that the culture industries are now "solely concerned with the production of cultural commodities that can be rapidly and easily consumed in any context, that is, cultural artifacts that are detached from any particular meaning frame. . . . These products are consumed not because consumers find them meaningful but because they appeal, directly, to the soma of the consumer" (1993, p. 4). The culture industries do attempt to bypass discursivity to channel desire into satisfaction through commodity consumption. But it is equally important to understand that an eroded lifeworld (the locus of identity formation, community, and meaning) abhors a vacuum. Television, radio and movies are the primary media for fostering a "bureaucratic society of controlled consumption" (Lefebvre, 1971). Advertising, electronic media, and mass publications assign new meanings to commodities, values to symbolically enriched packages of material life, and purposes to conventional scripts of personal improvement in advanced capitalism. Thus, values, meanings, and purposes are, for many, no longer produced and sustained through the everyday life rituals and communicative practices of family, neighborhood, church, or workplace. This commodification process is further evident in our public life. Timothy Luke speaks of the "televisual pre-fab quality of contemporary American politics," and Paul Piccone of the "spectacularization of politics" which requires the "prepackaging of whatever political issue is advocated to fit the media form" (Anderson et al., 1991, pp. 9, 5).

IN DEFENSE OF THE LIFEWORLD

A critical adult education privileges the realm of the lifeworld as site for learning to command our life situations. But under the conditions of late modernity, the colonization of the lifeworld has taken its toll. Here we can speak only of general tendencies within the global order. Within the liberal democratic welfare-states, the roles of worker and citizen have been severely disempowered. These roles do not tend to channel the influence of the lifeworld to the system. Now, the newly inflated roles of consumer and client channel the influence of the system to the lifeworld. This anti-normative inversion of human life "desiccates the communicative contexts of our common life and depletes nonrenewable cultural resources" (Fraser, 1987, p. 48). This invasion of the lifeworld generates several disturbing pathological conditions: personalities are destabilized, sources of meaning dry up, and communal bonds erode. Those with money and power stave off despair and lifeworld disintegration through the compensations of the commodified good life. Those in the underclass drop into an ever-deepening morass of violence, drugs, alcoholism, and criminality. UNESCO seminar talk of lifelong learning and empowerment seems like a cruel joke of new class ideologists. Nothing works very well anymore.

I have argued elsewhere that Habermas' theory helps us think about how adult educators can assist in creating developmental, learner-centered, and emancipatory institutions within which individuals can find purpose and identity. He believes that while all institutions are educative, not all are true communicative learning communities. He encourages us to ask whether our institutions, large and small, truly enable human beings to unfold their potentials (cognitive, moral, technical, aesthetic) in their daily routine interactions and deliberations (Welton, 1993a). I would like to explore what these rather pleasant-sounding phrases mean in relationship to the roles of worker and citizen in our dystopic world. The fate of critical adult education is tied closely to these two roles.

Expressed in a very elemental way, I have always thought that human beings living in a modern world must have good work and be able to be active citizens. Without good work and active citizenship, infused by a sense of the meaning of the whole, life goes sour and the pathological consequences reverberate in and out of the lifeworld. It is in the spirit of Habermas' work to argue that the human individuation process (the sustaining and opening-out of meaning, self-realization, and solidarity) must not be blocked within the domains of adult interaction. Cultural reproduction, social integration, and socialization continue throughout the life span; they do not end at adolescence. The actually existing structures of work may arrest adult development, with severe consequences for character development. We must be able to do and create useful things and services for others. And the public sphere is a fundamental space for adults to unfold and express their capacities as authentic speakers and decision-makers. If the system blocks meaningful work and citizenship, what happens, in effect, is the creation of a powerful dam within the lifeworld. This dam will build up and eventually burst its walls.

At first glance, it seems that Habermas banishes the redeeming power of reflection from the sphere of work itself (unlike the more romantic Marcuse [Agger, 1992, pp. 172–90]). To be sure, Habermas argues that the emancipatory interest manifests itself in the domain of work as humankind learns how to circumvent the constraints of nature and overcome material scarcity. The realm of work remains the "realm of necessity," and humankind's exercising of technical control over natural processes is bound up with "liberation from hunger and misery" (1973, p. 169). Habermas asserts immediately that this liberation, dependent upon cumulative learning processes in the sphere of work, does not converge automatically with "liberation from servitude and degradation." There is no "automatic developmental relationship between labor and interaction" (p. 169). This controversial conceptual move enables Habermas to explore why, in the modern welfare state, the coming-to-the-end of a "particular utopia that in the past crystallized around the potential of a society based on social labor" (1989a, p. 287) does not signal the exhaustion of "utopian expectations" as such. The idea of worker self-management, however, has lost its "persuasive power" to "project future possibilities for a collectively better and less threatened way of life" (p. 288).

There can be no doubt that Habermas tends to restrict the interest of reflective reason to the overcoming of material scarcity and suggests that emancipatory social learning processes outside the sphere of work itself could lead to the transformation of the organization of labor. The transformation of work into a realm of intersubjective communication depends, therefore, on the "organization of enlightenment" in workers' organizations or, more promisingly, in new social movements. The contemporary struggle in British Columbia's Clayoquot Sound between the forest industry and social movement activists of various stripe indicates that social learning processes within the lifeworld (new ways of understanding our relation to nature) can feed into the system domain of the instrumental organization of logging (in this case, of centuries-old Douglas Fir). Most of the workers within the forest industry have assimilated themselves to the logic of the corporate organization of this industry, and the British Columbian state-administrative apparatus has historically served big capital. Thus, here we see social learning processes originating outside the sphere of social labor precipitating reflective learning processes within the system domain itself, with the potential to create a more communicatively and ecologically attuned organization of work. But the impetus toward transformation of a fundamentally instrumental, exploitative relationship to nature is hardly emerging from within the capitalist mode of production itself. Still, having said that, one also knows that the depletion of meaning from contemporary work has created a seething restlessness in an extraordinary number of workplaces.

Habermas's depiction of work as a sphere of calculating, bureaucratic action—a domain into which "unfettered partnership or communication cannot enter," a realm of "dumb necessity," "solitary and silent" (Keane, 1984, p. 136) accurately captures the dominant historical tendency within the capitalist organization of work. This, too, is the central theme in Mechthild Hart's neo-Adornoian text, *Working and Educating for Life* (1992). But, in my view, Habermas tends to reify this process and, consequently, cannot argue that the sphere of work partially realizes (for a few) the radical human need for self-determination and could become an individuating structure for many more. This would require the "abolition of heteronomy" (lack of moral freedom or self-determination) from the sphere of work, which would depend upon the convergence of oppositional learning within and without the domain of work. Habermas can admit of the need to transform the goals orienting the labor process (e.g., the planned humanization of work conditions). But the "subjective, creative moment of labor (i.e., the autonomous development of producers' capacities) would always be subordinated to its objective aspects, namely, to the tasks of controlling nature through the fabrication of a world of artificial objects" (Keane, 1984, p. 206).

Habermas' dichotomizing of work and interaction, a crucial epistemological conceptual move, may obscure, however, the extent to which the social organization of technology and work by a small minority of "work designers" has been developed not strictly according to the value of efficiency (guided by the empirical-analytic sciences), but rather according to the particular interest in controlling and disciplining the labor force. Habermas does not believe, as Eyerman and Shipway think, that technological development is a "transcendent and neutral process" (1981, p. 563). But he chooses to downplay the old Marxian notion that the alienating experience of work itself may still generate the radical need to transcend the existent bureaucratic development of the productive forces for exchange. The concrete, historical evidence of workers' struggles indicates that producers' "consciousness of injustice" (Keane, 1984, p. 208) and moral-practical struggle emerges within the learning domain of work, and can serve as catalysts for collective social movements (Johnson, 1993).

John Keane argues that the "bureaucratic supervision within the workplace produces struggles for the questioning and abolition of bureaucracy. These moral-practical struggles against a labor process rationally planned and executed from above and outside embody an embryonic form of autonomous public life" (1984, p. 209). Eyerman and Shipway also think—and here I am in agreement—that the transition to a freer, more rational society is a task which "must contain as at least one of its goals an altogether different view of work, one which emphasizes reciprocal and collective relationships of worker control over technological growth, direction and productivity, and which will be goal-directed towards individual creativity and expressivity" (1981, p. 563). This goal—the "self-management of complex and socially necessary labor processes"—Habermas might view as "illusory and unrealizable" (Keane, 1984, p. 209). Habermas thinks that the very idea of self-determined activity requires sources of solidarity rooted in workers' subcultures. But, since these sources of solidarity have eroded, or disappeared under the onslaught of suburbanization and consumerism, the workplace lacks the power to create solidarity. We can no longer assume the "utopian idea of a laboring society" (Habermas, 1989a, p. 298). The possibilities of what I would call "developmental work" can now be posed only as a "theme for discussion" (p. 298). The potential of the workplace as a site for emancipatory learning remains at least partially open. We cannot close the case against the "introduction of public spheres of discussion and decision-making within the sphere of (socially necessary) production" because the "technical or means-oriented questions concerning tools, the design of work procedures, and so on nevertheless cannot be reduced to technical rules of decision making. If only because these rules do not reveal themselves spontaneously and transparently" (Keane, 1984, p. 209). The presence of emancipatory, reflective moments within the learning domain of work speaks of the necessity, within the Habermasian framework, of having "autonomous public communication enter the realm of the office, the factory, the department store, and the laboratory" (p. 210). Critical adult educators practice must be brutally realistic here: our mandate is to argue and struggle for workplaces that open up space for non-coerced, free communication pertaining to the organization, control, and purposes of work. We must search for "receptors for societal influence within the belly of the whale, as it were" (Arato and Cohen, 1992, p. 480). But the dice are loaded against us. The possibility of developmental work exists only for a relatively small percentage of employees whose workplaces demand increasingly complex forms of knowledge and call for the exercise of autonomy and collective responsibility (Zuboff, 1988; Hart, 1993).

Another fundamental task confronting critical adult educators is to work for new, communicative relationships between professionals and their clients. The professions, many of which are in crisis, still retain a stock of ethical commitment to serve others without being driven by the imperative of making more money. They are not totally instrumentalized. The painful social learning processes currently evident in the medical professions, for instance, has its primary roots in lifeworld rebellions against forms of domination exhibited by doctors. There are many other issues currently being debated, and critical adult educators ought to enter into dialogue with those who are experimenting with attempts to re-embed work in the lifeworld, those who are arguing for the sharing of ever decreasing waged work widely among society's members and those who are attempting to reinvent the meaning of work in a society of increased permanent unemployment and diminishing finances for the state-client system. Mechthild Hart's chapter in this book exemplifies this move to return work to the lifeworld. Richard Barnet maintains that: "In the end, the job crisis raises the most fundamental question of human existence: What are we doing here? There is a colossal amount of work waiting to be done by human beings—building decent places to live, exploring the universe, making cities less dangerous, teaching one another, raising our children, visiting, comforting, healing, feeding one another, dancing, making music, telling stories, inventing things, and governing ourselves. But much of the essential activity people have always undertaken to raise and educate their families, to enjoy themselves, to give pleasure to others, and to advance the general welfare is not packaged as jobs. Unless we rethink work and decide what human beings are meant to do in the age of robots and what basic economic claims on society human beings have by virtue of being here, there will never be enough jobs" (1993, p. 52). At each point in every debate, our standpoint is simply this: does the organization of work enable or constrain human beings to develop their capacities for speech and action? How can work become meaningful? If work is not meaningful, or increasingly unavailable, what are the consequences for the lifeworld?

Habermas believes that under the damaging conditions of late capitalist life, citizens have often been treated as objects of bureaucratic manipulation and administration. The counterbureaucratic goal of public, unrestricted communication in which people are involved in learning procedures of "discursive formation of will that put [them] in a position to realize concrete possibilities for a better and less threatened life, on their own initiative and in accordance with their own needs and insights" (Habermas, 1989a, p. 299) is posited as mandate for critical adult educators committed to a revitalized citizen role. Ben Agger (1981) believes that Habermas' theory of communicative competence and systematically distorted communication can be construed as "ideology critique" for the technocratic phase of capitalism. Technocratic capitalism, Agger says, legitimates the social order by requiring its people to relinquish an "active participatory role in the market place and in politics in exchange for greater material comfort and occupational security" (1981, p. 8). This ideology he labels "socially structured silence." Simply put, technocratic society is too complex for worker and citizen participation; the monopoly of capital goes hand-in-hand with the monopoly of information and dialogue chances. Our economic and political elites think that most issues are beyond citizen competence. Their specialized knowledge requires our silence; self-directing citizen action is deemed impossible or dangerous in a "complex world of institutional giants" (1981, p. 9).

From the perspective of a critical theory of dialogue, the fundamental problem with the political order is insufficient "dialogic justification" of elite decision-making and power. For Habermas, the entry into dialogue is a "deeply political action"—the "expressive form of critique" of a technocratic society (Agger, 1981, pp. 18–19). In Marx's time political enlightenment was triggered around "life-and-death matters of material deprivation" (p. 20). In our time the character of ideology has changed as we are presented with technocratic "laws" of socioeconomic complexity. This ideology sanctions (or used to sanction) elite governance through inhibiting participation. Dialogue, therefore, is placed squarely in the center of critical theory because the "loss of people's 'dialogue chances' is the most fundamental mode of ideological dominance in advanced capitalism" (p. 20).

It is only when citizens ask the power holders to engage in justificatory dialogues—What reasons can you provide us with that justifies our exclusion from dialogue? How can you justify your claim to have a superior conception of the good?—that possibilities for developmental citizenship open up. The recognition of the very possibility of dialogue ignites the political learning process, and immediately confronts us with the "real-world [of] exploitation, monopolies of power and wealth that do not admit of dialogic justification" (p. 12). Progressive adult educators like the American Eduard Lindeman believed that "intelligent participation" in the control of public affairs called for the production of a "large number of socially-sensitive, healthy-minded, progressive adults" (Stewart, 1987, p. 171). Lindeman insisted that adult education was a method that focused on the way adults could "discover the meaning of their experiences, analyze their situations, and plan actions to work through the situation" (Stubblefield, 1988, p. 143). Lindeman linked learning with the multiple realities of adult life, and sensed that adult "situations" had to be structured to permit and not hinder dialogue. How do individuals become public-spirited? How do they acquire the characterological traits of tolerance, respect for others, the ability to listen and to enter into dialogue (Gould, 1988)?

The emergence of the well-informed or activated citizen, whose education through participation spirals outward, reaching to new levels of political knowledge and competency, has emerged most decisively in our time on the terrain of civil society in *defense of the threatened lifeworld*. The new social movements (ecology, peace, women, local and personal autonomy) are privileged sites for the rebellious speech of citizens. These "new conflicts," Habermas observes,

> arise along the seams between system and lifeworld. . . . Alternative practice is directed against the profit-dependent instrumentalization of work in one's vocation, the market-dependent mobilization of labor power, against the extension of pressures of competition and performance all the way down into elementary school. It also takes aim at the monetarization of services, relationships, and time, at the consumerist redefinition of private spheres of life and personal life-styles. Furthermore, the relation of clients to public service agencies is to be opened up and reorganized in a participatory mode, along the lines of self-help organizations. It is above all in the domains of social policy and health policy (e.g., in connection with psychiatric care) that models of reform point in this direction. Finally, certain forms of protest

negate the definitions of the role of citizen and the routines for pursuing interests in a purposive-rational manner. (Habermas, 1987b, p. 395)

Andrew Arato and Jean Cohen argue in *Civil Society and Political Theory* (1992) that the new social movements ought to be understood as dynamic elements in social learning processes and identity-formation. These movements have the "potential to initiate processes by which the public sphere might be revived and discourses institutionalized, within a wide range of social institutions" (1992, p. 527). Critical adult educators have as their mandate the initiation of political learning processes that (1) target new political actors for recognition and inclusion within political society (a "politics of inclusion"), (2) aim to influence the "universe of political discourse to accommodate new need-interpretations, new identities, and new norms" (a "politics of influence"), and (3) attempt to create receptors within political institutions and to democratize political society (the "politics of reform" [Arato and Cohen, 1992, p. 526]). Thus, within our critical social learning paradigm, we can identify the collective learning processes occurring within the new social movements themselves as well as in a plethora of voluntary associations and the *mediational political learning processes* that manifest themselves when activated citizens engage the elite managers of economic and state steering media in dialogue and contestation. Critical adult educators would be committed to defending an autonomous and exuberant civil society.

CONCLUSION

In this chapter, I have argued that a critical adult education practice requires a social learning theory. This new social learning paradigm replaces the older andragogical paradigm in a historical epoch of the exhaustion of utopian dreams. No longer does the "myth of progress" grip our Western imagination. Habermas' theory retains a hopefulness in a disenchanted and despairing time. His model of system and lifeworld and manner of theorizing roles provides critical adult educators with a normative and theoretical frame for their practice in a complex and differentiated society. Critical adult education practice cannot be identified in conceptually sloppy and vague ways with "education for social transformation." Societies are not undifferentiated wholes, and no educational practice ever transforms society! But if we understand that the fundamental task of critical adult educators is to preserve the communicative infrastructure of the lifeworld and extend communicative action into state or economic institutions, then we are able to speak in determinate and realistic ways about the enlightenment and empowerment of persons who occupy different roles with different potential for collective self-determination through communicative action.

6

Declining Opportunities:
Adult Education, Culture, and Postmodernity

Donovan Plumb

Few concepts are as central to the so-called "critical" forms of adult education[1] as is culture. Critical adult education positions itself in society as a cultural practice and depicts its practitioners as "cultural workers" (Westwood, 1980, p. 44). The tools it uses are deemed to be cultural and its aspiration is "cultural freedom" (Freire, 1985). All too often, however, it is forgotten that critical adult education's understanding of what culture is and of what role it plays in society is inseparable from the larger socio-historical developments that have transfigured our world over the past two centuries. Critical adult education's representation of its relationship with culture and its depiction of itself as a cultural practice are forms of thinking that are clearly modernist. It is precisely these modernist forms of thought that have come under scrutiny in recent years in the heated discourses of postmodernism. For many postmodernists who are sceptical of the assumptions of modernity, the concept of culture, which critical adult educators seem to take for granted, is highly problematic. Postmodernist discourses suggest that rapid social changes are transforming what constitutes culture and are refashioning its place in contemporary society far beyond what is depicted in modernist discourses. Not only is culture being commodified to an unprecedented degree, its form is changing from one that is essentially discursive to one that is increasingly figural, which, in turn, transforms its social role. Some postmodern discourses, particularly those tracing their heritage to post-structuralism, celebrate this change as a final end to the oppressive emancipatory hopes of modernity. Others, especially Marxist discourses, despair over the bleak options left for an emancipatory politics. The cultural changes transpiring in postmodernity represent a disconcerting challenge for the modernist and emancipatory discursive formation of critical adult education.

CULTURE IN MODERNITY

We must keep in mind that complex and heavily used concepts like culture cannot be fully circumscribed. Only through mining the varied discourses that thematize culture can we gain a sense of how its "meaning is embedded in actual relations as well as processes of social and historical change" (Easthope and McGowan, 1992, p. 258). Raymond Williams provides a serviceable depiction of culture when he contends that it is "a whole way of lifewhich expresses certain meanings and values not only in art and learning, but also in institutions and ordinary language" (Williams, cited in Hebdige, 1976, p. 6). Williams' broad definition corresponds more with the anthropological sense of the word than it does with narrowly construed notions of culture such as 'high culture' or 'popular culture'. Culture is not a particular set of manners or habits or, as Williams writes in relation to 'working-class culture', "proletarian art, or council houses, or a particular use of language" (Williams, 1992, p. 229). Rather, it refers to a broad fabric of meanings and interpretations that members of a social group can draw upon to make sense of and share their lived experiences.

Concurring with Williams' definition, Habermas agrees that culture is "the stock of knowledge from which participants in communication supply themselves with interpretations as they come to an understanding about something in the world" (1987b, p. 138). In traditional societies, culture provides a vast and complete framework of interpretations (a worldview) that "secures the unity of the collectivity and largely suppresses conflicts that might arise from power relations and economic interests" (p. 87). In modern societies, however, culture loses its taken-for-granted status. Individual cultural elements—knowledge, representations, symbols—no longer hold a sacred, binding power on individuals and no longer smoothly coordinates action (Lash, 1990, p. 45). Instead, as a result of a general evolutionary process that Habermas (1987b) identifies as the "linguistification of the sacred," cultural elements assume the status of validity claims and, for the first time, become susceptible to critique (pp. 77–111). Once an all-powerful and all-inclusive force for action coordination, in modernity culture now assumes the new role of providing a background of interpretations that discourse participants can draw upon to work out action coordinating understandings.

In modernity, culture undergoes other changes. Whereas, in traditional societies, culture is undifferentiated, in modern society, three different cultural spheres emerge and gradually gain autonomy from one another: the theoretical, the ethical, and the aesthetic cultural spheres. In each sphere, people evaluate cultural elements according to how well they meet discursive criteria specific to that sphere. In the theoretical sphere, people assess cultural elements according to the accurateness of their representations. Institutions of science emerge to produce their cultural products—representations. In the ethical sphere, people assess cultural elements according to their congruence with legitimate moral codes. Legal institutions emerge to produce their products—laws and judgments. Finally, in the aesthetic sphere, people evaluate cultural elements according to their expressiveness and beauty. Institutions of art and art criticism emerge to produce art objects and art critique (Habermas, 1990, pp. 17–18).

Despite these changes, one aspect of culture stays the same: it remains the backdrop for the symbolic reproduction of society. Lifeworld members refresh and reproduce that stock of interpretations as they draw upon the cultural stock of interpretations to work out common situation definitions, to affirm the norms governing social integration, and to socialize their young. *"Cultural reproduction* ensures that (in the semantic dimension) newly arising situations can be connected up with existing conditions in the world; it secures the continuity of tradition and a coherency of knowledge sufficient for the consensus needs of everyday practice" (Habermas, 1987b, p. 343). It is important to appreciate the above evolutionary characteristics of modern culture. But our understanding will remain incomplete if we do not, at the same time, understand the historically contingent characteristics culture assumes when considered in light of the dramatic relationship between system and lifeworld that distinguishes modernity.[2] The process of lifeworld rationalization increasingly burdens people with working out action coordinating agreements through communication and creates pressure to find other, less risk-prone means of action coordination, particularly in the area of *material reproduction*. The emergence of alternate steering-media like money and power disburden the lifeworld of the need to coordinate select actions. Unlike communicative action, these media do not require culture to coordinate actions for material production. Their emergence and their subsequent organization as sub-systems of action coordination initiates a long and complicated interaction between system and lifeworld. Within this interaction, culture assumes an important if somewhat peculiar role.

Habermas notes that Marx's analysis of the commodity recounts how the economic sub-system removes the process of action coordination from the worker's lifeworld. Marx's analysis provides the basis for

clarifying the role culture plays in modernity. He begins his account of
the commodity by distinguishing two different ways the value of products are assessed.[3] The use-value of a product, he contends, is derived
from the utility it has for its consumer. The use-value of a coat, for
instance, is assessed according to the way it satisfies the complex needs
of its wearer—it may provide warmth, draw glances, become a good
pillow. According to Marx, "this usefulness doesn't dangle in mid-air.
It is conditioned by the physical properties of the commodity, and has
no existence apart from the latter" (1977, vol. 1, p. 126). Marx's statement does not imply that a thing can only be considered to have use-
value if it satisfies a *physical* need. It does not matter from where the
needs arise, Marx insists, "whether they arise, for example, from the
stomach or the imagination, makes no difference" (p. 125). Marx is
aware that, whatever the need, it is always the result of a complex process of social interaction (vol. 3, p. 282). On the other hand, however,
as the following passage discloses, he is also convinced that use-value
emerges in relation to biological, if not primordial, human needs:

> The labour-process, resolved as above into its simple elementary
> factors . . . is human action with a view to the production of use-val-
> ues, appropriation of natural substances to human requirements; it is
> the necessary condition for effecting exchange matter between man
> and nature; it is the everlasting nature-imposed condition of human
> existence, and therefore is independent of every social phase of that
> existence, or rather, is common to every social phase. (Marx in Sayer,
> 1989, p. 43)

Marx believes that the value of a thing exchanged in the market (a
commodity) is assessed very differently from its use-value. The
exchange-value of a commodity has nothing to do with its utility or with
any needs it might satisfy. When the exchange-value of a commodity is
assessed, "all its sensuous characteristics are extinguished" (vol. 1, p.
128), including any knowledge of who made it, under which conditions,
who might consume it, and why. Instead, its value is assessed solely its
exchange value in the market. The concrete social relations governing
production and consumption are made abstract and mystified by the
process of commodification. As Marx writes:

> The mysterious character of the commodity-form consists therefore
> simply in the fact that the commodity reflects the social characteristics
> of men's own labour as objective characteristics of the products of

labour themselves, as the socio-natural properties of these things. Hence it also reflects the social relation of the producers to the sum total of labour as a social relation between objects, a relation which exists apart from and outside the producers. (vol. 1. p. 165)

Marx realizes that the capitalist system does not employ abstract labor power. It employs complete human beings who are born and raised within a cultural context. Labour power, a fundamental and inseparable part of every human being, is abstracted in the capitalist labor process and transformed into a commodity to be sold on the marketplace. Marx's primary concern, however, is to reveal how the commodification of labor is, in itself, sufficient to mystify the inequitable relations that lie at the base of capitalism.

The limitations of Marx's analysis of the relationship between exchange-value and use-value begin to become apparent if we reinterpret this relationship in Habermasian terms. For Habermas, the emergence of money provides a new basis for organizing people's actions for material production. The valuation of objects is abstracted by means of commodification from the cultural contexts of workers and carried out within the restricted and objectifying value sphere of the economy according to the cold, passionless calculations of mean-ends rationality.

A very different process is used for the valuation of objects within the lifeworld. The use-value of a thing and the actions required to produce it are not determined abstractly outside of the cultural context. Rather, the use-value of a thing is determined through a process in which social actors either position it in an existing interpretive framework (culture)—Marx identifies this framework as "social needs"—or, drawing upon the interpretive framework of culture, communicatively work out new agreements about its value. From this perspective, the label 'use-value' appears to be somewhat of a misnomer. Its utility does not determine the value of a thing in the lifeworld; rather, value is determined by the meaning it accrues within a cultural context. Something may not have much utility (in the sense that its physical presence does not gratify any concrete needs) but still be valued highly because within that cultural context it is an item of great meaning.

Jean Baudrillard makes this difference clear in his critique of Marx's concept of use-value. In his essay, "Beyond Use Value," Baudrillard (1981) states that the same critique that Marx levels at exchange-value—that it is an abstraction that fetishizes the commodity as an object independent of social relations—can also be applied to Marx's own notion of use-value (pp. 130–32). Marx posits use-values as derivable from the simple relationship of a product to primordial human needs, "a universal and immediately transparent relation that expresses the true being of productive labour beyond all historical or cultural determinants" (Bogard, 1988, p. 230). Then, with use-value as his benchmark, Marx argues that exchange-value is a synthetic way of assessing value that has less to do with "true" human needs than it does with the desire of capitalists to make money from commodity exchange. Marx fails to subject the notion of use-value (and especially his assumptions about true human needs) to the same critique he applies to exchange-value.

Baudrillard, however, makes such a critique. Beginning with needs, he contends that they are not natural and ahistorical. In the words of Pefanis (1991), "[f]ar from being the objective and natural effect of the commodity system (or any system for that matter), needs themselves are the product of a system that inscribes utility at the heart of the object and a productivist mentality in the individual" (p. 74). Marx overlooks the fact that utility as the basis of product valuation is itself the outcome of a particular social and historical context: namely, a point in the development of capitalism when basic physiological requirements are only barely being met, and where the commodities produced are very basic (food, clothing, shelter, fuel, transportation). Baudrillard points out, however, that people "need" objects for many reasons other than their usefulness. Following Thorstein Veblen, he observes that very often people consume objects not because they need them but because they *do not* need them. They consume them, in other words, to distinguish themselves as possessing certain characteristics or to exhibit social status.[4] This is only possible because, in addition to having a material presence, objects have the capacity to signify and to communicate meaning. Applying a structuralist analysis, Baudrillard says that an object's meaning results from the same semiotic process that provides other signs with meaning: the meaning of the object/sign is derived from the relationship it has to other signs, and, ultimately, from its position within large sign systems that comprise our culture.[5] Thus he writes that "[a]n accurate theory of objects will not be established upon a theory of needs and their satisfaction, but upon a theory of social presentations and signification" (Baudrillard, 1981, p. 30).

Baudrillard's contention that Marx's utility notion of social need obscures other reasons people might consume commodities (consumption of commodities as "terms within a complex social code" [Bogard, 1988, p. 231]) overlaps, in interesting ways, with Habermas' contention that "social needs" are worked out in processes of discursive will formation. In his theory of communicative action, Habermas posits that, when people assert the validity of a claim (a claim about the value of an object, in this instance), they can expect to defend not only why they think their claim is true, but also why they believe it to be morally right (i.e., accords with a cultural code regulating intersubjective interactions) and sincere (Habermas, 1984, p. 307). Baudrillard's criticism that Marx mistakenly interprets the socio-historically privileged term "utility" in his depiction of use-value can be rewritten in Habermasian terms as follows: Marx is duped by the very form of rationality he is trying to escape (means-ends rationality of the system) when, in his analysis of use-value, he imputes this same form of instrumental rationality to the lifeworld (value as utility) (Habermas, 1987b, p. 342).[6] The process of valuation that would take place in contexts of communicative action does not restrict itself to questions (claims) of whether an object has utility. It also is open to claims about the place the object holds in the complex system of norms and values.

In the end, Marx's analysis of the commodity as the basic social form through which capitalists exploit living labor, obscures culture's continued role in modern society. Marx wants to find positive grounds for critiquing the social relations of capitalism. Rather than conceptualizing culture as reproducing itself in an on-going process of signification, he posits a naturalistic representation of human needs which he can then condemn the market for ignoring. While Marx's vision of capitalist society is two-leveled,[7] dead and abstract labor on one side and living and concrete labor on the other, his representation of living labor is not a cultural but a naturalistic representation.

In Habermas' estimation, Marx's chief failing is his inadequate differentiation of *material reproduction* and *symbolic reproduction*.[8] While the systems of money and power are well able to take over the task of coordinating action for the material reproduction of society, only communicative action can reproduce the cultural elements—information, representations, symbols—necessary for the continued integration of the lifeworld. In failing to make this distinction, Marx finds himself forced to locate the normative foundation for his critique of capitalism

in the idea that, in depriving people of the fruits of their labor, capitalism cuts people off from their true nature as beings of praxis. In making
this move, however, Marx not only leaves himself open to the construc-
tivist critique that he is simply erecting another abstracted and naturalistic representation of true human nature (Baudrillard). He also fails to
do justice to the complex *symbiotic* relationship that develops in modernity between system and lifeworld. Whereas the lifeworld becomes reli-
ant on the economic sub-system for material reproduction, the economy
also remains dependent on the capacities of the lifeworld for symbolic
reproduction. Marx focuses on neither the symbiotic relationship
between system and lifeworld, nor the degree to which the system might
be compelled to intervene in the lifeworld's culture in order to guarantee its own continued existence.[9]

Not until the 1920s and 1930s did the economistically foreshortened
analyses of Marx (warped even more drastically in this direction by the
Second International) come under fire by a cluster of theoreticians like
Georg Lukács, Karl Korsch, Max Horkheimer, and Antonio Gramsci.[10]
Gramsci, in particular, provided a much needed elaboration of Marx's
sketchy analysis of the relationship between capitalism and culture. He
understood very clearly that the abstract relations that emerged with commodification were insufficient to guarantee an unproblematic regulation
of the labour force. While many aspects of the worker's life had been
sucked into the objectifying relations of the market, working-class cultures were still enough intact to pose a serious threat to bourgeois domination (witness the massive labor unrest of the mid-nineteenth century).
Incapable of operating independently of or even finally disposing of
working-class cultures, leading factions of the bourgeoisie were forced
to invest considerable resources producing ideology to achieve a hegemony most conducive to capital accumulation. Drawing on the work of
Horkheimer and Adorno, Sut Jhally (1989) reconceptualizes Gramsci's
notion of hegemony as the *formal* subsumption of culture. Extending
Marx's concept of the 'formal subsumption of labour,' Jhally relates how,
"the *formal* subsumption [of culture] refers to a situation where an area
of society becomes vital for the functioning of the economic system without actually taking on the structures of the economic system" (p. 72).[11]
In this situation, capitalism invests in producing cultural goods (information, representations, symbols) not as commodities for exchange but
to create a cultural climate (legitimations, norms, values, personalities,
motivations) conducive to capitalist enterprise.

I should take a moment, at this point, to clarify the difference between 'cultural goods' and 'material goods'. Both cultural goods and material goods possess a use-value (Marx) and a sign-value (Baudrillard). The use-value refers to the goods' capacity to meet a need; the sign-value refers to the goods' position in a system of semiotically evolving signs. Thus: "In material goods, the use-value lies in the material properties of the good, and the sign-value in its signifying properties. In cultural goods both use-value and sign-value are inherent in the objects' signifying properties" (Lash, 1990, p. 43–44).

The relative strength of the use-value component or the sign-value component of a good varies from context to context. In Marx's time, for example, material needs were so great and physical goods so simple (limited signifying properties) that much more emphasis was placed on a good's use-value than its sign-value (to the point that Marx could not even discern that material goods have sign-value).

With this distinction in mind and drawing on Habermas again, it is possible to augment Jhally's presentation of the formal subsumption of culture. Habermas argues that the media of money and power originally emerged to coordinate actions required for material reproduction. Material production and not symbolic production constituted the domain of the early capitalist economy for several reasons. For one, "functions of material reproduction . . . do not *per se* need to be fulfilled by communicative action" (Habermas, 1987b, p. 350). The media of money could successfully interweave the teleological actions of workers to produce material goods. Symbolic reproduction, on the other hand, can only be accomplished by communicative action. The economy focused on material reproduction for another reason. At the end of the eighteenth century, traditional cultures were still relatively intact and there was very little market for cultural goods (capitalism had yet to ignite the mountains of coal that would fuel the industrial revolution and transform what was still a largely agricultural world into a world of factories and urban sprawl). The cultures themselves were able to produce a plethora of interpretations sufficient to guarantee enculturation, social integration, and adequate socialization. The same cannot be said for material reproduction. The massive dislocations leading up to the industrial revolution actively forced people from the land and deprived them of their traditional means of material reproduction. During the eighteenth century, for instance, capitalists initiated a conscious political struggle to dismantle the medieval institutions that impeded increased productivity in Britain's fledgling manufacturing industries (Larrain, 1989). They challenged and overturned feudal restrictions, such as those on free trade, personal freedom of workers, practices of guilds, and usury, initiating in the process a capitalist revolution that spawned an era of unprecedented economic growth. In less than a century, radical political reforms "freed" rural populations from their feudal ties with the land, while fundamental economic reforms that fostered mass production rapidly transformed Britain from an agrarian to an industrial society. The result was massive social upheaval as rural populations, stripped of the means of providing their own sustenance—the land— converged on the industrialized centers to "freely" exchange their only remaining possession—their labor—for wages. In this regard, the bourgeoisie and their allies were able to create the social conditions where material reproduction required the services of the economy.

No *market* for cultural goods, however, did not mean that the bourgeois was spared the task of producing these goods. On the contrary, the relative health of traditional cultures and the new and increasingly communicative cultures of the industrial working class meant that the bourgeois had to expend considerable resources producing ideology to contest cultural norms and values not in their best interests.[12] It must be recalled, moreover, that ideology is comprised, not only of a set of ideas, but also of a range of cultural goods and services that require real resources (materials and labor) to produce. Bourgeois law, parliamentary governments, educational systems, museums and libraries, and so on, as well as the cultural goods they produce (knowledge, representations, symbols), are the result of deliberate and costly productive activities.

Although the bourgeois became involved in the production of cultural goods and services to foster cultural forms conducive to capital accumulation, they did not produce cultural *commodities*. A commodity, it must be remembered, is a good that is produced for exchange on the market and valued in relation to the criteria of exchange. People produce and exchange commodities, in other words, to make money. This was not the motive that drove the bourgeois to produce cultural goods. In Marxian terms, the bourgeois investment in cultural products was done with their use-value in mind, not their exchange value. The motive was to create the kind of interface between system and lifeworld wherein, at the same time as they could draw upon the reproductive accomplishments of the lifeworld, the media of economy and state could coordinate action effectively free from the unruly demands of traditional or modern normative codes. This interface, itself, needed to be constructed of norms and, therefore, could only be located in the lifeworld. As with all norms, though, it was subject to the critical power of communicative action. Jhally states that, as long as the bourgeois resorts to the manipulation of culture to ensure its perpetuation, it risks being challenged. The attempts by the bourgeoisie to forge a hegemony are actions that are perceivable as *political* actions. Alternate groups and classes can create interpretations, norms, roles, or institutions to oppose the social relations these actions perpetuate. The history of capitalist modernity has, in fact, been one in which anti-capitalist forces have occasionally mustered powerful ideological campaigns to contest capitalist hegemony.

To summarize, the modernist notion of culture that prevails in critical adult education cannot be completely grasped if one ignores the historical interaction between the system and the lifeworld. Certainly, one need understand the modernist view of culture as a body of interpretations open to linguistic appraisal within differentiated cultural spheres. In addition, though, the modernist view of culture is an essentially contested terrain where the drama of hegemony is played out. An important part of understanding the modernist concept of culture is understanding the central role modernists believe culture has in contemporary society.

Before proceeding, I would like to make one more set of observations about the nature of culture in modernity. In his *Sociology of Postmodernism*, Scott Lash (1990) claims in 'ideal-typical' fashion, that cultural forms in modernity tend to be 'discursive'. He lists the basic characteristics of what he means by discursive in the following passage:

> [T]he discursive (1) gives priority to words over images; (2) valuates the formal qualities of cultural objects; (3) promulgates a rationalist view of culture; (4) attributes crucial importance to the *meanings* of cultural texts; (5) is a sensibility of the ego rather than of the id; (6) operates through a distancing of the spectator from the cultural object. (p. 175)

While Lash's first characteristic is fairly clear (words are linguistic utterances that privilege speaking and hearing; images are pictures that privilege seeing), others require elaboration. His claim that discursive cultural forms evaluate the formal qualities of cultural objects means that people in these cultures approach cultural objects as representations of reality and they assess the formal characteristics (truth, rightness, comprehensibility, sincerity) of that representation be it theoretically, ethically, or aesthetically. His claim that discursive cultural forms are rationalist suggests that people settle disputes about the formal characteristics of a cultural object through the process of argumentative discourse. Lash's suggestion that discursive cultural forms emphasize the meanings of cultural objects means that people do not take the surface presentation of a cultural object for granted. Rather, they endeavor to seek out its underlying meaning through processes of interpretation. His argument that discursive cultural forms are ego-oriented refers to the capacity of language to discharge id energy (frustrated by constraints of social reality) through a secondary process of transformation and verbalization. The ego emerges as a feature of the personality to manage this socially acceptable process of id gratification. Drawing on Lyotard (1984), Lash describes the ego's reliance on language as follows:

> Discourse . . . must proceed according to a set of obstacles, a set of rules, that is , through a "process of selection and combination of language," which itself is more bound than mobile in language's articulated and differential nature. Similarly, in the secondary process the investment of energy is canalized by rules, by obstacles, that the defense mechanisms of the ego construct, which subordinate the possibility of energy discharge to the "transformation of the relationship between the psychic apparatus and the external world." (Lash, 1990, p. 178)

The ego mediates between the id and reality. It sets the human subject back from direct contact with reality from where she or he can objectively and rationally work out appropriate forms of intervention with the world. Thus, as Lash relates in his final point, discursive culture is characterized by the psychic distance it generates between spectator and cultural objects.

All of these characteristics of discursive culture are consistent with our account of culture in modernity. The linguistification of the sacred, the differentiation of cultural realms, the linguistic reproduction of culture, the overburdening of communication as a form of action coordination, the reliance of the system on the communicative capacities of the lifeworld, and the ideological battle for cultural control, all presuppose that culture possesses the six discursive characteristics outlined by Lash. As will be seen below, it is these very presuppositions that postmodernism calls into question.

CRITICAL ADULT EDUCATION AND CULTURE
IN MODERNITY

For the sake of clarity, I will examine the ways critical adult education presumes a modernist notion of culture. While one might think that culture would be commonly discussed in critical adult education literature, it is, in fact, barely thematized. It is true, of course, that many critical adult educators are aware that culture is important to their field. As early as 1970, for instance, Paulo Freire identified critical adult education as "Cultural Action for Freedom" (in Freire, 1985). Even earlier, in the mid-1950s, Raymond Williams, although never part of the adult education establishment, noted the importance of cultural struggle for critical adult education (John McIlroy [1991] makes this observation in his assessment of Williams' contribution to critical adult education). More recently, Tom Lovett (1988) speaks of critical adult education struggling for "cultural democracy" (p. 143), and Wendy Ball (1992), garnering an insight from Alain Touraine, argues that culture is important to adult education because "political struggle to transform society takes place at the cultural level" (p. 6). While these scattered references to culture indicate its underlying importance, to date, critical adult educators have been rather quiet on the topic. To my knowledge, a systematic exploration of the important place of modern culture in critical adult education has yet to be done. For now we will be content with a few general observations to lay a basis for exploring the consequences of postmodernism's position on culture for critical adult education.

From the outset, critical adult education held a modernist view of itself as a cultural practice that pursues symbolic reproduction through the process of communicative action. Its prime referent is the stock of interpretations (primarily knowledge, but including representations, and symbols) that comprise our culture and its prime task is to reproduce culture to ensure that people continue to have a basis for coordinating actions. However, unlike traditional practices of symbolic reproduction, which do not question the sacred, binding power of traditions, critical adult education holds a modern view of culture as a background of interpretations that people in communication can draw upon to achieve action coordinating understandings. Individual cultural elements are not held as sacred but are understood as validity claims open to assessment.

Critical adult education also presumes the modernist differentiation of culture into three specialized realms, and understands that the form

of knowledge developed in each realm is distinct. Critical adult education has resisted the contention that the only legitimate cultural realm in
which social learning can take place is the theoretical realm where all
things are evaluated according the criteria of truth. It has insisted that
the ethical realm is also a sphere of social learning in which critical
adult education should be involved. Long-standing debates between
adult educators who insist that adult education should be value free and
those who insist on its political nature reveal the modern awareness of
different cultural realms.[13] Perhaps one key aspect of critical adult education's adherence to a modernist understanding of culture is its awareness of culture as an important site of struggle. Critical adult education
has long construed itself as a critical practice that contests the cultural
products of the bourgeois. With the emergence of Gramscian analytical
tools, it increasingly understands itself as a counter-hegemonic enterprise that positions itself in the contested terrain of culture.[14]

Finally, critical adult education's view of culture is modernist in that
it understands culture as discursive. Critical adult education upholds each
of the characteristics of discursive culture outlined by Lash. From the
outset, critical adult education has been oriented to language. Its on-going
focus on dialogue as a principal pedagogical device is a case in point.
From Grundtvig and the Danish folk schools, from the Workers' Education Association to Paulo Freire and his pedagogy of the oppressed,
critical dialogue has been the principal tool for social learning. Knowledge is not viewed as something to be passively consumed but actively
examined and criticized before being accepted as valid.

For the most part, critical adult education's assumptions about the
nature of culture have served it well. Let us now turn and examine concerns postmodernism raises about the modern understanding of culture.
The challenges postmodernism issues, it turns out, have dramatic implications for critical adult education.

CULTURE IN POSTMODERNITY

In this section, we must begin with a hesitant step. The very suggestion
that postmodernism challenges the modernist notion of culture pushes
us immediately into a methodological quagmire. How is it possible to
understand the kinds of cultural changes transpiring in postmodernity if
our conceptual tools are deeply impacted by these very cultural

changes? It would be nice, somehow, to be able to get beyond the horizon of our culture (setting aside for a moment the whole question of understanding culture as a unified entity) and to locate those shady external forces that are guiding our entrance into postmodernity. If we heed the concerns of the postmodernists, however, we can no longer rest easy with this strategy. We are left with the uncomfortable suspicion that social theorists are no more than hucksters advertising their culture-bound representations of society as something transcendental.

But, there is a difference, I think, between offering an explanation, as if it actually provides a true and objective representation of reality, and speaking a metanarrative, knowing it is just a story, but believing, at the same time, that it offers some kind of guiding insight into reality. The narrative approach does not maintain the pretense of eternal and universal validity that the postmodernists so virulently condemn. At the same time, though, neither does it give up altogether and wallow in the contingency of the particular as many postmodernists would have us do. Rather, it imagines theory as a "guiding thread" (Marx in Sayer, 1987, p. 1) which can foster our understanding of our world. It is only when we begin forcing the world to fit our truth that the "violence of abstraction," as Derek Sayer (1987) identifies it, is perpetrated.

This said, I would like in the following passages to begin my analysis by offering a "guiding thread" for understanding culture change in postmodernity. The basic plot of this narrative is that the rapid and pervasive commodification of culture and the growing predominance of the image over discourse is producing a dramatic de-linguistification, de-differentiation, and de-politicization of culture. I will end the story with an account of the varied postmodernist responses to this narrative.

Recall my above contention that one of the key reasons capitalism did not move immediately into the production of cultural commodities is that, until quite recently, the lifeworld was so capable of reproducing an ample supply of interpretations and meanings that there was simply no market for such products. The twentieth century, especially the past twenty years, has changed all that. John Tomlinson (1991), in his discussion of Cornelius Castoriadis' critique of modernity, argues that the advance of capitalism has created a cultural void at the center of contemporary society, noting that "what Max Weber first called the 'disenchantment of the world'—the breaking of the spell of traditional belief and practices—leaves a hole at the centre of culture, which Castoriadis believes cannot be adequately filled with stories of growth or development" (p. 164). Similarly, Habermas (1987b) argues that the gradual imposition of the imperatives of money and power on the lifeworld impair its capacity to reproduce the stock of cultural interpretations [see also Welton's arguments in chapter 5—Ed.]. This, he argues, is experienced by people as a growing sense of meaninglessness and detachedness (p. 327). Thus, while in the nineteenth century capitalism had a limited market for cultural commodities, in the late twentieth century such a market abounds.

Capitalist enterprises are rushing to fill the cultural void created by the forces of late capitalism. Jhally (1989) suggests this signals a *real* subsumption of culture. Expanding on Marx, he argues that "real subsumption . . . refers to a situation where the media [and other cultural institutions like adult education] become not ideological institutions but economic ones. That is, investment in the media is not for the purpose of ideological control but for the purpose of reaping the biggest return. Culture is produced first and foremost as a commodity rather than as ideology" (p. 73).[15]

It is important to think for a moment what the commodification of culture actually means and to tease out its various nuances. Previously, I noted that people consume material objects not only because of their utility but because through consumption people are able to display a particular social standing. Thus, material products not only meet people's physical needs but are a sign that people can display to communicate something about themselves, typically about their social status, to others—a hat, for instance. One of the reasons a person wears a hat is because its physical properties provide protection from the elements. Another reason is that a hat has the capacity to signify. What exactly the hat is meant to signify depends on the system of signs in which the hat as signifier is located. A hat is a police hat, for instance, because it is different from other signifiers: fire-fighter's hat, a cowboy hat, and so on. A person who wears a hat that looks like a police hat communicates that she or he is not a cowboy or a fire-fighter but a police officer. A thing like a hat can signify numerous and subtle differences depending upon the system of signs in which it is located. A police hat can signify on officers detachment, his or her name, and his or her rank. In this case, a person would value the hat for its capacity to signify the social role she or he plays. All material objects have a similar capacity for signification.

As I have noted, capitalism's early commodities were consumed primarily for their use-value. By the end of the nineteenth century, however, with the breakdown of traditional ways of life and of the semiotic landscape they prescribed, commodities began to accrue meanings unintended by the market: they began to take their place as signs within the cultures of working-class and bourgeois consumers. People in these cultures revealed their adeptness at attributing increasingly sophisticated layers of meaning to seemingly innocuous items. In a fascinating study of the Italian motor scooter, for instance, Dick Hebdige (1988) explores how the efforts of manufacturers to control the various meanings the scooter were constantly outflanked by meaning-giving capacities of varied sub-cultural groups (the Mods in Britain, for instance) who consumed the machines.[16] Scooters were just one of a proliferating number of products that were attributed ever finer layers of meaning by cultural groups who used them as signs to differentiate social standing.

Even though a commodity is consumed as a sign, culture has not yet been subjected to commodification. The meanings that cultural groups assign to commodities is derived either from the positioning of the commodity as sign within a traditional signification system or through the communicative achievements of cultural members themselves who together attribute a meaning to the commodity. In neither case is the meaning of the product a motive for their production. The commodification of culture only occurs when capitalists realize that money can be made producing signs and when they actually begin to produce them as commodities.

The first significant instances of cultural commodification took place at the end of the nineteenth century—in bourgeois culture with the end of the patron system of painting and architecture and in mass culture with the emergence of such phenomena as "music halls, popular spectator sports, the fish and chip shop in England, vaudeville, etc." (Lash, 1990, p. 51). Industrial designers did not focus on enhancing the signifying capacity of commodities through innovations like streamlining and decoration until the 1930s (Hebdige, 1988, pp. 58–59). Simultaneously, a whole new focus in advertising on the sign-value of products, began to promote an increasing differentiated sign-system that "detached the reproduced object from the dimension of tradition" (Benjamin in Hebdige, 1988, p. 72). The flood of new signifiers produced according to the logic of the market, quickly outstretches any culture's capacity to integrate these signs into meaningful systems of signification. As Baudrillard (1983a) relates in his essay, "The Implosion of Meaning in the Media," the proliferation of information and sign (largely produced by the various media) extinguishes meaning by trivializing and homogenizing all content. In the end, this results in not only a collapse in meaning but a blurring of the distinction between representations and reality. He writes:

> The loss of meaning is directly linked to the dissolving and dissuasive action of information, the media, and the mass media. . . . Information devours its own contents; it devours communication and the social. . . . Instead of causing communication, *it exhausts itself in the act* of staging the communication; instead of producing meaning, it exhausts itself in the staging of meaning. It is a gigantic process of simulation with which we are very familiar. (pp. 96–98)

The new economy of the sign—"an economy of consumption, of the signifier, of endless replacement, supercession, drift and play" (Hebdige, 1988, p. 71)—replaces lost and damaged traditional cultures with a detached and fragmented collage of unrelated sign systems drawn from around the globe and transported by the sophisticated technologies of mass communication and transport. The new economy cannot replace the shared meaning frames that constitute the social realities that late capitalism is destroying. Habermas (1987b), for one, is singular in his insistence that a culture cannot be reproduced from outside the horizons of the lifeworld. A way of life can only be reproduced through the communicative accomplishments of the lifeworld's participants (p. 350). But as David Harvey (1989) notes, capitalist enterprises, in fact, have no real interest in creating integrated worldviews. They are concerned solely with the production of cultural commodities that can be rapidly and easily consumed in any context, that is, cultural products that are detached from any particular meaning-frame (p. 286). Such products can be consumed in any cultural milieu, dramatically increasing the size of the market. As Jameson (1991) relates, however, when the chain of significations that comprise culture snaps, then "we have schizophrenia in the form of a rubble of distinct and unrelated signifiers" (p. 26).

The proliferation of cultural commodities has occurred simultaneously with a drift from discourse to the image as the principle means of signification in our society. Discourse and image both represent reality. They are similar in that both require physical media for their expression (these media can be as simple as sound waves or beams of light) and hence require resources for their production (Harvey, 1989, p. 289). In many other ways, however, they are quite different. Scott Lash (1990) summarizes the characteristics of image as a form of signification. He suggests that this form of signification:

> (1) is a visual rather than a literary sensibility; (2) devalues formalisms and juxtaposes signifiers taken from the banalities of everyday life; (3) contests rationalist and/or 'didactic' views of culture; (4) asks not what a cultural text 'means', but what it 'does'; (5) in Freudian terms, advocates the extension of the primary process into the cultural realm; (6) operates through the spectator's immersion, the relatively unmediated investment of his/her desire in the cultural object. (p. 175)

As we found for Lash's corresponding depiction of discursive culture, the first of these characteristics is fairly straightforward; the others require comment. When he contends that "figural" forms of signification devalue formalisms he is referring to the tendency of people to approach images aesthetically without feeling a requirement to assess its theoretical or ethical qualities using formal procedures. Images do not need to be presented sequentially or concurrently to make sense—powerful images can be comprised of juxtaposed signifiers from daily life piled together in a pastiche. Lash also relates how images do not appeal to reason: even though they are representations of reality, they do not present themselves as validity claims open to rational appraisal.[17] Neither do they claim to be part of larger systems of meaning: they do not demand to be examined for the meaning that lies behind them but communicate through direct appeal to the observer's emotions. The fleeting images, infobytes, clichés, fashions, and sound effects that are flooding into the cultural void of late capitalism are consumed, not because consumers find them meaningful, but because they appeal directly to the soma of the consumer. Consumers are motivated to watch TV, listen to CDs, change fashions simply because it feels good, not because it makes sense. In this sense, mass images bypass the ego as the personality-construct mediating between the id and reality. Images present themselves to the person *as if the images are reality* and, rather than discharging id energy through a secondary process of transformation and verbalization, discharge it directly in an ecstatic outburst of gratification.[18] No distance is required between the spectator and the spectacle for the image to do its work. No contemplation or discussion

is required in its presence. Rather, the image draws the spectator into
itself, where his or her desire is directly assuaged.[19]

Images are now ubiquitous. As Angela McRobbie (1989) laments:

> Images push their way into the fabric of our social lives. They enter
> into how we look, what we earn, and they are still with us when we
> worry about bills, housing and bringing up children. They compete for
> attention through shock tactics, reassurance, sex, mystery and by
> inviting viewers to participate in series of visual puzzles. Billboard
> advertisements showing an image without a code, impose themselves,
> infuriatingly, on the most recalcitrant passerby. (p. 172)

The incorporation of the image into the exchange economy represents
an increase in the power of capital to produce commodities that require
no mediation by culture. Representations produced as images are consumed without making sense. With the emergence of vastly powerful
technologies of representation, image commodities become so appeal-
ing that they eclipse all other forms of social reality. The fleeting
romances of the "soaps" are of more importance to many viewers than
their own lives, CNN's high-tech rendition of the Gulf War became, for
the many who experienced it on TV, the "real" war,[20] Stephen Spielberg's (1993) *Jurassic Park* enables us to virtually experience Tyranno-
saurus rex, watch spellbound as it captures its prey, and shudder at the
sound of his terrifying, CD-generated roar. The power of the commodified image is now such that Jean Baudrillard, perhaps the most vision-
ary of contemporary social theorists, goes so far as to suggest that reality no longer exists. We now all live in a virtual reality, a simulacra of
fleeting images.[21]

The swing to the image merges with rampant processes of cultural
commodification to blast away at the ragged shards of tradition that still
remain and to sunder people's capacity to use discourse to coordinate
actions. Let us tally up the changes all of this entails for culture in
modernity.

De-linguistification: Observers of culture note the growing inun-
dation of non-discursive cultural products—image-driven advertising,
spectacles like sporting events, MTV, tourism,[22] hi-tech movies, shopping malls, Nintendo games, rock music, comic books—that are dis-
placing traditional and more discursive cultural elements.[23] Whereas in
modernity, cultural products present themselves as validity claims open
to discursive appraisal, in postmodernity, cultural products come to us

not as claims, not even as representations, but as images that "seduce" us into a simulacrum more real than reality itself (Baudrillard, 1990).

De-differentiation: We noted how in modernity, culture increasingly differentiates into three separate cultural spheres, each with its own means of assessing the validity of cultural elements. Scott Lash (1990) contends that a primary feature of postmodernity is the de-differentiation that occurs amongst these realms (pp. 11–12). Mike Featherstone (1991) understands this de-differentiation as the result of an aestheticization of all features of life that accompanies the growing predominance of figural over discursive cultural elements. He notes five ways this de-differentiation proceeds. The first is the historic breakdown of the distinction between high and low art. This undermines the institutionalization of aesthetic discourse and blurs "the distinction between art and everyday life. In effect, art is everywhere: in the street, the refuse, the body, the happening" (p. 124). The second element in the aestheticization of life is the growing emphasis in contemporary society of an aesthetic of sensation, "an aesthetics of the body which emphasizes the immediacy and unreflexiveness of primary processes" (p. 124). The third element is the antifoundationalist critique of all metanarratives and the critique of consensus (exemplified by Lyotard's critique of Habermas). "Knowledge henceforth should be nomadic and parodic. It should playfully emphasize the discontinuities, openness, randomness, ironies, reflexivity, incoherences and multiphrenic qualities of texts which can no longer be read with the intention of extracting a systematic interpretation" (p. 124). Fourth, is the "transformation of reality into images, and the fragmentation of time into series of perpetual presents" (p. 124). Fifth, is the overall aestheticization of experience in which art becomes "the master paradigm for knowledge, experience and sense of life-meaning" (p. 124). The growth of aesthetic modes of experience breaches the boundaries between the artistic realm and the theoretical and moral realms eroding their normative bases for evaluation and action coordination.

Lash contends that, as this de-differentiation develops, the distinction between the cultural and the social becomes hazy (p. 11). In Habermasian terms, the lifeworld is becoming so impaired by the colonizing effects of the system that cultural reproduction is jeopardized. It may be, in effect, that the aestheticization of everyday life is equivalent to the annihilation of culture. Finally, Lash notes that another element of de-differentiation is the blurring of distinctions between signifier, signified, and referent which was a key feature of the modern view of culture. In a world in which images are so pervasive, signifiers become referents for other signifiers which claim no meaning.[24] Reality loses its definition and there is an implosion of meaning. Society evaporates to leave a hyper-real simulacrum of society in its place.

De-politicization (The annihilation of culture): All of these changes impact culture's position in contemporary society. Recall Habermas' contention that, while the systems of money and power are capable of coordinating the material reproduction of society, symbolic reproduction is a cultural activity that transpires within the horizons of the lifeworld. The lifeworld is dependent on the system for the production of material forms of sustenance, the system is also dependent on the lifeworld for ensuring the reproduction of cultural forms conducive to capitalist accumulation. Thus, social factions who benefit from the relations of capitalism must struggle to contrive a social formation in which cultures, social relations, and personalities beneficial to capitalism prevail. As we noted above, the cultural terrain in which hegemony is waged is one of struggle and contestation.

As early as 1968, however, Habermas realized that there was no necessity that this arrangement persist. Reflecting on the increasing number of techniques for behavioral and personality change, he suggests that they point:

> to an area of future possibilities of detaching human behavior from a normative system linked to the grammar of language-games and integrating it instead into self-regulated subsystems of the man-machine type by means of immediate physical or psychological control. Today the psychotechnic manipulation of behavior can already liquidate the old fashioned detour through norms that are internalized but capable of reflection. Behavioral control could be instituted at an even deeper level tomorrow through biotechnic intervention in the endocrine system, not to mention the even greater consequences of intervening in the genetic transmission of inherited information. If this occurred, old regions of consciousness developed in ordinary-language communication would of necessity completely dry up. At this stage of human engineering, if the end of psychological manipulation could be spoken of in the same sense as the end of ideology is today, the spontaneous alienation derived from the uncontrolled lag of the institutional framework would be overcome. (1970, pp. 117-118)

While he anticipated the continued growth of biological and genetic engineering, Habermas did not anticipate how the growth of media technologies could achieve the same power to liquidate the "old fashioned detour through norms." The capacity of images to slip by the mediating presence of the ego and to directly slake the desires of the id offers new possibilities to the creators of these images to manage motivations. "At the technological level," writes Debord (1990),

> when images chosen and constructed by *someone else* have everywhere become the individual's principal connection to the world he [*sic*] formerly observed for himself, it has certainly not been forgotten that these images can tolerate anything and everything; because within the same image all things can be juxtaposed *without contradiction* [emphasis added]. The flow of images carries everything before it, and it is similarly someone else who controls at will this simplified summary of the sensible world; who decides where the flow will lead as well as the rhythm of what should be shown, like some perpetual, arbitrary surprise, leaving no time for reflection, and entirely independent of what the spectator might understand or think of it. (pp. 27–28)

The commodification of culture generates such a proliferation of signifiers that it undermines the capacity of individuals or groups to locate themselves in an action-coordinating system of norms. The deterioration of discourse as a prime cultural element strips away people's capacities for communicative action. Fragmenting personalities and impoverished cultures provide ever less protection from the intrusive power of media-technic regulation. One might criticize this rather Baudrillardian vision of society as unrealistically pessimistic, and suggest, as does Zygmunt Bauman (1992), that it can only be held by someone who watches entirely too much TV and who fails to get out enough into the fresher light of reality. Considering that the average adult in the United States now watches 32 hours of television per week,[25] not to mention the additional time spent shopping, listening to the stereo, playing video games, going to movies, or the countless other hours spent consuming the images of postmodernity, one wonders, even if we did manage to get out into the light of "reality," who exactly we might find there.

Whereas, at one time, culture represented a terrain of intense struggle, where different social factions fought over the governing norms of society, now it represents something quite different. It is true, of course, that culture is still a site for struggle. Discourse as a means of action coordination still exists. It is just that, in light of all of the above changes, the struggle that transpires in culture is now less ferocious than it was before.

The symbiosis between system and lifeworld, which placed culture in such an important and contradictory position in modernity, is breaking down. The system no longer requires the lifeworld *to the extent it once did* to perform the tasks of social integration and motivation formation.[26] One can imagine, with Baudrillard, that a time might come when culture will lose its functionality for the system and when we might find ourselves in the fragmented and alienating cultural landscapes portrayed in Bladerunner (Perenchio, Yorkin, and Scott, 1982) or *Robocop* (Schmidt and Verhoeven, 1987) or by William Gibson (1984; 1986; 1988) in his cyberpunk novels.[27] I do not believe that this has happened yet (this dystopia is still in the realm of science fiction— we all still inhabit lifeworlds). What has happened, though, is that the role of culture in the drama of social struggle has weakened. As it turns out, the implications of this cultural weakening are traumatic for critical adult education.

SUBPLOTS: CULTURAL STUDIES, MARXISM, POST-STRUCTURALISM

Before moving on to my final reflections on postmodern culture and critical adult education, I wish to issue a reminder that not all theorists of postmodernity would tell the same the story of postmodern culture as the one I just narrated. While I do not wish to consider them in detail, I think it is important to sketch a few alternate scenarios—introduce them as subplots, as it were—to enrichen, perhaps de-simplify, the previous narrative.

Some theorists, like John Fiske (1989a, 1989b), would probably not agree that culture is threatened by commodification or by the turn to the image anywhere near to the extent indicated in the forgoing narrative. His studies of people's reception of cultural products convince him that "culture industries" have no more capacity now to *determine* forms of sociation than any time before. With a eye keen to the multitude ways cultural groups attribute meaning to the varied cultural products of postmodernity and resist the attempts of commodity producers to dominate the process of signification, Fiske resolutely insists that postmodernity is not undermining culture as the arena in which our social forms emerge.

It is important to keep Fiske's perspective in mind. The extent and nature of lifeworld colonization and of the resultant destruction of culture varies tremendously according to the specific history of contact between system and specific portions of the lifeworld. It is presumptuous to claim, like Baudrillard, that we now live in a pure simulacrum. As Manuel De Landa (1982) contends, if this were so, why is such a massive system of surveillance and police/military force still being deployed? Fiske's insistence on the capacity of cultures to resist domination and to appropriate cultural commodities for their own uses stands as an important counterweight to Baudrillard's pessimistic prognosis. On the other hand, though, Fiske's perspective downplays a host of social transformations that are hard to ignore. While it may be true that culture still stands as an important site of hegemonic struggle, it must be admitted that other mechanisms of domination—surveillance, simulation, and intimidation—that do not attempt to dispute meanings but that assert their force directly on people's bodies, have diminished the importance of culture as an arena of contestation. The subplot to our narrative offered by theorists like Fiske and other culture studies theorists like Dick Hebdige (1979) and Richard Dyer (1982, 1986) restrain us from an overhasty pronouncement that culture is now terminal. But they provide little indication of the deep wounds that have already been inflicted on its corpus.

Marxist theorists like Fredric Jameson, David Harvey, and to some extent, Douglas Kellner are not quite so blasé. They believe that postmodernity is wreaking profound changes that threaten to destroy modern forms of culture. The subplot that they provide is that the complexity of late capitalism is outstripping people's capacity to understand and hence to resist new forms of domination that capitalism is producing. The fragmentation of culture produced by commodification and by the turn to the image further undermines people's ability to trace their experiences of oppression to their root causes. Just under the surface of their earnest warnings about the collapse of culture is a panicked realization that the metanarrative of Marxism is now being overwhelmed by the vast transformations of contemporary society. Harvey's impulse is to refurbish the sagging structure of Marxism with a host of new explanations that can harden the resistive capacity of weakened cultures. Jame-

son questions whether Marxism can continue to carry the torch of emancipation. He does argue, though, that people need to re-map the world
of multinational capitalism with new totalizing schemas which can
coordinate their resistances to its unruly imperatives (1991, p. 54). The
Marxists' contribution to the story of culture in postmodernity is their
realization of the depth to which late capitalism devastates culture. The
panic they display reinforces the desperate difficulty of achieving a perspective on these changes that can assure continued and effective opposition to the imperatives of late capitalism. For critical adult educators
still believing in the potential of culture to oppose the excesses of
modernity, the Marxist postmodernists' dire observations are deeply
disconcerting.

Post-structuralist theorists like Jean-François Lyotard offer a very
different subplot. While Lyotard might agree that modern cultural
forms are being transformed in postmodernity, he does not agree that
this is such a bad thing. In Lyotard's (1984a) view, the transformations
accompanying the information age (in particular the proliferation of
cultural forms) do not undermine the capacity of modern theories to
adequately represent reality. Rather, these transformations reveal that
modern theories *never did* possess this capacity. Lyotard is pleased with
the postmodern turn because it represents the rapid delegitimation of the
metanarratives of modernity which he contends obscured the relationship between knowledge and power (p. 37). This includes, not just the
metanarratives perpetrated by capitalism, but the whole metanarrative
project, including the shameful totalizations of Marxism which, in their
Stalinist expression, caused so much grief for so many people (pp. 12–
13). While Lyotard recognizes that dramatic changes in cultural production (including the commodification of knowledge, pp. 4–5) are transforming the world, he is not as convinced as David Harvey, for instance,
that postmodernity can simply be attributed to changes in capitalist
forms of production (p. 38). Rather, he contends that the postmodern
condition has emerged because scientific skepticism has undermined
people's belief in metanarratives. According to Lyotard: "That is what
the postmodern world is all about. Most people have lost the nostalgia
for the lost narrative. It in no way follows that they are reduced to bar-
barity. What saves them from it is their knowledge that legitimation can
only spring from their own linguistic practice and communicational
interaction" (p. 41). Cultural vitality (including concepts like justice)
emerges with the institution of genuinely communicative practices.

Exactly what these practices are, however, depends on the language game (culture) in which a person finds themselves. Lyotard refuses to acknowledge Habermas' assertion that cultural differences can be resolved within communicative contexts oriented toward consensus. Consensus, for Lyotard, smuggles a disguised and unwarranted will to unity back into the situation. Postmodernity is positive because it offers no such pretenses. As Lyotard writes:

> A recognition of the heteromorphous nature of language games is a first step in that direction. This obviously implies a renunciation of terror, which assumes that they are isomorphic and tries to make them so. The second step is the principle that any consensus on the rules defining a game and the "moves" playable within it *must* be local, in other words, agreed on by its present players and subject to eventual cancellation. The orientation then favors a multiplicity of finite meta-arguments, by which I mean argumentation that concerns metaprescriptives and is limited in space and time. . . . This orientation corresponds to the course that the evolution of social interaction is currently taking. (p. 66)

Lyotard contends that the oppressive metanarrative of modernity is in need of destruction (deconstruction) so that new, less rigid, more heterogeneous forms of sociation can emerge. Post-structuralist theorists celebrate the commodification of culture and the turn to the image as a new opportunity for humanity to escape the stultifying and oppressive conditions of modernity.

The contribution of Lyotard to our story, is twofold. Firstly, it calls into question the impulse toward emancipation (my own admitted impulse) that persists throughout the other parts of the narrative. It challenges its half-spoken assumption that the destruction of culture is a bad thing, that modernist forms of cultural resistance are all that beneficial, and that new totalizing visions must be developed to refurbish culture's lost vitality. Secondly, and perhaps more importantly, it introduces a level of skepticism toward the entire thrust of the main part of the narrative. It calls into question its seeming desire to explain away the complexities of postmodernity by locating their origin in the commodification of culture and the turn to the image. It has us wonder if, once again, the intent of the analysis is to repress the heterogeneity of contemporary social existence for the sake of another metanarrative. This, I think, is an important contribution. It refocuses our attention on the limits of reason and of totalizing discourse, it reminds us that the validity claims the narrative advances are not inscribable as transcendental truths, and it denies us the dangerous belief that we have escaped the narrow horizons of our specific language game.

DECLINING OPPORTUNITIES: CRITICAL ADULT EDUCATION, CULTURE, AND POSTMODERNITY

Critical adult education's modernist view of culture is insufficiently flexible to disclose the full implications of cultural commodification for its cultural practices. I do not want to assert that culture has been destroyed by processes of commodification. Nor that critical adult education, without being aware that it has even happened, has already ceased to exist as a meaningful enterprise. I do believe, however, that, as a realm of symbolic reproduction, culture is now far less important and more questionable in postmodern society than it was previously. Postmodernity, I suggest, constitutes an environment of declining opportunities and increased uncertainties for counter-hegemonic cultural practices like critical adult education. As a result, critical adult education is confronted with the uncomfortable prospect of finding new ways to constitute itself as a viable cultural enterprise in postmodern times.

Critical adult education is deeply affected by cultural commodification. One of the most important reasons for this is that knowledge, the cultural element of central significance for critical adult education, is susceptible to commodification. Critical adult educators view knowledge as a body of interpretations that lifeworld members can draw upon in their efforts to reach communicative agreements. Specific interpretations are viewed as validity claims that are open to criticism by any concerned lifeworld member. For critical adult education, knowledge is valued according to its capacity to motivate communicative understandings. The assault of the system on the lifeworld and the subsequent erosion of the capacity of the lifeworld to reproduce itself through communicative action is what critical adult education emerges to oppose. It struggles to foster the rationalization of the lifeworld and its capacity to resist the deleterious intrusions of the system by fostering contexts of open and unhindered discursive will formation.

The view of knowledge prevailing in this schema is rendered problematic by commodification. Like other cultural products, knowledge can be incorporated by the system and exchanged on the market. And like other products, its consumption is motivated not just by its use-value but also by its sign-value. For example, postmodernism itself seems to be enjoying a fairly high sign-value right now. While the hippest 'theory consumers' now no longer like to associate with the term, in many contexts postmodernism still is quite fashionable. On the other hand, while Althusserian structuralism was once so popular that almost every self-respecting Marxist identified him or herself as an Althusserian, its sign-value is now abysmally low. In less than twenty years, it has almost disappeared from academic discourses.

The movement of the market into knowledge production enhances the ephemerality and fragmentation of knowledge. Knowledge elements are stripped out of their constitutive lifeworld contexts and exchanged on the market like soft drinks or vacuums. Increasingly, their value is determined not by what they disclose about the world, about social relations, or about beauty and expressiveness (i.e., their use-value), but by the number of books they sell, by the audience they gather, by the corporate contracts they attract, or, even more simply, by the money they make.

As noted in the preceding account of postmodernity, the entry of the market into cultural production vastly increases the number of circulating signifiers. Market-driven knowledge production floods culture with information that it has little chance of assimilating. Instead of providing a backdrop of commonly held interpretations against which understandings can be worked out, information increasingly becomes background noise which interferes with the process of discursive will formation. In this context, individual information elements are not produced or consumed as validity claims open to contestation by lifeworld members, but increasingly as commodities valued only according to their market worth.

It is interesting to note that instrumental forms of adult education adapt easily to the changing nature of knowledge in postmodernity. The commodification of knowledge provides new and unforeseen opportunities for previously unprofitable adult education enterprises to make good money. Over the past twenty years, instrumental adult education has transformed from a collection of practices located in large state-funded educational institutions (technical institutes and community colleges that aimed to meet the legitimation and accumulation needs of capitalism) into a diverse array of small and mid-sized entrepreneurial enterprises which produce and disseminate information, skills, and even entertainment for profit.[28] The function of adult education is no longer to produce knowledge that may be generally useful but to produce knowledge that specific purchasers are willing to buy. To make this possible, knowledge is packaged into discrete, measurable bundles of information that can be sold for specific sums of money. Many of these companies maximize earnings by focusing on short-cycle programming or tailored-to-fit training packages. Other "knowledge" products include courses, credentials, patents, processes, computer programs, research innovations, and so on. Computers, video, and telecommunications play a key role increasing the effectiveness of information dissemination.

Critical adult education has not experienced a similar positive transition. Instead, cultural commodification dangerously undermines the fund of interpretations that critical adult education draws upon to foster the health of the lifeworld. What is happening, in effect, is that commodification is destroying culture faster than restorative cultural practices like critical adult education can reproduce it. While it may be true that lifeworld rationalization is required to stop system colonization, lifeworld destruction may already have eroded the basis for the discursive practices required for this rationalization—including, most notably, the activities of critical adult education. The proliferation of market-stimulated information, unassociated with any integrated and culturally sustained meaning-frame, is not produced to undergird processes of communicative action. Information elements are not valued for their capacity to motivate discursive agreements. Rather, they are valued solely for the profits they can earn. Detached from the communicative contexts of life, they heed only the imperatives of the market. The commodification of culture means that critical adult education must make its way in an environment impoverished by the intrusive steering mechanisms of the system. All that remains of once integrated and vital cultures is the "rubble of distinct and unrelated signifiers." The notion of culture presumed by critical adult education offers little insight into how it might continue to foster the healthy discursive institutions that were once the pride and aspiration of modernity.

If critical adult education is incapable of accommodating the vicissitudes of cultural commodification, it is even less capable of dealing with the unruly implications of the drift from discourse to the image as the main means of signification in our society. Note once again that critical adult education presumes a discursive notion of culture and envisions itself as a dialogical cultural practice that fosters the communicative capacities of the lifeworld. The growing ability of the mass-media to produce representations that seem more real than reality itself undercuts the modernist notion of culture as a discursive fund of interpretations that mediate the actions of lifeworld members. Figural forms of signification devalue the kinds of activities promoted by critical adult education. Images do not present themselves as validity claims open to dialogue, they do not call upon formal procedures for assessing their worth, and they do not inspire inquiry into their underlying meaning or significance. Rather, they present themselves as if they are "reality" and gratify needs directly without requiring people to deliberately coordinate their actions. Why should adult learners engage in critical discourse when it is so much easier and pleasurable and even more real to just go shopping?

Again it is interesting to note that instrumental adult education is not deleteriously impacted by this transformation. The "knowledge products" produced by adult education companies are increasingly image-oriented. This is particularly apparent in skills training where much learning is carried out utilizing simulations of actual job situations. Computers and video technology make it possible for airline pilots, electronic engineers, auto-mechanics, data-entry operators, and physicians to receive extensive training through simulation. Critical adult education, on the balance, does not fare so well with the rise of the image. Representations produced as images require no mediation by culture. While it may be true that culture still exists, the extensiveness of its influence is dramatically reduced in a society dominated by powerful media images. The pervasiveness of the image reduces the discursive territory within which critical adult education can operate. The modernist notion of culture as a terrain of action coordination is rendered partially incomplete with the upsurge of a world connecting directly with the consumer's soma.

The de-linguistification of culture that accompanies commodification and the rise of the image undermines the basis for critical adult education's dialogical practices. Whereas in modernity, critical adult education could engage lifeworld members in a critical appraisal of validity claims, in postmodernity, critical adult education is left without the discursive resources required to confront the validity of simulacra that seem more real than reality itself. Critical adult education's belief that culture is differentiated into three separate realms no longer quite holds.

The aestheticization of everyday life and the breakdown of the boundaries between aesthetic, moral, and theoretical realms overruns this
understanding of culture. In postmodernity, all claims are assessed
according to their sensational impact. Deliberative discourse in moral
and theoretical realms is depreciated. The concomitant blurring of the
distinction between society and culture also has an impact on critical
adult education's understanding of culture. No longer is culture seen as
a distinct location for symbolic reproduction. The manufacture of representations as cultural commodities destabilizes the discursive sphere
where critical adult education implements its practices.

All told, the commodification of culture confronts critical adult
education with declining opportunities to engage in its political aspirations as a counter-hegemonic cultural enterprise. Critical adult education pins its emancipatory intentions on the modernist idea that culture
is a key site of social contestation. In postmodern times, however, the
process of cultural commodification significantly lessens the importance of culture as a place where different social agents struggle over the
norms and values governing society. Critical adult education is outflanked by these developments and, given its modernist theoretical
foundations, is incapable of mustering an adequate response.

Even more unsettling, however, are the questions post-structuralism raises about the desirability of critical adult education's emancipatory agenda in the first place. Not only is critical adult education overwhelmed by transformations that commodification wreaks on culture, it
is also challenged by the post-structuralist contention that the destruction of culture as a realm of legitimation provides new opportunities for
less rigid and more heterogeneous social forms to emerge. Critical adult
education has devoted itself to the idea that rational discourse can provide the basis for consensus about which norms should prevail in society. Post-structuralism raises the uncomfortable notion that critical adult
education is just another means by which the heterogeneity of social life
is suppressed. Locked into a modernist conceptual framework that posits social struggle in terms of the struggle for hegemony, critical adult
education is poorly equipped to articulate how it can persist as a meaningful emancipatory practice without reinscribing itself as an institution
that suppresses heterogeneity and difference.

In some ways, I hesitate to take the next step and sketch out a possible
path forward for critical adult education. My principle intent in the fore-
going has been to disclose the unsettling nature of postmodernity for crit-

ical adult education. In my mind, the most immediate need is for critical adult educators to absorb the magnitude of postmodernity's implications without rushing to find answers. While mindful that it is easier to disassemble an existing theoretical construct than it is to create a new one, I would still be satisfied, at this stage, if my study were to have a deconstructive effect and challenge the coherency of critical adult education's underlying assumptions about culture. My hope is that people might find my analysis disturbing, that it might rock complacency, that it might prompt a second look at taken-for-granted assumptions. Only in Hollywood movies and soap commercials do things come out unequivocally right in the end. An essay like this need make no such gesture.

Still, I cannot suppress a feeling of resolute optimism that critical adult education does have a way forward, that it still has an important role to play, despite the profundity of postmodernity's aporias. So great are the challenges that confront us that Frederic Jameson's impassioned plea for us to develop new cognitive maps of our world seems hopelessly feeble. In the thick of the fight to preserve the few remaining fortifications protecting the frightened encampments of our culture, it is hard to develop new ways to ward off the enemy or of imagining our enemy anew. Rather, our impulse is to resort to old and habitual ways of struggling, to close off to the need for taking any additional risks, and, so armed, to battle to the bitter end. But even if we were to admit the validity of Jameson's contention, and agree that we must reconstitute how we view ourselves and our world in postmodern times, could we possibly take the next and perhaps most painful step and acknowledge that we can no longer rely on the hard and glistening logic of instrumental reason to help us form these new maps? Faced with the urgency of change required, faced with the danger of cultural destruction, can we admit that the struggle to map postmodernity must now transpire in the verdant and dangerous terrain of communicative action?

In some strange way, I think critical adult education is particularly capable of offering an affirmative response to this question. While its heritage, its aspirations, its conceptual foundations, and its self-understanding are all bound up in the project of modernity, there is a sense in which critical adult education has always resisted embracing wholeheartedly the role of cultural legislator. Critical adult education has always been shot through with ambiguities that belie its recognition of radically democratic forms of sociation. Critical adult education has always been attracted to the terrible terrain of dialogical action. It already possesses considerable resources to sustain the tension of discourse and action, of openness and resolve, of the variegated boundaries, of the heterogeneity that prevail in postmodern times.

NOTES

I would like to thank Derek Briton for his help in developing this paper. He and I have published a paper entitled, "The Commodificaton of Adult Education" in the *Proceedings of the 33rd Annual Adult Education Research Conference* (1993) that expores additional dimensions of culture and adult education.

1. "Critical adult education" has become the conventional term for designating that loose collection of adult education theories and practices that aspires to such ideals as freedom, justice, and equality. Claiming a heritage that includes such notable and varied adult educators as Paulo Freire, Myles Horton, and Father Moses Coady, and such movements as the Danish folk schools, Canada's Women's Institutes, and British labor education (including the Worker's Education Association), contemporary critical adult educators (like most of the contributors to this volume) draw on theorists in critical theory, feminism, and cultural studies to promote adult education for progressive social change.

2. Habermas has long been concerned to differentiate *universal* lifeworld structures from those specific to the historical emergence of capitalism. For a discussion of this difference, see *The Philosophical Discourse of Modernity* (Habermas, 1987a, pp. 344–45).

3. He conducts this famous analysis in the opening chapter of *Capital, vol. 1.*

4. See Pierre Bourdieu's *Distinction: A Social Critique of the Judgment of Taste* (1984) for a similar analysis.

5. With this move, Baudrillard shifts the discussion from one that is political-economic to one that is post-structuralist. Eventually, this leads him to reject Marxism as naturalistic and fetishizing. Charles Levin (1991) relates the implications of Baudrillard's post-structuralism as follows: "The problem with Baudrillard's later work is that what began as a critique of naturalistic categories has grown steadily into an obsession, a kind of desire to expunge nature itself, or more precisely, to convert it into an enormous and meaningless cycle of collapsing culture" (p. 180).

6. David Frisby and Derek Sayer (1986) argue likewise and relate that "there is an inconsistency in Marx himself—testimony to a 'capturing', perhaps,

of his own analytic framework by dominant, self-understood forms of social life akin to the ideological distortions he himself analyzed in others" (p. 104).

7. Habermas (1987b) identifies the two-level structure of Marx's theory as perhaps its greatest contribution (p. 342).

8. Frisby and Sayer (1986) make a similar contention when they write that, "Marx's concept of production effectively reduces to that of production of material goods alone. Yet in reality, production of *people* is as fundamental to the possibility of social existence as production of their means of subsistence. They have to be produced, moreover, as *social* individuals. Marx recognized this in general terms, but this recognition did not extend to how he actually analyzed modes and relations of production" (p. 104).

9. As Habermas notes in *Knowledge and Human Interests* (1972), Marx is much more guilty of this in his analysis of development of economic formations of society than he is in his concrete historical analyses. *"At the level of his material investigations,* Marx always takes account of social practice that encompasses both work and interaction" (p. 53). See in particular *The German Ideology* (1968) and *The Eighteenth Brumaire of Louis Bonaparte* (1963).

10. Albrecht Wellmer (1985) provides a good account of summary of this critical movement in his chapter, "Reason, Utopia, and the *Dialectic of Enlightenment.*" For another interesting account, see Scott Warren (1984), *The Emergence of Dialectical Theory.*

11. Marx distinguishes the formal subsumption of labor as follows: "The form based on absolute surplus-value is what I call the *formal subsumption of labour under capital.* I do so because it is only *formally* distinct from earlier modes of production on whose foundations it arises spontaneously (or is introduced), either when the producer is self-employing or when the immediate producers are forced to deliver surplus labour to others. All that changes is the compulsion is applied, i.e. the method by which surplus labour is extorted" (1977, p. 1025).

12. Marx, himself, was well aware of the deliberate efforts expended by the bourgeoisie to build and sustain a culture in their best interests. For a good analysis, see *The German Ideology* (1968).

13. See R.W.K Paterson's (1989) paper "Philosophy in Adult Education" for a clear account of the need for neutrality in adult education. In the same collection of essays see Colin Griffin (1989) "Cultural Studies, Critical Theory, and Adult Education" for an argument for adult education to be political.

14. For a clear expressions of this awareness see Paula Allman (1988), "Gramsci, Freire, and Illich: Their Contributions to Education for Socialism"

and Sallie Westwood (1980), "Adult Education and the Sociology of Education: An Exploration."

15. See Marx's discussion of the real subsumption of labor in *Capital*, *vol. 1*, pp. 1034–38 (1977).

16. John Fiske (1989b) reasserts the meaning attributing power of popular culture when he writes: "Popular culture is made by subordinated peoples in their own interests out of resources that also, contradictorily, serve the economic interests of the dominant. Popular culture is made from within and below, not imposed from without or above as mass cultural theorists would have it. There is always an element of popular culture that lies outside social control, that escapes or opposes hegemonic forces" (p. 2). While he agrees in part with this perspective, Graham Turner (1990) also submits that one must be careful not to romanticize popular cultures. Today's mass media have tremendous power to "manufacture consent" (to use Noam Chomsky's phrase).

17. Although, as Michael Shapiro (1990) argues in his essay "Strategic Discourse/Discursive Strategy: The Representation of 'Security Policy' in the Video Age," even the most high-tech video presentations of the U.S. federal government still are subjected to a nuanced and reflective reception by a suspicious and "image-wise" public. In the closing paragraph of his paper he includes a letter from a nine-year-old boy to the Pentagon stating that they were mistaken in saying that the missile that shot down the Libyan war plane was a Sparrow missile when anyone could see from the battle video that it was a Phoenix missile! (p. 339). This point is also contested by numerous culture studies theorists who argue that the public is far more critical in its reception of media presentations than people like Baudrillard would ever admit. See, for instance, John Fiske's (1989b) *Understanding Popular Culture.*

18. Lyotard (1984b) explores how the ego is bypassed in postmodernity in *Driftworks*. Deleuze and Guattari (1977) develop the theme extensively in *Anti-Oedipus: Capitalism and Schizophrenia.*

19. See Guy Debord (1990), *Comments on the Society of the Spectacle.*

20. Baudrillard (1991) makes this point in the extreme in his controversial essay, "The Gulf War Has Not Taken Place." For one of many reactions to this essay, see Christopher Norris (1991), "The 'End of Ideology' Revisited: The Gulf War, Postmodernism, and *Realpolitik.*"

21. Baudrillard develops this theme most fully in his book *Simulations* (1983b). Douglas Kellner offers an insightful analysis of this and many other of Baudrillard's ideas in his intellectual biography, *Jean Baudrillard* (1989).

22. Jameson (1979) writes of travel as commodity as follows: "The American tourist no longer lets the landscape 'be in its being' but takes a snap-

shot of it, thereby transforming space into its own material image. The concrete activity of looking at a landscape is thus comfortably replaced by the act of taking possession of it and converting it into a form of personal property" (p. 131).

23. Some worthwhile examples of the vast literature that examines these new cultural products includes: Henry Jenkins (1992), *Textual Poachers: Television Fans and Participatory Culture*; E. Ann Kaplan (1987), *Rocking Around the Clock: Music Television, Postmodernism and Consumer Culture*; Douglas Kellner (1990), *Television and the Crisis of Democracy*; Annette Kuhn (ed.) (1990), *Alien Zone: Cultural Theory and Contemporary Science Fiction Cinema*; Janice Radway (1992), "Mail-Order Culture and Its Critics: The Book-of-the-Month Club, Commodification and Consumption, and the Problem of Cultural Authority"; Maureen Turim (1991), "Cinemas of Modernity and Postmodernity"; and Andrew Wernick (1991), "Promotional Culture." For a panoply of analyses of different cultural products, from comics to magazines to popular music, see Dick Hebdige's (1988), *Hiding in the Light*.

24. In *Jurassic Park*, for instance, the dinosaurs are representations of artist's representations of paleontologist's representations of how they may have looked in the past. Our expostulations about how 'real' the dinosaurs look are to a large extent our affirmation that Spielberg's signifiers accurately represent other signifiers and not that they represent reality.

25. Kellner (1990) details television consumption patterns in his book, *Television and the Crisis of Democracy*.

26. I would like to remain clear, here, that I am talking of tendencies and not, as Baudrillard and his followers often do, of a "done deal." However, just as in the case of the ozone layer, in which the CFCs already released into the atmosphere should, over the next few decades, be sufficient to seriously deplete ozone concentrations, it may be that tendencies toward cultural disintegration may already be in motion which, over the next few decades (that is, a short time), can deeply undermine the integrity of contemporary cultures.

27. Disturbed by the inflationary language Baudrillard uses to characterize modernity, Douglas Kellner (1989) contends that it is much better to view Baudrillard as a science-fiction writer rather than as a social theorist. Not only does this guard against taking some of his outlandish views as actually descriptive of reality, but it also makes us more willing to entertain his profound insight into trends in contemporary society (pp. 203–8).

28. A very successful Toronto-based adult education firm realizes they can make money providing training programs that do not provide information or skills but that engage students in an emotionally satisfying or relaxing afternoon. They call their company "The Entertrainers."

Conclusion

Dialogue, Encounters, and Debates

MICHAEL COLLINS:
IN THE WAKE OF POSTMODERNIST SENSIBILITIES
AND OPTING FOR A CRITICAL RETURN

I want to avoid, as much as possible, framing a response that merely seeks to justify the overall tack of my response in light of what the other contributors have said. (We were each given plenty of leeway.) However, their chapters are instructive for me. I am obliged to think carefully about the adequacy, and appropriateness, of my emphasis on the *agency* of adult education and adult educators. Is it any longer *meaningful* to think in terms of a practice of adult education guided toward *reasonably* determined goals? From the critical perspectives described in our text, does it still make sense to talk about the role of the adult educator?

For sure the skepticism of later Frankfurt School critical theory, characterized in the bourgeois intellectual aestheticism subsequently adopted by Adorno and Horkheimer, makes such questions appear overdetermined. And an appreciation for postmodernist thought (which attempts to evade appropriation) renders problematic any discourse around the agency or role of the adult educator. A postmodernist sensibility, regardless of whether or not it opts for consistency, unsettles any ambition to provide reasons for mediation implicit in the way we write, even from a critical theory perspective, about adult education and adult learning. For Baudrillard, and other postmodernist thinkers, such an ambition is self-delusory and the discourse on adult education a symptom of this delusion. Have we overstated our case for identifying an object of systematic study, relevant pedagogical contexts, a theory of practice, and a vocation we call adult education?

As contributors to this book, we are not happy with the way that conditions under late capitalism (mis)shape social learning processes, determine the goals of our institutions, and restrain the creative impulses of ordinary men and women. In this regard, our unhappiness with the way things are constitutes, if I can draw on Michael Welton (invoking Brian Fay), a shared perspective we bring to the contemporary critical discourse on adult education research and practice. This critical perspective we share highlights a significant area of concern about the ways *alienation* is manifested within the everyday lifeworld of ordinary men and women. *Alienation* refers us to conditions under early and late, corporate and state (eg., China and the former USSR), capitalism which effectively block the realization of human activity (learning and working) "where [citing Mechthild Hart] the involvement in body and mind, in nature and culture, is not devalued, impoverished, and exploited but seen as creating and nourishing life." Accordingly, our critical commentaries on adult education and adult learning are informed by our views on the global pervasiveness of a corporate (market-driven) ethos, the relentless commodification of vital lifeworld (cultural) forms of communication, the prevailing levels of exploitation and violence, the seemingly diminished capacities of adults to think for themselves, and the incapacity of those who understand where our collective interests lie to organize effectively in the cause of a more just society. These concerns are sufficiently exemplified, in one form or another, throughout this collective work on *critical adult education* which Donovan Plumb identifies, quite rightly in my view, with the project of modernity.

To my knowledge the term *critical adult education* has only recently emerged within the lexicon of modern adult education practice and research. At this juncture, there are relatively few adult educators whose work could be located within an area of practice designated as critical adult education. And it is not clear that many of these adult educators whose work is informed by critical theory (or critical theories) are wedded to the notion of carving out critical adult education as a distinctive field of theory and practice. I would, however, eschew any notion of the inevitable commodification of adult education within this particular legacy. We do need to seek even further self-clarification around the notion of critical adult education.

Donovan Plumb's analysis is timely and remarkably thought-provoking. It points us to the enduring relevance of Marx's insights into commodity fetishism. We now have to consider such eventualities as the commodification of critical theory, the commodification of cultural studies . . . the commodification of postmodernist thought.

The unhappiness we share about prevailing conditions under late capitalism might well be the significant impulse connecting the chapters of this book. Yet this "existence of feelings of unhappiness," as a relevant dimension of our critical theorizing (Welton, chapter 1), does not lead us as a collectivity to envisage prospects for the revolutionary overthrow of institutions and vested interests through which deeply rooted conditions of alienation are sustained. (Although, in her chapter, Mechthild Hart does allude, and very tentatively, to the possibility of envisioning a revolution.) In fact most of the important arguments explaining the absence of a potentially revolutionary agency and the skepticism about prospects for revolutionary praxis are cogently represented within the text. By and large I think our text envisages, in its most optimistic vein, perspective and institutional transformations within the nexus of prevailing economic, political, and social arrangements. (Our discourse on culture and postmodernity falls within this nexus.)

In these circumstances, I find Jack Mezirow's chapter very pertinent to what our critical perspectives on adult education are about. Mezirow's on-going research project around perspective transformations and adult learning have provided, within institutionalized forms of adult education, prospects for alternatives to the sterile functionalist approaches exemplified in pre-packaged curriculum. I would not question the usefulness of Mezirow's continuing attachment to the Habermasian project, especially around notions of communicative competence. And the recent incorporation of insights from Vygotski into a theory of adult learning seems to be a relevant development. However, Mezirow's chapter reinforces my view that his work is an invitation, even though he himself may not want to offer it in this way, to looking at adult learning again within the radically democratic tradition of John Dewey (from whom there are citations in Mezirow's chapter), William James, and Alfred North Whitehead. In my view, a critical theoretical— and not just a Habermasian—investigation of the way these educational theorists thought about the learning processes and everyday reality could contribute significantly to the reconstruction of adult learning theory. With the demise of andragogy as the guiding technology of adult education (could we be right in this regard?), Jack Mezirow's work on transformative learning becomes even more meaningful within the context of modern adult education practice and research.

In a critically informed transformative theory of adult learning, however, questions to be addressed concern the material and ideological circumstances which restrict the development of emancipatory learning processes envisaged by adult educator Thomas Hodgskin (cofounder of the mechanics' institutes movement and author of a sterling source of reference for Marx—*Labour Defended Against the Claims of Capital*) and, more recently, by Paulo Freire. What economic, political, and social factors prevent the acquisition of communicative competence and the realization of an ideal speech situation?

I think Michael Welton is right when he identifies Jürgen Habermas as the primary theorist whose work has influenced the recent critical turn in modern adult education practice. Welton's main argument in the opening chapter "that the critical theoretical tradition from Marx to Habermas has much to teach us about adult learning" is nicely sustained. We are reminded that the Habermasian project, though of major significance, draws on a rich legacy of Marxian theory and practice which is still in process.

Welton illuminates our text from the outset with a substantial narrative which places Frankfurt School critical theory and, subsequently, the Habermasian project on a trajectory from classical Greek philosophy and Renaissance thought through to Kant and Hegel, and then to Marx. My only concern would be that in enthroning "Habermas' giant presence," and in elevating Frankfurt School critical theory, we are overlooking other important trends of democratic Marxist thought; the intellectual work and political activities from which Euro-Marxism have emerged, for example. The Frankfurt School intellectuals were not the first leftist thinkers to acknowledge the abandonment of the socialist project in the USSR, and to identify those aspects of its form of state (bureaucratic) capitalism which pre-figured Stalin's repressive command economy. This oppositional critique within the Marxian legacy did not, and still does not, entail a rejection of reasonable prospects for the working class to realize itself as a revolutionary force. (And the concept of class remains a major category for the purposes of critical analysis.) It is quite feasible, then, to conceive of Frankfurt School critical theory, and the Habermasian project which has given it further dimensions, as a challenging eddy to be explored at a juncture in the mainstream of the Marxian legacy. Whatever the outcome of this conceptualization, however, Welton effectively explores Habermas' research project as a means for helping us understand the nature of social learning processes in these times.

The juxtaposition of lifeworld and system concepts is clearly significant in enabling us to "think deeply and realistically about the systemic blockages to the achievement of a more fully democratized society." So far the lifeworld/system analysis in adult education literature seems to be privileging "new social movements" as sites of emancipatory pedagogy, although recent critically oriented commentaries on the workplace as a site of learning suggests that the balance is shifting. I think that Mechthild Hart's essay with its focus on the workplace and family is significant in this regard. A concern I have about an overburdening of new social movements with our aspirations for the construction of an emancipatory pedagogy is conjectural but not, I hope, too premature in the absence of a substantial analysis which would be too lengthy an undertaking for this essay. Suffice it to say that I remain convinced that conventional institutions and points of production still constitute the most promising locations for progressive initiatives in line with our aspirations around an emancipatory pedagogy.

Donovan Plumb's essay is important because it represents a significant move to up the ante on theoretical discourse in adult education. In particular, Plumb obliges us to focus on the ways that the concept of culture is misappropriated within contemporary North American adult education discourse. The tendency towards cultural commodification, illuminated by Baudrillard, Lyotard, and other postmodernist thinkers in Plumb's essay, is readily understood via the leading concepts of Marx (especially from his investigations on commodity fetishism and alienation) and from the Habermasian lifeworld/system differentiation. The same goes for an apprehension of the *consequences of cultural commodification* in which either a Habermasian or Marxian analysis could bring into account the differences between Baudrillard, Lash, and Lyotard noted by Plumb. For Plumb the significant differences between a Marxist (including "neo-Marxist") and deconstructionist understandings of culture commodification reside in the fact that the former examine culture as an aspect of modernity while the latter are "postmodern." A lot hinges on the notion, and the location, of postmodernity. And even so, apart from the question of emphasis, a Marxist can reasonably ask, "so what is fundamentally novel about postmodern culture critique?"

The limitations in Marx's analysis of the relationship between exchange-value and use-value (which Plumb posits as a problem for Marxist culture critique) are apparent only if these concepts are (mis)apprehended—as with Baudrillard, for example—in a way that does not account for the philosophy of internal relations. Shorn of this understanding (which is central to the philosophy of Bradley and Whitehead as well as that of Hegel and Marx) about the external and internal connectedness of events, Marx's concepts are *represented* (postmodernly) in a much more limited way than is intended. It is ironic, though not surprising, that Baudrillard's brilliant insights lend

theoretical support to North American mass cultural theorists who interpret popular culture, *monolithically*, as being imposed from above.

In these regards British cultural studies, with discernible connections to adult education through the founding work of Richard Hoggart
and Raymond Williams, have offered a more sophisticated and hopeful
conception of culture than that of mass cultural theorists. In the light of
Plumb's critique, contemporary British cultural studies, though losing
some of the original impetus, still constitute a critical source of reference for North American adult educators. Plumb is strong on "declining
opportunities" but he tantalizes himself, and us, with the prospects for
"a meaningful emancipatory practice" within the realm of culture.

Reference to these "postmodernist times" is fairly pervasive within
our text. Taken literally (that is, semantically), the term is immediately
problematic. Yet our postmodernist tendencies, drawing aesthetic and
moral authority in the *modern era* from the philosophy of Nietzsche,
have a history. For example, the early years of the Bolshevik era in the
USSR witnessed a brilliant flowering of postmodernist art forms and
architectural designs which extended into the Stalinist era.

I am inclined to agree with the sentiments on postmodernism
expressed by Richard Johnson in his farewell speech ("Good-bye Cultural Studies, Hello . . . ?") given at Birmingham University in the
spring of 1993. He suggested that postmodernist thought still merits
attention in the field of cultural studies. My proviso is that postmodern
sensibilities should now be critically assessed within the project of
modernity which they cannot realistically evade anymore than could
Bush's "New World Order" signify the end of history.

One of the most unreal postmodernist prognostications in recent
times was made by Jean Baudrillard. Just before the outbreak of hostil-
ities he insisted that the Gulf War could not happen (*The Guardian*, 11
January 1991). Subsequently, he has tried to explain that it was not
really a war. At what stage does intellectual foreplay around *deconstruction* and *representation* become a touch obscene? In any event, on
the European continent from which the brilliant writings on the most
recent outbreak of postmodernism have emerged, there are *signs* that
the sparkle has disappeared from postmodernist pop.

The potential of making gender a primary analytical category,
incorporating an effective political agenda, is nicely elucidated in
Hart's "Motherwork.". If gender is addressed in a way that attends dialectically to the other major concepts of critical theory—class, com-

modity, race, surplus value, and so on—Hart's proposal assumes revolutionary proportions. It brings closer together working activity and creativity as the means towards a more fully human, joyful existence.

Hinging our critical discourse about production and reproduction onto a central concern for the care of children, "motherwork" invokes a moral and political force that can only be contained under advanced capitalism through ideological co-optation. Sexism and racism, as Hart demonstrates, are endemic to everyday life under advanced capitalism. These alienating tendencies remain integral to the fragmentation of social learning processes which prevent us (ordinary men and women from different ethnic backgrounds) from acting collectively in our best interests. For Hart's proposal to be realized, the revolutionary changes in institutional arrangements, political organization, and working-class consciousness will entail continuous struggle. Inevitably, there will be resistance from vested interests—beginning at the level of ideological co-optation, and then escalating. It will be interesting to see what forms the struggle can take and how adult educators of the critical persuasion are able to position ourselves in regard to Hart's challenging proposal.

Mechthild Hart's references are impressively up-to-date. Would it be out of place to suggest that the early political work of Alexandre Kollontai, and of Clara Zetkin and other women socialists, prefigure in a substantial way the integral aspects of Hart's proposal?

Aspirations around the advancement of (collective) communicative competence among ordinary men and women call for the effective *teaching* (in Heidegger's sense of the vocation) of fundamental skills and knowledge. At the same time, from the perspective of a critically informed emancipatory pedagogy which is, admittedly, very much constrained, it is possible for adult educators to get into the real world and engage in real struggles. Postmodernist sensibilities notwithstanding, we still live in a class-divided international society. For a critically informed practice of adult education in these times an aspiration to be politically and theoretically correct is no bad thing.

MECHTHILD HART:
WHOSE KNOWLEDGE? WHAT KIND OF KNOWLEDGE?

It is difficult to write a commentary on the contributions of this book. It is not difficult because all of my colleagues are clearly contributing to our on-going learning process, an imperative they have taken quite seriously. Instead, the difficulty is rooted in two different (but related) issues: First, I am the only woman contributor, and of white skin color on top of it. This makes me wonder whether I am a token feminist who is to give a "feminist touch" to critical theory, but also whether we can afford to leave out a "non-white," that is, a black, anti-racist perspective which would shed some undoubtedly important new light on critical theory. And this brings me to the second difficulty. Can we still talk about "the adult" in an essentially asexual, color-blind way (for which Mezirow is a prime example)? Can we as adult educators disregard the immense body of knowledge created by people of color (women and men in different parts of the world)? Which, of course, brings up the question whether the field (and profession) of adult education indeed has to remain within its professional context, that is, must stay away from social (including cultural), political, and economic analyses that are not directly related to the (professional) field itself.

As my colleagues (including myself) in this book have shown, it is impossible to engage in the theory and practice of education without being influenced by and paying tribute to theories that are trying to contribute to our understanding of the current turbulent changes in the world. All contributors are grappling with a multitude of changes, be it the commodification of culture and the movement of the market into "knowledge production" (Plumb), the development of a "high-risk society" where "survival issues" have become important for adult education (Mezirow), or the "convulsive global changes" (Welton) or "pressing global circumstances" (Collins) whose magnitude is articulated with severity. These larger social perspectives are accompanied by a critique of the professionalization of our field, its history, and its more current trends toward making a "corporate pedagogy" fit an "increasingly competitive global marketplace" (Collins).

Seen within this larger framework, it is impossible to disregard analyzing the role of *education*, because it is a developing theory of education rather than a theory of *learning* which is capable of taking a larger social context into consideration. Of course, this is already a move away from the context and history of professionalized adult education. Its traditional emphasis has been on "adult learning," supported by cognitive psychology, and anchored in andragogy and self-directed learning. This allegedly politically neutral concentration on the "individual adult learner" has been complemented by the more current component of "learning for earning," with its behaviorist agenda and its "focus on the guided responses of the individual adult learner" (Collins). It is even hard for Mezirow to insist that it is "the nature of adult learning" where questions concerning the role of transformative adult education in a risk society have to be grounded. He is taking recourse to Habermas' universal ideal of rational discourse, clarifying the "professional commitment" of adult educators as fostering "individual transformations toward more inclusive, differentiating, permeable, and integrative meaning perspectives and schemes." Despite his mentioning of a number of social problems (like poverty and homelessness), Mezirow can only keep his focus on adult learning by making sure that adult educators remain politically neutral.

Unfortunately, no matter how hard we try to hide behind the veil of political neutrality, we always take sides in a world marked by glaring forms of domination, injustice, and exploitation. This is my point of departure for these brief and highly selective comments, which undoubtedly are doing injustice to the many interesting and stimulating points made in this book: If we want to develop a critical perspective within and for our field, we have to be open and articulate about the sides we are taking, theoretically and practically. And this leads me back to my above-mentioned difficulties, now phrased slightly differently.

Is it possible to make a few (scant) references to feminist theories, and basically leave out anti-racist and anti-imperialist theories? For instance, can anyone criticize Marx's theories without mentioning feminist and Third World theories of 'labor'? Clearly, the "worker" is taken for granted as the male model of "modernist" theory. What about analyzing the patriarchal dimension of the Marxist (and mainstream) concept of worker—which is modern *and* postmodern? Despite his sophisticated criticism of modernity, Plumb does fall victim to the modern ideology of progress by not considering the spread of poverty and the destruction of colonized people during the very modern rise of capitalism as an essential component of the Western concept of progress. What "we" have done to the colonies is now catching up with "us" in the (old) First World, in what is now called postmodernism. To ask a simple and (I admit) highly polemical but telling question: From where do postmodern theories originate? Who developed them? Is it Native American people, or African-American women? Are they behind the times, have not caught up with theories, and are therefore in need of critical adult educators?

To make this question more general, let's look at the issue of knowledge production. Is it sufficient to criticize the move of the market into its basic sites of production (Plumb) without asking *whose knowledge* has been allowed to enter these sites before the market took over, and *what kind of knowledge* we talking about? And there are many more questions. Where are the areas of knowledge that are still vital, that never have been (officially and professionally) produced but denied, devalued, ignored, or silenced by the representatives of the production sites? Do we have to follow the tradition of academic debates, that is, leave out epistemological questions that are related to "non-white" and "non-male" populations—to their ways of living and producing knowledge? To use a key word of Habermas' theories, we are here dealing with "lifeworld contexts" that have *never* become important aspects of knowledge production, but have been labeled in the typical Western (white, masculinist) way as "traditional" societies, which were "premodern," "pre-capitalist," and "undeveloped." And despite a number of disagreements I have with Mezirow's ideas, his call on adult education "to counter a trend toward the deterioration of traditional communities by supporting new forms of community" clearly supports my asking the above questions.

However, despite their sharp criticism of the professionalization of adult education, the contributors to this book remain dependent on an institutionalized view of the professional adult educator. For instance, Collins writes about the "collective capacity of ordinary men and women." If we ask the questions of where important sources of knowledge are to be found, and if we take Collins' idea of a "collective capacity" of ordinary people seriously, we cannot at the same time consider the academy the "undoubtedly" most likely source of valid knowledge. Maybe this is the class bias that is implicitly manifested by all contributors, a bias which has a standing in the field of adult education. Even where adult education is connected to "popular education " and "community-based initiatives" (Collins), there is no real attempt to put into words what it would mean for "us" adult educators to learn from "ordinary men and women." For example, despite his attempts to break through the confines of rational discourse thinking, Mezirow refers to the "ignorant homeless," and to the role of adult education to develop the capacity for critical reflexivity. He manifests a standpoint that would keep the oppressed, exploited, dominated, and others from ever *wanting* to participate in a discourse that reinforces the ideological view of the "marginalized" as suffocated non-communicators. What about their knowledge, survival skills, insights "we" in the middle-class professions need to learn?

It seems that "we" are going back to "primary" issues of physical survival. Plumb's referral to Marxism's "uneasy but resilient interpretive framework for understanding capitalism" which is now being "overwhelmed by the vast transformations of contemporary society" has been thoroughly questioned by other "marginalized" thinkers for decades. However, questions have been asked in ways that were far from refurbishing "the sagging structure of Marxism" (Plumb), but different languages, languages which are grounded in very different experiences and modes of thought and action. For someone profoundly interested in education's assistance in "emancipatory" or "transformative" practice, it is hard to neglect these documents, as it is those who could lead us out of the Western quagmire of refurbishing new dichotomies and hierarchies even in our attempts to criticize (Marxist and non-Marxist) Western beliefs.

For instance, Welton places the importance of dialogue at the center of his critical perspective of adult education. But what about acknowledging a more dialectical relationship between "primary," vital, life-giving issues and communication? He touches upon the idea, but only touches upon it by calling the defense of an "autonomous and exuberant civil society" the prime task of critical adult education, a task that is meant to preserve the communicative structure of the lifeworld and to extend communicative action into state or economic institutions. But this needs to be taken further.

Similarly, Welton does criticize Habermas for setting up a dichotomy between work and interaction. He does have a pessimistic but realistic view of how limited the possibilities are for creating developmental workplaces. And he does write about the necessity of rethinking work. But he and the authors he quotes entirely leave out the relationship to *nature*, and nature is more than the geese flying above our heads but includes the material we are taking from nature *and* our bodies—the physical foundation of our existence—as well. Especially in his first essay Welton develops a more disembodied and ultimately "head"-bound approach to critical adult education, where "rational self-clarity and collective autonomy" are primary values of critical theory. But how do we interact with nature? Is this vital form of interaction excluded from rational discourse, communication, or rational self-clarity? What is not addressed by Habermas' model, and why?

If we look at the body, at physical foundations and issues of survival as crucial, as being of vital interest, we are moving into a very different conceptual and critical framework. This framework would not set up another dichotomy and thereby another hierarchy between modernist and postmodernist, First World (including the "new" First, former "Second" World) and Third World, heterogeneity (difference) and commonality, public and private, and so on. By refusing to consider myself an exception because reality is not a "simulacrum" that seems "more real than reality itself" (Plumb), by learning from other cultures and people, by refocusing on my own potential of having knowledge reside in the body (yes, female, white), and by considering issues of survival not simply "basic" and "primary" but highly complex and symbolically mediated although irreducible to "virtual realities"—I arrive at a dialectical framework. This framework does not "expunge" (Baudrillard) the physical foundation of anything alive, and it does not reduce it to the "id" either, but it simultaneously affirms and transcends it. And this process is founded upon "integrative values" that go beyond but do not contradict the rationalist impetus of discourse (and communication). These are the values of cooperation, nurture, connection, reciprocity. (These ideas have been given to me by Angela Miles; they are discussed in her forthcoming new book on *Integrative Feminisms*.) When we focus on the issue of nurture, we are dealing with a complex topic that leaves out neither communication nor physical well-being. Welton mentions the importance of a "developmental nurturing environment" as a lifeworld prerequisite, but his comments are brief. What would our critical perspective look like if we put a view at the center that affirms individual and cultural differences *and* transcends them by seeing and developing commonalities—which includes the differences and commonalities between body and mind? As Angela Miles points out, it is easier to see differences than commonalities in a society that is divided by racism, sexism, homophobia, and class. But a criticism of the postmodern ease of celebrating heterogeneity and difference without transcending these differences gives us a sense of the magnitude of our task as educators: As many ideas presented in this book made clear, the idea of rational consensus and discourse should not be thrown away. But it needs to be looked at, reevaluated and transformed in light of other, especially non-Western theories that help to acknowledge differences but do not neglect the tremendous relations of power that are woven into any differences. To recognize issues of power makes it impossible to stay politically neutral, or to ignore that we cannot keep power in abeyance in our educational endeavors, especially not in our decidedly *critical* attempts. And, as everybody interested in any critical perspective and practice should know, "we" in the West can learn a lot about these issues from other, "non-Western" cultures. And maybe it is not a matter of developing new and heterogeneous narratives to the modernist metanarrative (Lyotard), but of trying to relearn our ability to always see the connection of learning and education to something vital, something *living*.

DONOVAN PLUMB:
THE VARIEGATES OF POSTMODERNITY

As a relatively recent participant in the discursive formation of adult education, I would like to begin my response by commending my fellow contributors to this volume. Each thinker has done an exemplary job of deepening the theoretical foundations of adult education. They have refused to be swept aside by the strong anti-intellectualist currents which exist in our field and have rapidly shaped a body of theory that affords new and powerful insights into the difficult issues that increasingly confront adult educators. As intellectual scouts, they have revealed conceptual pathways linking adult education to some of the most impressive theoretical developments of the twentieth century: to critical theory, to feminism, and to cultural studies. In the essays in this volume, Welton, Mezirow, Collins, and Hart challenge us once again to reflect on the pragmatic, ethical, and moral underpinnings of our field.

Michael Welton has distinguished himself as an historian and theorist of adult education. He has worked hard to reveal adult education's rich historical context. In typical fashion, he has pursued his two contributions to this book with unrelenting theoretical rigor. Historically, one of the most debilitating aspects of adult education has been its persistent refusal to subject its foundational presuppositions to thorough-going intellectual examination. Welton's work has always been refreshing to me because he has never yielded to the pressure to keep complex things simple.

In his opening essay, for example, he explores the robust lineage of the term "critique" in order to locate the complex points of intersection that exist between critical theory and adult education. In particular, he argues that the "learning turn" in critical theory and the "critical turn" in adult education are symptomatic of a historical and conceptual development of profound significance: the emergence of a social learning paradigm. Armed with a clear grasp of this paradigm, Welton is able, once again, to demonstrate the relevance of critical theory's most important insights for the theory and practice of adult education. Welton's second essay is even more ambitious. Here he contends that the social learning paradigm, especially as it is outlined by Habermas, can provide a normative and theoretical foundation for adult education equal to the aporias of contemporary life. Welton argues that adult education should take as its "fundamental task" the defense of the lifeworld and the fostering of communicative action.

Welton intends his essays to inspire and to uplift: he wants to point out a positive path for adult education in what he knows are desperate times. In his efforts to be upbeat about the future of adult education, though, Welton underplays the unrelenting challenges that confront it in postmodernity. Digging into the sociological dimensions of postmodernity, for instance, would disclose the scale and power of cybernetic action systems which imperil communicative action in new and unanticipated ways. Further pursuing the philosophical discourses of postmodernity would reveal that Habermas, himself, does not believe that critical theory can be grounded ontologically and that we must seek other, more hazardous foundations. As much as Welton's essays steer adult education in a very promising direction, much remains unsaid about the perilous fate of the social learning paradigm in postmodernity.

I was very pleased with Jack Mezirow's decision to flesh out the *psychological* underpinnings of his "transformation theory of adult learning." From the beginning, Mezirow's intent has been to explore the nature of significant learning episodes in individual adults. His forays into critical theory were inspired not by a desire to understand collective learning processes but to understand the social and cultural conditions most conducive for an individual's perspective transformation. As consequential as these forays have been, it is my view that his focus in this essay on cognitive and developmental psychology enables him to advance his theory of adult learning in particularly important ways. It is in the arena of psychology that the theory of perspective transformation has always found its most comfortable home.

In this essay, Mezirow's lucid depictions of the different means by which people can construe meaning (presentational, propositional, and intentional) and his account of the origins and varieties of meaning-perspectives place him in a position to offer fresh insight into the events and processes (both internal and external) which precipitate and sustain transformations in meaning-schemes and meaning-perspectives. Working up the psychological dimensions of his theory also has the rather interesting effect of enabling Mezirow to clarify the links he sees between his transformation theory and communicative theories like Habermas'. For instance, his analysis of the psychological process of perspective transformation enables him to illuminate the extent to which interpersonal communication both stimulates and influences transformational learning. Mezirow can now comfortably contend that it is through dialogue that people test the adequacy of their meaning schemes and transform them if they are found wanting. He can also point out how some dialogical situations are more conducive to authentic forms of transformation than are others.

Even though Mezirow develops a means for highlighting the links between perspective transformation and Habermas' critical theory, it would be a mistake to assume that his transformation theory of learning is a social learning theory. Aside from agreeing that communicative distortions can be traced to inequitable relations of power in society, he shows very little interest in the shape, the content, or the history of structures of power. Mezirow is not a sociologist or an historian. He does not analyze capitalism, racism, patriarchy, modernity, or postmodernity. These terms, if they are mentioned at all, are floated like insubstantial chimeras in his text. Unlike Welton, he does not trace the historical convergence of critical theory and adult education. Unlike Collins, he does not pursue the power relations of society expressed in developments like competency-based education. Unlike Hart, he does not explore the complex relationship between work and gender. And I do not think he needs to. Mezirow offers a fascinating *psychological* theory of adult learning—well researched, carefully considered, useful. There is little problem unless we forget (or he forgets) that his transformation theory of adult learning can only constitute one small part of a much broader theory of adult education.

Over the past few years, Michael Collins has begun to question whether any such broad theory is possible (or even desirable). He has become suspicious of the motives of "academic" adult educators who create big theories and, ever sensitive to the class interests of most academics, doubts the capacity of the university to bring about emancipatory change in the world. Collins' aspirations for adult education in the academy are much more modest. Rather than producing theories which, like the tonics of traveling medicasters of times gone by, promise to heal all the ills of contemporary society, Collins believes that academic adult educators should adopt a far smaller, contextual, and more *ethical* focus.

To make his point, Collins shows how good and noble academic initiatives of the past—initiatives like andragogy, professionalization, self-directed learning, competency-based education, and human resource development—have served only to draw adult learners deeper into the mire of oppressive social relations. He is more optimistic about the potential of the critical turn in adult education. Eschewing its more "abstract formulations" and "constructs," Collins contends that critical traditions (critical theory, feminism, postmodernism) offer university adult educators the means for developing analyses and strategies which are truly practical for adult learners. They provide a basis for revisiting what it is that constitutes an ethical practice of adult education.

I admire Collins' desire to foster forms of adult education which can contribute honestly to building good lives for people. I also tend to agree that, in general, universities are difficult places from which to conduct an emancipatory practice of adult education: many big and elaborate schemes of the past did result in more harm than they did good. I wonder, though, if this necessarily means that academic adult educators should get out of the business of big theorizing. As Habermas points out in his recent book, *Justification and Application* (1993), there are many ways to conceptualize being practical. Collins' perspective is that to be truly practical adult educators should help people realize the "good life," however they might define it. This, he asserts, cannot be achieved in the abstract. An ethical notion of what is practical demands that adult educators stick to the specifics of people's lives, keep their aspirations modest, and make their plans small. It is my belief, though, that being ethical is just one way an adult educator can be practical. Another way is to help people realize *just* ways of living together. In this case, discerning the moral life demands we forego the specifics of the personal life, propel ourselves into an abstract realm where all humans are considered equal, and make judgments the size of universal truths. My feeling is that our society is far from being a just place, that there is still plenty of room for big theorizing in adult education, and that universities still can become an important sight for moral discourse. The obvious importance of realizing the good life need not be stacked up against the more abstract importance of achieving human justice.

In her contribution to this book, Mechthild Hart continues her challenging exploration of women's lifeworlds within the twisted configuration of power relations in contemporary society. Her task is to sort out how the abstract relations of capitalism have articulated with normative power structures like patriarchy and racism to produce the gradients of opportunities, violence, and deceits that women must somehow negotiate in their daily lives. Her specific task in this paper is to explore the vicissitudes of a specific point of articulation between capitalism and patriarchy—the "binary" notion of work/family—and to spell out the ways this articulation subordinates, impoverishes, and violates specific social groups (women, minorities, immigrants, and children). Hart systematically reveals how dominant conceptions like the "monolithic family" are tightly intertwined with the world of work to produce a structure which focuses its deprivations on women. She contends that only when adult educators burst through the bonds of monolithic conceptions of family and workplace and begin to validate previously suppressed actions and agents (symbolized by her concept of "mother-work") can they develop pedagogical strategies to truly revolutionize the lifeworld contexts of both women and men.

Hart has contributed significantly to the difficult task of sorting out the articulations of capitalism and patriarchy (racism is only briefly considered in her analysis). She has provided a penetrating analysis of the way gender is mobilized to sustain profitability and the way the workplace is utilized to enhance patriarchal dominance. My only concern is that the lucidity of her argument and forthrightness of her claims serve to underestimate the complexity of the world in which we now live. Critical adult educators are confronted now by a recalcitrant world where domination is affected by new and ethereal means. Hart contends that it is the ideology of the workplace and the monolithic family that continues to constrain women's lives. I would submit that, in postmodernity, ideology is declining as a central strategy of social control. Rather than unifying ideologies, it is fragmentation that now sustains the world's most powerful regimes (bureaucracies and corporations); surveillance increasingly replaces normative regulation as the way for controlling social space; capitalism floods indigenous cultures with meanings which can never be sorted or contextualized or understood; desires are ecstatically gratified by the great imaging machines of postmodernity; people are seduced by the proliferation of commodities that inundate their daily lives. In postmodernity, gender, race and the myriad other discriminators of social privilege no longer form a unified front. Capitalism, augmented with newfound cybernetic capacities, no longer needs to generate cultural uniformities (like work/family) to sustain its profit-making enterprises. With its sensors and probes it can seek out the most nuanced markets for the production and consumption of its products.

One cannot accuse either Collins or Hart of ignoring the social contexts of adult education. In fact, both take dead aim at the abstract theorizing that obsesses many critical social theorists (most notably, those working with the notion of postmodernity) and call for specific analyses and interventions to combat concrete instances of domination. As much as I agree with their insistence that we attend to the particulars of domination in our society, this should not be our only focus. As Fredric Jameson (1991) insists, the dimensions of postmodernity are far and above what we might ever hope to grasp through our everyday experience or oppose through everyday action. As difficult and as abstract as it might seem, it is still possible to reach out with our imaginations and to map the broad contours of postmodern existence. Somehow we must assure that our specific acts of resistance are not simply part of broader more obscure forms of social control.

At the same time as I take inspiration from the many important ideas articulated in this book, I believe that the theoretical foundations of critical adult education are in far greater need of revision than most of the preceding essays suggest. While all of my colleagues admit that we do indeed live in strange and rapidly changing times, none of them really bear down and examine the transformations that now reverberate through our world. I am now convinced that "postmodernity" can no longer be written off as the fantasy of a few cultural visionaries. Rarely has a concept spurred such heated debate across a range of disciplines or stimulated such rethinking of some of the most cherished ideas in contemporary society. The term "postmodernity," with all its inconsistencies and ambiguities, with all its wildness and despair, powerfully designates the world in which we live, a world in which many of critical adult education's most deeply held assumptions can no longer be taken for granted—including its conceptions of culture, time and space, identity, power, and politics. If critical adult education is going to continue to exist as a meaningful enterprise, it needs to begin paying a great deal more *specific* attention to the variegates of postmodern times.

JACK MEZIROW: BEING CLOSE TO HOME

As an adult educator from the United States, inspired by the ideas of John Dewey, Eduard Lindeman, and Myles Horton, I read Welton's introductory chapter on the history and nature of critical theory with its many references to contemporary European social theorists with a feeling of being far from home. It seems to me that critique, discourse, and critical education need to be understood also as an indigenous American tradition.

My colleague and friend, Maxine Greene, (1986) has seen this most clearly. She traces the critical impulse in America to Plato, Socrates, Bacon, Hume, Blake, (who wrote of "mind-forg'd manacles" which not only shackle consciousness but assured the continuation of institutionalized systems of domination), and J. S. Mill to make us see and to defamiliarize our commonsense worlds. This legacy of resistance to the systems of domination of church and state, of land-holding arrangements and the armed forces over the lives of individuals was a founding influence in America.

Greene writes of an atmosphere created by rational, autonomous voices engaged in dialogue for the sake of bringing into being a public sphere. Rights, sanctioned by natural and moral laws, were being violated.

> Among these rights were "life, liberty, and the pursuit of happiness," which (especially when joined to justice or equity) remain normative for this nation. . . . Liberty, at the time of the founding of our nation, meant liberation from interference by the system in the lives of citizens. For some . . . liberty also meant each person's right to think for himself or herself, "to follow his intellect to whatever conclusions it may lead" in an atmosphere that forbade "mental slavery." (Greene, 1986)

Central to an American tradition of critical reflection and dissent through discourse are the contributions of Emerson, Thoreau, William

James, and John Dewey and the tragic literature of Twain, Melville, Crane, Wharton, Hemingway, and Fitzgerald whose vision was "of a dream betrayed, of a New World corrupted by exploitation and materialism and greed. In background memory, there are images of Jeffersonian agrarianism, of public spheres, of democratic and free-swinging communities. We do not find these in European literature, nor in the writings of the critical theorists" (Greene, 1986). (It was Fitzgerald whose "test of a first-rate intelligence" sounds remarkably like a test of critical reflection and rational discourse: "the ability to hold two opposed ideas in the mind at the same time, and still retain the ability to function").

Throughout our history there have been frequently recurrent calls for justice and equality and resistance to materialism and conformity. Civil rights have been central to the meaning of democracy in the United States. "Great romantics like Emerson and Thoreau gave voice to the passion for autonomy and authenticity. Black leaders, including Douglass, W.E.B. DuBois, the Reverend Martin Luther King and Malcolm X, not only engaged dialectically with the resistant environment in their pursuit of freedom; they invented languages and pedagogies to enable people to overcome internalized oppression" (Greene, 1986). James Madison realized that to resolve the dilemma of people being both sovereign under our Constitution but also subject to the law, it was essential to allow the fullest possible freedom to engage in deliberative discussion on political issues. Madison's view of a deliberative democracy was predicated upon citizens exercising critical reflection, participating fully and freely in rational discourse and taking reflective action to effect change. One is also reminded of the critical journalistic tradition of dissent personified by the likes of William Cowper Brann, who founded and edited *The Iconoclast* in Waco, Texas in the latter part of the last century. The collective perspective transformations associated with the Holocaust and the civil rights, anti-Vietnam War, the women's movements, and the social activism of the 1960s are fresh in our memories.

Greene reminds us that our critical tradition in education includes the work of Jane Addams and Lillian Wald, who pioneered education for immigrants and the urban poor and supported union organization with "an explicitly political awareness of what they were about in a class-ridden society" (Greene, 1986) and Francis Parker, who educated teachers at the end of the century. There is a proud history of educators hostile to regimentation and manipulation, critical of constraints of consciousness. The central themes of critical pedagogy found a strong voice in the 1930s in the publication *The Social Frontier* at Teachers College, Columbia University. Workers's education through the labor movement was a significant contributor to the tradition of critical adult education in the United States.

John Dewey envisioned using education to create a social democracy. He clearly understood the meaning of what later was to be called the "hegemony" of the dominant ideology of a society when he wrote of the "religious aureole" protecting institutions like the Supreme Court, the Constitution, and private property. He was particularly aware of previously unexamined assumptions behind the public school curriculum. In *The Public and Its Problems* (1927), Dewey wrote of a "social pathology" which distorts inquiry into social institutions and conditions. It manifests itself in a thousand ways:

> in querulousness, in impotent drifting, in uneasy snatching at distractions, in idealization of the long established, in a facile optimism assumed as a cloak in riotous glorification of things "as they are," in intimidation of all dissenters—ways which depress and dissipate thought all the more effectively because they operate with subtle and unconscious pervasiveness. (Cited in Greene, p. 434)

The radical critique of American schools by libertarians, Marxists, critical theorists, romantics, and democrats has been built upon our earlier tradition of dissent. Greene observes; "Without an Emerson or a Thoreau or a Parker, there would not have been a Free School movement or a "deschooling" movement. Without a DuBois, there would not have been liberation or store front schools. . . . Without a social reformist tradition, there would have been no Marxist voices. . . . Without a Dewey, there would have been little concern for 'participatory democracy,' for 'consensus,' for the reconstitution of a public sphere."

Eduard Lindeman, perhaps the most influential founder of adult education as a field of study and practice in the United States, was profoundly influenced by Dewey. Lindeman's vision of adult education—and the practice of "The Inquiry," a group of prominent educators he organized—was of adult education as a critical pedagogy. Critical reflection and discourse were central, as reflected in this often quoted definition:

a cooperative venture in non-authoritarian, informal learning, *the chief purpose of which is to discover the meaning of experience; a quest of the mind which digs down to the roots of the preconceptions which formulate our conduct*; a technique of learning for adults which makes education coterminous with life and hence elevates living itself to the level of adventurous experiment. . . . Rather than studying 'subjects,' the learner begins with his or her immediate problems impeding self-fulfillment. The teacher moves from acting as an authority figure to become . . . the guide, the pointer-out, who also participates in learning in proportion to the vitality and relevance of his facts and experiences. (Brookfield, 1987, p. 4; author's italics)

Paulo Freire, the Brazilian author of the seminal *Pedagogy of the Oppressed* (1970), has been accorded a near icon status in both Latin and North American, an indication of the receptivity of American educators for critical pedagogy. But perhaps the American tradition of critical adult education is perhaps best exemplified by Myles Horton, who founded the Highlander Folk School in 1932. Highlander was a leader in introducing the organized labor and the civil rights movements in the South.

Of Myles, Bill Moyers writes, "Few people I know have seen as much change in the American South, or helped to bring it about, as Myles Horton. He's been beaten up, locked up, put upon and railed against by racists, toughs, demagogues, and governors. But for more than fifty years now, he has gone on with his special kind of teaching—helping people to discover within themselves the courage and ability to confront reality and to change it" (Horton, 1990, preface). As an educator, Horton's goal was social democracy "right down into the home and into children's lives. It's got to be everywhere" (p. 172). He wrote, "My position was that I believed in changing society by first changing individuals, so that they could then struggle to bring about social changes" (p. 184). *Transformation theory* supports the validity of this conviction. Critical reflection, discourse, solidarity, and reflective action are cardinal themes at Highlander.

Thousands of ordinary people came to Highlander to learn from each other and from Myles to think critically about common problems and to find the self-confidence and skill to together challenge entrenched social, economic, and political structures of a segregated and often exploitative society. In so doing they learned the meaning of democracy. They also experienced the mutual respect, equality, freedom, responsibility, compassion, solidarity, and reflective rationality this idea implies. Those who came experienced a democratic community, exemplifying the society of Myles' dream. Many of us who share that dream came by our convictions within a uniquely American tradition of critical thought and educational practice.

I would like to close with a few comments on Michael Collins' contribution to this book. In his chapter on the role of the adult educator, Collins (1) identifies professionalism with technical rationality and with the system (vs. the lifeworld), (2) dichotomizes professionalism and social action, (3) dichotomizes professionalism and independent learning, and (4) differentiates professionalism from unspecified "other forms of organization that could be more empowering." There are undoubtedly concepts of professionalism in adult education which fit this description. An alternative definition of professionalization in adult education, more consistent with critical education, might refer to a process whereby adult educators learn to understand how adults learn, how to help them learn, and how to learn with them.

If the process of adult learning is centrally concerned with critical reflection, rational discourse, and reflective action, and the ideal conditions of discourse are also ideal conditions of adult education, as I have suggested, then professionalization takes on a different meaning—that of precipitating, encouraging, and facilitating this kind of learning.

Over the past fifty years or so, we who are paid professionals have come to recognize a common core of normative practices which constitute a coherent and distinctive professional perspective. As I point out in my chapter, more than a decade ago Suanmali demonstrated empirically that these practices enjoyed a near unanimous endorsement by professors of adult education in the United States, one of the most influential groups of professionals. These practices cannot be interpreted as reflective of either instrumental learning or the characteristics selected by Collins to depict professionalism in adult education, nor are they reflective of professionalization in other fields, including that pertaining to other levels of education. Indeed, this evidence suggests that the core concepts of adult education or andragogy, as endorsed by professors of adult education, are entirely consistent with good critical pedagogy and with *transformation theory*. What Collins depicts as professionalism is a stereotype and just bad adult education.

Equating facilitating adult education with knowing nothing and consumerism is also a bit much. For me, facilitating learning means precipitating and fostering critical reflection, discourse, and reflective action—an extremely demanding and sophisticated professional role and the defining role of an adult educator. As with professionalism, let us not confuse the baby with the bath water.

MICHAEL WELTON:
WE NEED TO HAVE A RADICAL LEARNING THEORY

I have some questions to address to my colleagues, and in the spirit of continuing the conversation, would like to proceed somewhat informally to pursue several themes with them.

To begin with, Collins and I agree with the shortcomings of the andragogical model, and I applaud his emphasis on teaching. He is profoundly skeptical of the label of "facilitator," gutting as it does any ethical commitment from the practice of the teacher. To facilitate can mean accommodating our practice to someone else's agenda and interests. Teaching as a communicative practice is circumvented. This bypassing of teaching as a moral-practical activity is the main reason Collins rails against competency-based training and the ideology of self-directed learning. And I think he is a little leery of the emphasis on adult *learning* in our field (Mezirow and I certainly exemplify this) because this seems to remove the process from cognitive, ethical, and aesthetic scrutiny. He argues that the "case for adult education as a distinctive field of practice can be advanced" around the "agency of the adult educator."

In my view, adult education as a distinctive field of practice must be grounded in a social theory of adult learning. The agency of the individual adult educator is not sufficient anchoring. The *agency* of the *critical* adult educator must needs be grounded in a theoretical understanding of ideologies, structures, and movements—to what extent are these structures and movements enabling or disenabling of human individuation, learner-centeredness, and emancipation? Thus, the agency of the critical educator would necessarily be linked dialectically to the current possibilities inherent in the roles of child-rearer, worker, citizen, client, or consumer. I fear that Collins' emphasis on the agency of the individual teacher will not enable him to explore the way, in Mezirow's evocative phrase, the "nature of adult learning itself mandates participatory democracy as both the means and the goal" of our practice.

I would like to argue, too, that the "vocation" of the adult educator cannot be restricted to that of thoughtful pedagogue. The new social learning paradigm opens up space for us within the university as *critical intellectuals*. We, as university-based teachers of adult education, often occupy marginal spaces within the academy. Our assignment within the increasingly mind-numbing university is to focus on pedagogic techniques. But this assigned role only makes sense within the old andragogical model. When we conceptualize all of society as a vast school, we clear the way for the entry of the critical adult educator into the current social dialogue about the future of our society. We as professors of adult education ought not be silent witnesses to the degradation of our times. Here I recall how Gramsci helped me to see that pedagogical relationships could not be restricted to the conventional space of the formal school. He shifted our thinking about curriculum away from the narrow confines of the school to the culturally formative spaces of material and symbolic production and reproduction. We need to have a radical learning perspective on how society organizes its learning—this is the basis for our engagement with our times. One can only hope that a radical social learning perspective would be widely adopted as an orienting frame for an increasing number of thinkers who are now trapped within hermetic fiefdoms in the university. There is already considerable evidence that a social learning perspective is diffused throughout the university, rendering the traditional Department of Adult Education (with its imperialistic claims) obsolete and ineffective. And it is also increasingly evident that governments are interested in adult learning but not particularly in "adult education." It appears to me that a social learning perspective is converging with major trends in the society and university.

Each time we read one of Mezirow's essays he takes us down another track or adds another brick or two to his intricate transformative learning theory. It seems very much in keeping, for instance, that Mezirow would grapple with the implications of the learning challenges posed by Ulrich Beck's notion of the "risk society," and would be on the alert for new challenges for the adult educator. Indeed, if we follow Mezirow that the cardinal task of the adult educator is to foster critical self-reflection, then it clearly makes sense that he wants us to address the survival problems, the existential problems, and the persistent problems of social inequality in our societies. It does seem, though, that Mezirow's learning theory is more comfortable with the existential problems experienced by individuals in our liberal-democratic risk societies (where the atomization, or "singularization" [Habermas 1992, pp. 195–200] of individuals expands simultaneously with the loosening of social bonds) than it is with the unruly world of structures of domination and oppression.

I think that Mezirow and I have somewhat different approaches to how we ought to think about the constitution of meaning and the transformation of a person's "meaning perspective." I am much more inclined by academic training as an anthropologist, historian, and social theorist to feel rather uncomfortable with Mezirow's tendency to isolate the "individual" from "structure." It is not that he is unaware of the enormous constraining power of large-scale institutions on the learning processes of adults or that our meaning perspectives are constituted socially. But it sometimes feels very much as if, in constructing the formal properties of the transformation of "meaning-schemes" and a "meaning-perspective," that we have moved inside the cognitive-psychic processes of the individual subject and have forgotten that forms of knowledge are embedded in, and constitutive of, the actions "we carry out" in and through social practices (Giddens, 1986, p. 536).

Social theorists slide between two poles—structure (objectivism) and agency (subjectivism)—when they attempt to understand "meaning" and "forms of consciousness." Mezirow's strong emphasis on intentionality, agency, and reflexivity places him close to the subjectivist pole. I tend to work closer to the other pole. I certainly do not want to dissolve subjectivity into structure, but I think one can only get at the constitution of meaning, and its possible transformation, by conceptualizing structure as "both the medium and the outcome of the human activities which it recursively organizes" (Giddens, 1986, p. 533). Structures both create and constrain us simultaneously, and meaning is produced and challenged within the contexts of social life. My notions of "developmental work" and "developmental citizenship" are attempts to formulate an adequate account of the *social structuration* of adult learning. "Disorienting dilemmas" are always social in origin (and here we need socially attuned crisis theory), although they reverberate through our cognitive processes.

Hart's essay carries me back to the early 1970s in Toronto, Ontario, when the "wages for housework" movement burst on to the scene, and the Marxian notion of class was deemed as inadequate to account for the full range of women's exploitation and oppression. Feminists like the late Maggie Benston (1969) insisted that women's unpaid domestic labor was crucial to the reproduction of capital, and many thousands of words were expended in learned journals about whether Marx's notion of reproduction included the work of caring for children. From the mid-to-late 1970s, radical ideas about the importance of men sharing the care of children (Dinnerstein 1976; Balbus 1982) circulated among small groups of American and Canadian leftists. But the radical reform of child-rearing was not on the agenda through the 1980s (although the issue of universal day-care certainly was). Now, in the desperate 1990s, Mechthild Hart argues that women's work (motherwork) must be central to the agenda of the global critical adult education movement.

This is a bold and not overly popular move within the North American adult education scene. At the moment, even the liberal wing of adult education has jumped aboard the HRD bandwagon and embraced the reveries of diversity and participative management. By focusing on the feminization of poverty—the gendered nature of the welfare system and labor markets—Hart demythologizes the bitter realities of many women's lives. In a sense, Hart's text calls adult educators, particularly those who are still critically oriented, to stand with the poorest. It is there, she says, "where we find the true answers to the question of what this society is all about."

Hart's main message, though, is that if we are to even know where to look to see the poor, we must cut through a heavy ideological curtain veiling their reality. The masculinist construction of work and the normalization of the monolithic family obscures the misery of women's lives and continues to degrade their work of nurturance. Hart wants us to reframe the meaning of productivity away from its present connotation (learning for earning, for the bottom line) toward a reconstituted notion of productivity as the production and enhancement of life itself. It is not that I disagree with the radical transformation of our present notion of "production," or with the idea of "bringing the issue of children into the 'world of work'." But I remain unclear, within our present understanding of late modernity, about what reasons and what forces would, in fact, carry the issue of children into the world of work in an emancipatory way. Hart appears not to be particularly concerned with providing us with a social theoretical justification and dialectical argument for her defense of "motherwork." Her affirmation of motherwork is neither situated within the history of debates about domestic labor nor articulated within an adequate understanding of the system-lifeworld interplay.

These questions suggest themselves. Does the idea of "motherwork" have enough revolutionary force to challenge our social system?

Where is there evidence that it does, in history or in our contemporary world? Does the notion of motherwork harbor essentializing notions of women, a position akin to Gilligan and other ethicists of caring? How does the actual, concrete work of mothering escape deformation by the system? What would enable an expanded notion of work (something like Hart's) to be channeled from the lifeworld to the system? Any expanded notion of work, it seems to me, would have to differentiate caring for children (which ought not to ever be fully incorporated into wage labor) and other forms of caring, for example, pedagogical caring for one's students. There is no undifferentiated notion of caring, and one can hardly argue, in any realistic sense, that the parent's care for a helpless child is transferable, and relevant, to the kind of care that ought to be exhibited between cultural groups in a nation-state. Hart's position seems resolutely ethical, but more in the sense carried by the utopian socialists criticized by Marx in the mid-nineteenth century.

Donovan Plumb's essay is very disconcerting for critical adult educators. His main argument is that critical (or radical) adult education was grounded in a "modernist view of culture" and that modernist critical adult education could understand its project as counter-hegemonic because culture was reproduced through communicative contestation over norms and values. Plumb argues that the "drift from discourse to the image as the principle means of signification in our society" undermines the foundation of a critical practice. There can be no doubt that, over the last three decades, we have been "dominated by the reign of images" (Gross, 1992, p. 59). For those who uphold the value of critical theories and humanistic studies, this reign of the image is unpleasant news. Images float free from any attachment to tradition; they are unstable and open to infinite association; they supersede textuality (the word). If Plumb's thesis is anywhere near accurate, then it is "conceivable that the capacity to reason and conceptualize may actually be eroding, which necessarily means a drying up of the sources of negativity and more uncritical adaptation to existing social processes" (Gross, 1981, p. 97). Following Gross, and probably hordes of old humanists, I am inclined to think that the "written word is essential for critical reflection, not only because it permits a certain distance from the material confronted, but also because it allows a reader to engage a work, dispute with it, and enter into a sustained dialogue with its essential themes" (p. 97).

Plumb points to tremendous variations in the extent of the decline of our will to fight over the "governing norms of society." This, I think,

is a plea for us to interrogate our culture—its cracks, nooks, crevices—
for indications of otherness. I would like to point to four sources (of
many) for the sustenance of communicative action. First, I have argued,
following Habermas, that world-religions can no longer claim to unify
the lifeworld. It is important, however, to realize that Judaism and
Christianity (and other religions as well) still function as "communities
of interpretation" for many people in North America. The dominant tendency in our postmodern, commodified religious culture, to be sure, is
to embrace consumerism with open arms. But Judaism and Christianity—as texts and practices—are replete with what David Gross (1992)
calls "noncontemporaneous otherness" (they have resources that can
always be mobilized against instrumental rationality, erosion of com-
munality, and the possessive, calculating individual). Second, even
though the liberal-democracies are characterized presently by widespread apathy and resignation, the new social movements (peace, ecology, women, identity) are still important sites for oppositional forms of
learning. It also appears that some movements—such as ecology—have
the earmarks of new attempts to unify the lifeworld. Third, history contains sources of non-contemporaneous otherness. Subversive and alternative traditions can maintain an underground existence (this appears to
be the case with some aboriginal traditions), dissenting traditions can
exist at the margins of a culture for a very long time, and, in the spirit
of Walter Benjamin, it is always possible to retrieve a fragment from the
past that beams critical light on the dark surfaces of the present. Fourth,
one can never discount the sheer resilience of human beings who can
always say no.

REFERENCES

Abramovitz, M. (1991). Putting an end to doublespeak about race, gender, and poverty: An annotated glossary for social workers. *Social Work*, 5, 380–84.

Adorno, Theodor (1950). *The Authoritarian Personality*. New York: Harper.

——— (1973). *Negative Dialectics*. New York: Seabury Press.

Agger, Ben (1981). A critical theory of dialogue. *Humanities in Society*, 4, 1, 7–30.

——— (1992). *The Discourse of Domination: From Frankfurt School to Post-modernism*. Evanston, Illinois: Northwestern University Press.

Allman, Paula (1988). Gramsci, Freire, and Illich: Their contributions to education for socialism. In Tom Lovett, ed., *Radical Approaches to Adult Education: A Reader*. London: Routledge.

——— and Wallis, John (1990). Praxis: Implications for "really" radical education. *Studies in the Education of Adults*, 22, 1, 14–30.

Altenbaugh, Richard J. (1990). *Education for Struggle: The American Labor Colleges of the 1920s and 1930s*. Philadelphia: Temple University Press.

Amott, T. L. and Matthaei, J. A. (1991). *Race, Gender, and Work: A Multicultural Economic History of Women in the United States*. Boston: South End Press.

Anderson, Richard (1991). The empire strikes out: A roundtable on populist politics. *Telos*, 87, 3–36.

Appelbome, P. (1993). Deep south and down home, but it's ghetto all the same. *The New York Times*, 21 August.

Arato, Andrew (1972). Georg Lukacs: The search for a revolutionary subject. In Dick Howard and Karl Klare, eds., *The Unknown Dimension: European Marxism since Lenin*. New York: Basic Books.

——— and Cohen, Jean (1992). *Civil Society and Political Theory*. Cambridge, Mass.: MIT Press.

Aronowitz, Stanley and Giroux, Henry (1985). *Education Under Seige: The Conservative and Radical Debate*. Hadley, Mass: Bergin and Garvey.

—————— (1993). *Education Still Under Seige: The Conservative, Liberal and Radical Debate*. Toronto: OISE Press.

Balbus, Isaac (1982). *Marxism and Domination*. Princeton: Princeton University Press.

Ball, Wendy (1992). Critical social research, adult education and anti-racist feminist praxis. *Studies in the Education of Adults*, 24, 1, 1–25.

Barnet, Richard (1993). The end of jobs. *Harper's*, September, 47–52.

Baudrillard, Jean (1981). Beyond use value. In C. Levin, ed., *Critique of the Political Economy of the Sign*. St. Louis, Mo.: Telos Press.

—————— (1983a). The implosion of meaning in the media. In Jean Baudrillard, *In the Shadow of the Silent Majorities, or, The End of the Social and Other Essays*. New York: Semiotext(e).

—————— (1983b). *Simulations*. New York: Semiotext(e).

—————— (1990). *Seduction*. Montreal: New World Perspectives.

—————— (1991). La guerre de Golfe n'a pas eu lieu. *Liberation*, 29 March.

Bauman, Zygmunt (1992). *Intimations of Postmodernity*. London: Routledge.

Beck, Ulrich (1993). *The Risk Society; Toward a New Modernity*. Newbury Park, Cal.: Sage.

Bell, Brenda, Gaventa, John, and Peters, John, eds. (1990). *We Make the Road by Walking*. Philadelphia: Temple University Press.

Bell-Scott, P., Guy-Sheftall, B., Royster, J. J., Sims-Wood, J., DeCosta-Willis, M., and Fultz, L. P., eds. (1993). *Double Stitch*. New York: HarperPerennial.

Bellah, Robert and Associates (1985). *Habits of the Heart*. Berkeley: University of California Press.

—————— (1991). *The Good Society*. New York: Alfred A. Knopf.

Benhabib, Seyla (1981). Modernity and the aporias of critical theory. *Telos*, 49, 38–59.

—————— (1984). The Marxian method of critique: Normative presuppositions. *Praxis*, 4, 3, 284–98.

—————— (1986). *Critique, Norm and Utopia: A Study of the Foundation of Critical Theory*. New York: Columbia University Press.

Benston, Maggie (1969). The political economy of women's liberation. *Monthly Review*, 21, 4, 13–27.

Bergmann, B. (1986). *The Economic Emergence of Women*. New York: Basic Books.

Bernstein, Richard (1983). *Beyond Objectivism and Relativism: Science, Hermeneutics, and Praxis*. Philadelphia: University of Pennsylvania Press.

———— (1991). *The New Constellation: The Ethical-Political Horizons of Modernity/Postmodernity*. Cambridge, Mass.: MIT Press.

Blum, L. M. (1991). *Between Feminism and Labor*. Berkeley: University of California Press.

Bobbio, Norbert (1991). The upturned utopia. In Robin Blackburn, ed., *After the Fall: The Failure of Communism and the Future of Socialism*. London: Verso.

Bogard, William (1988). Sociology in the absence of the social: The significance of Baudrillard for contemporary thought. *Philosophy and Social Criticism*, 13, 3, 227–42.

Borgmann, Albert (1993). *Crossing the Postmodern Divide*. Chicago: University of Chicago Press.

Bourdieu, Pierre (1984). *Distinction: A Social Critique of the Judgement of Taste*. Cambridge, Mass.: Harvard University Press.

Boyd, R. D. and Myers, J. G. (1988). Transformative education. *International Journal of Lifelong Education*, 7, 261–84.

Brandtstadter, Jochen (1990). Development as a personal and cultural construction. In Gun Semin and Kenneth J. Gergen, eds., *Everyday Understanding*. London: Sage.

Braverman, Harry (1974). *Labor and Monopoly Capital: The Degradation of Work in the Twentieth Century*. New York: Monthly Review Press.

Briton, Derek, and Plumb, Donovan (1993). The commodification of adult education. *Proceedings of the Adult Education Research Conference*. University Park, Pa.: Pennsylvania State University.

Brookfield, Stephen (1985). *Understanding and Facilitating Adult Learning*. San Francisco: Jossey-Bass.

———— (1987). *Learning Democracy*. London: Croom Helm.

———— (1993). Self-directed learning, political clarity, and the critical practice of adult education. *Adult Education Quarterly*, 43, 4, 227–42.

Brown, E. B. (1993). Mothers of mind. In P. Bell Scott et al., eds., *Double Stitch*. New York: HarperPerennial.

Bruner, Jerome (1990). *Acts of Meaning*. Cambridge,Mass.: Harvard University Press.

Burbules, Nicholas C. and Rice, Suzanne (1991). Dialogue across differences: Continuing the conversation. *Harvard Educational Review*, 61, 393–415.

Burnham, M., Clayton, C., Gresham, J. H., Height, D., Waters, M., Wattleton, F., Wilkerson, M., with Davis, O. (1989). Scapegoating the black family. *The Nation*, 249, 24/31 July (special issue).

Cafferella, Rosemary and Merriam, Sharan (1991). *Learning in Adulthood*. San Francisco: Jossey-Bass.

Calhoun, Craig, ed. (1992). *Habermas and the Public Sphere*. Cambridge, Mass.: MIT Press.

Candy, Phil (1991). *Self-Direction for Lifelong Learning: A Comprehensive Guide*. San Francisco: Jossey-Bass.

Carnevale, A., Gainer, L. J., and Meltzer, A. S. (1988). *Workplace Basics*. Alexandria, Va.: The American Society for Training and Development.

Celis, W., III (1993). Study says half of adults in U.S. can't read or handle arithmetic. *The New York Times*, 9 September, A1, A16.

Cervero, Ron (1992). Adult and continuing education should strive for professionalization. In M. Galbraith and B. Sisco, eds., *Confronting Controversies in Challenging Times: A Call for Action*. San Francisco: Jossey-Bass.

Children's Defense Fund (1992). *Vanishing Dreams: The Economic Plight of America's Young Families*. Washington, D.C.: Children's Defense Fund.

Chilman, C. S. (1993). Parental employment and child care trends: Some critical issues and suggested policies. *Social Work*, 38, 451–60.

Chynoweth, J. K. (1989). *Enhancing Literacy for Jobs and Productivity*. Washington, D.C.: The Council of State Policy and Planning.

Clark, Carolyn and Wilson, Arthur (1991). Context and rationality in Mezirow's theory of transformational learning. *Adult Education Quarterly*, 41, 2, 75–91.

Coady, Moses (1939). *Masters of Their Own Destiny: The Study of the Antigonish Movement*. New York: Harper & Row.

———— (1971). *The Man from Margaree: Writings and Speeches of M.M. Coady, Educator*. Toronto: McClelland and Stewart.

Cobble, D. S., ed. (1993). *Women and Unions: Forging a Partnership*. Ithaca, N.Y.: ILR Press.

Cockburn, C. (1991). *In the Way of Women: Men's Resistance to Sex Equality in Organizations*. Ithaca, N.Y.: ILR Press.

Cohen, Jean (1987). *Class and Civil Society: The Limits of Marxian Critical Theory*. Amherst: University of Massachusetts Press.

Collard, Sue and Law, Michael (1989). The limits of perspective transformation: Further perspectives on Mezirow's theory. *Adult Education Quarterly*, 39, 2, 99–107.

Collins, J. (1985). *Between Women*. Philadelphia: Temple University Press.

Collins, Michael (1985). Jürgen Habermas' concept of communicative action and its implications for the adult learning process. *Proceedings of the 25th Adult Education Research Conference*. Tempe, Ariz.: Department of Higher and Adult Education, Arizona State University.

——— (1987). *Competence in Adult Education: A New Perspective*. Lanham, Md.: University Press of America.

——— (1988a). Prison education: A substantial metaphor for adult education practice. *Adult Education Quarterly*, 38, 2, 101–10.

——— (1988b). Self-directed learning or an emancipatory practice of adult education: Re-thinking the role of the adult educator. *Proceedings of the 28th Adult Education Research Conference*. Calgary, Alberta: University of Calgary.

——— (1991). *Adult Education as Vocation: A Critical Role for the Adult Educator*. New York: Routledge.

——— (1992a). Adult and continuing education should resist further professionalization. In M. Galbraith and B. Sisco, eds., *Confronting Challenges in Challenging Times: A Call for Action*. San Francisco: Jossey-Bass.

——— (1992b). Critical trends in adult education: From self-directed learning to critical theory. Paper presented to Association of Process Philosophy of Education, American Philosophical Association. Louisville, Kentucky.

——— and Plumb, Donovan (1989). Some critical thinking about critical theory and its relevance for adult education practice. *Proceedings of the 30th Annual Adult Education Research Conference*, Madison, Wis.: University of Wisconsin.

Collins, P. H. (1993). The meaning of motherhood in black cultures and black mother-daughter relationships. In P. Bell-Scott et al., eds., *Double Stitch*. New York: HarperPerennial.

Commons, M. L., Richards, F. A., and Armon, C., eds. (1984). *Beyond Formal Operations: Late Adolescent and Adult Cognitive Development*. New York: Praeger.

Connerton, Paul (1976). Introduction. In P. Connerton, ed., *Critical Sociology*. Harmondsworth: Penguin Books.

————— (1980). *The Tragedy of Enlightenment: An Essay on the Frankfurt School*. Cambridge: Cambridge University Press.

Cultural Studies (Birmingham) Group II (1991). *Education Limited: Schooling and Training and the New Right since 1979*. London: Unwin and Hyman.

Cunningham, P. M. (1992). From Freire to feminism: The North American experience with critical pedagogy. *Adult Education Quarterly*, 42, *3*, 180–91.

————— (1993). The politics of worker's education. *Adult Learning*, *5*, 13–14.

Dallmayr, Fred (1984). *Polis and Praxis: Exercises in Contemporary Political Theory*. Cambridge, Mass.: MIT Press.

Davenport, Joseph (1993). Is there any way out of the andragogy morass? In Mary Thorpe, Richard Edwards, and Ann Hanson, eds., *Culture and Processes of Adult Learning*. London: The Open University Press.

De Landa, Manuel (1982). Policing the spectrum. *Zone 1/2*.

Debord, G. (1990). *Comments on the Society of the Spectacle*. London: Verso.

Deleuze, Gilles and Guattari, Félix (1977). *Anti-Oedipus: Capitalism and Schizophrenia*. Minneapolis: University of Minnesota Press.

DeParle, J. (1992). Incomes in young families drop 32% in 17 years, study finds. *The New York Times*, 15 April, A15.

Dewey, John (1916). *Democracy and Education*. New York: Macmillan.

————— (1927). *The Public and Its Problems*. New York: Henry Holt.

————— (1939). *Freedom and Culture*. New York: Capricorn Books.

Diggins, Jack (1994). *The Promise of Pragmatism: Modernism and the Crisis of Knowledge and Authority*. Chicago: University of Chicago Press.

Dinnerstein, Dorothy (1976). *The Mermaid and the Minotaur*. New York: Harper & Row.

Dole, E. (1989). America's competitive advantage: A skilled work force. *Adult Learning*, 1, 12–13 September.

Draves, William (1980). *The Free University: A Model for Lifelong Learning*. Chicago: Association Press.

Dugger, C. W. (1992). Tiny incomes, little help for single mothers. *The New York Times*, 31 March, A1, A16.

Dyer, Richard (1982). *Stars*. London: BFI.

———— (1986). *Heavenly Bodies: Film Stars and Society*. London: BFI.

Dykstra, C. (1993). Keywords: The dilution of social change language in adult education. *Proceedings of the 34th Annual Adult Education Research Conference*. University Park, Pa.: Pennsylvania State University.

Eagleton, Terry (1991). *Ideology: An Introduction*. London: Verso.

Easton, Lloyd and Guddat, Kurt, eds. (1967). *Writings of the Young Marx on Philosophy and Society*. New York: Anchor Books.

Ehrlich, E. (1988). For American business, a new world of workers. *Business Week*, 19 September, 112–14, 118, 120.

Ellsworth, Elizabeth (1989). Why doesn't this feel empowering? Working through the repressive myths of critical pedagogy. *Harvard Educational Review*, 59, 297–312.

Evans, S. M., Nelson, B. J. (1989) *Wage Justice*. Chicago: `University of Chicago Press.

Eyerman, Ron and Shipley, David (1981). Habermas on work and culture. *Theory and Society*, 10, 4, 547–66.

Fay, Brian (1987). *Critical Social Science: The Limits of Liberation*. Ithaca, N.Y.: Cornell University Press.

Featherstone, Mike (1991). *Consumer Culture and Postmodernism*. London: Sage.

Finger, M. (1989). New social movements and their implications for adult education. *Adult Education Quarterly*, 40, 15–21.

Fiske, John (1989a). *Reading the Popular*. Boston: Unwin Hyman.

———— (1989b). *Understanding Popular Culture*. London: Routledge.

Foley, Griff (1993). Adult education research as interpretive activity and social production. *Studies in Continuing Education*, 15, 2, 75–79.

Forester, John (1989). *Planning in the Face of Power*. Berkeley: University of California Press.

Fraser, Nancy (1987). What's critical about critical theory? The case of Habermas and gender. In Seyla Benhabib and Drucilla Cornell, eds., *Feminism as Critique*. Minneapolis: University of Minnesota Press.

Freire, Paulo (1973). *Education for Critical Consciousness*. New York: Seabury Press.

——— (1974). *Pedagogy of the Oppressed*. New York: Seabury Press.

——— (1978). *Pedagogy in Process: The Letters to Guinea-Bissau*. New York: Seabury Press.

——— (1985). *The Politics of Education: Culture, Power and Liberation*. South Hadley, Mass.: Bergin and Garvey.

Frisby, David and Sayer, Derek (1986). *Society*. Sussex, England: Ellis Horwood.

Funiciello, T. (1990). The poverty industry. *Ms.*, November/December, 1, 33–40.

——— (1993). *Tyranny of Kindness*. New York: The Atlantic Monthly Press.

Garson, B. (1989). *The Electronic Sweatshop*. New York: Penguin Books.

Gelpi, B. C., Hartsock, N. C. M., Novak, C. C., and Strober, M. H., eds. (1986). *Women and Poverty*. Chicago: University of Chicago Press.

Gergen, Kenneth J. (1982). *Toward Transformation in Social Knowledge*. New York: Springer.

Gibson, William (1984). *Neuromancer*. NewYork: Ace Books.

——— (1986). *Count Zero*. New York: Ace Books.

——— (1988). *Mona Lisa Overdrive*. New York: Bantam.

Giddens, Anthony (1984). *The Constitution of Society*. Berkeley: University of California Press.

——— (1986). Action, subjectivity, and the constitution of meaning. *Social Research*, 53, 3, 529–45.

——— (1991). *Modernity and Self-Identity: Self and Society in the Late Modern Age*. Stanford: Stanford University Press.

Goleman, D. (1990). Studies offer fresh clues to memory. *New York Times*, 27 March.

Gordon, L. (1992). Family violence, feminism, and social control. In B. Thorne and M. Yalom, eds., *Rethinking the Family*. Boston: Northeastern University Press.

Gould, Carol (1988). *Rethinking Democracy: Freedom and Social Cooperation in Politics, Economy and Society*. Cambridge: Cambridge University Press.

Gould, Roger (1978). *Transformations: Growth and Change in Adult Life*. New York: Simon and Schuster.

Gouldner, Alvin (1976). *The Dialectic of Ideology and Technology*. New York: Seabury Press.

Grabowski, Stanley (1981). Continuing education in the professions. In S. Grabowski et al., *Preparing Educators of Adults*. San Francisco: Jossey-Bass.

Greene, Maxine (1986). In search of a critical pedagogy. *Harvard Education Review*, 56, 427–41.

Griffin, Colin (1983). *Curriculum Theory in Adult and Lifelong Education*. London: Croom Helm.

——— (1987). *Adult Education and Social Policy*. London: Croom Helm.

——— (1989). Cultural studies, critical theory and adult education. In Barry Bright, ed., *Theory and Practice in the Study of Adult Education: The Epistemological Debate*. London: Routledge.

Gross, David (1981). On critical theory. *Humanities in Society*, 4, 1, 89–100.

——— (1992). *The Past in Ruins: Tradition and the Critique of Modernity*. Amherst: University of Massachusetts Press.

Guglielmino, L. and Guglielmino, P. (1982). *Learning Style Assessment*. Baton Rouge, Fla: Guglielmino and Associates.

Habermas, Jürgen (1970a). On systematically distorted communication. *Inquiry*, 13, 3, 205–18.

——— (1970b). *Toward a Rational Society: Student Protest, Science, and Politics*. Boston: Beacon Press [German text, 1968].

——— (1972). *Knowledge and Human Interests*. London: Heinemann.

——— (1973). *Theory and Practice*. Boston: Beacon Press.

——— (1974). The public sphere: An encyclopedia article. *New German Critique*, 1, 3, 749–57.

——— (1975). *Legitimation Crisis in Late Capitalism*. Boston: Beacon Press.

————— (1979). *Communication and the Evolution of Society*. Boston: Beacon Press.

————— (1981). New social movements. *Telos*, 49, 33–37.

————— (1984). *The Theory of Communicative Action (Vol. I)*. Boston: Beacon Press.

————— (1985). Questions and counterquestions. In Richard J. Bernstein, ed., *Habermas and Modernity*. Cambridge, Mass: MIT Press.

————— (1987a). *The Philosophical Discourse of Modernity*. Cambridge: MIT Press.

————— (1987b). *The Theory of Communicative Action (vol. II)*. Boston: Beacon Press.

————— (1989a). The crisis of the welfare state and the exhaustion of utopian energies. In Seidman, Steven , ed., *Jürgen Habermas on Society and Politics: A Reader*. Boston: Beacon Press.

————— (1989b). *The Structural Transformation of the Public Sphere: An Inquiry into a Category of Bourgeois Society*. Cambridge, Mass.: MIT Press.

————— (1990). *Moral Consciousness and Communicative Action*. Cambridge, Mass.: MIT Press.

————— (1991). What does socialism mean today? The revolutions of recuperation and the need for new thinking. In Robin Blackburn, ed., *After the Fall: The Failure of Communism and the Future of Socialism*. London: Verso.

————— (1992). *Postmetaphysical Thinking: Philosophical Essays*. Cambridge, Mass.: MIT Press.

————— (1993). *Justification and Application: Remarks of Discourse Ethics*. Cambridge, Mass.: MIT Press.

Hacker, A. (1992). *Two Nations*. New York: Ballantine Books.

Hagen, J. L. (1992). Women, work, and welfare: Is there a role for social work? *Social Work*, 37, 9–14.

Hake, Barry (1992). Remaking the study of adult education: The relevance of recent developments in the Netherlands to the search for disciplinary identity. *Adult Education Quarterly*, 42, 2, 63–78.

Hart, Mechthild (1985). Thematization of power, the search for common interests, and self-reflection: Towards a comprehensive concept of emancipation. *International Journal of Lifelong Education*, 4, 2, 119–34.

———— (1990a). Critical theory and beyond: Further perspectives on emancipatory education. *Adult Education Quarterly,* 40, 3, 125–38.

———— (1990b). Liberation through consciousness raising. In Jack Mezirow, ed., *Fostering Critical Reflection in Adulthood.* San Francisco: Jossey-Bass.

———— (1992). *Working and Educating for Life: Feminist and International Perspectives on Adult Education.* London: Routledge.

Hart, M. (1993). Educative or miseducative work: A critique of the current debate on work and education. *The Canadian Journal for the Study of Adult Education*, 7, 21–38.

Hartsock, N. C. M. (1985). *Money, Sex, and Power.* Boston: Northeastern University Press.

Harvard Business Review (1991). Ways men and women lead. *Harvard Business Review*, January-February, 150–60.

Harvey, David (1989). *The Condition of Postmodernity.* Cambridge: Blackwell.

Hebdige, Dick (1979). *Subculture: The Meaning of Style.* London: Routledge.

———— (1988). *Hiding in the Light.* London: Routledge.

Held, David (1980). *Introduction to Critical Theory: Horkheimer to Marcuse.* London: Hutchinson Press.

Hendrickson, William (1959). William Hendrickson Papers, box 14, October. Syracuse University Archives.

Hensel, N. (1991). *Realizing Gender Equality in Higher Education. ASHE-ERIC Higher Education Report No. 2.* Washington, D.C.: George Washington University, School of Education and Human Development.

Heron, J. (1988). Validity in cooperative inquiry. In P. Reason, ed., *Human Inquiry in Action: Developments in Paradigm Research.* London: Sage.

Hochschild, A. and Machung, A. (1989). *The Second Shift.* New York: Viking.

Honneth, Axel and Joas, Hans (1988). *Social Action and Human Nature.* Cambridge: Cambridge University Press.

————, eds. (1991). *Communicative Action.* Cambridge, Mass.: MIT Press.

Horkheimer, Max (1947). *Eclipse of Reason*. New York: Oxford University Press.

――― (1976). Traditional and critical theory. In P. Connerton, ed., *Critical Sociology*. Harmondsworth: Penguin Books.

――― and Adorno, Theodor (1972). *The Dialectic of Enlightenment*. New York: Herder and Herder.

Horton, Myles, Kohl, Judith, and Kohl, Herbert (1990). *The Long Haul*. New York: Doubleday.

Hossfeld, K. J. (1990). "Their logic against them": Contradictions in sex, race, and class in Silicon Valley. In K. Ward, ed., *Women Workers and Global Restructuring*. Ithaca, N.Y.: Cornell University Press.

Houle, Cyril (1956). Professional education for educators of adults. *Adult Education*, 6, 3, 131–41.

Howard, Dick (1988). *The Politics of Critique*. Minneapolis: University of Minnesota Press.

Humphrey, Nicolas H. (1992). *A History of the Mind*. New York: Simon & Schuster.

Husper, Michael (1991). Taking aim on Habermas's critical theory: On the road toward a critical hermeneutics. *Communication Monographs*, 58.

Illich, Ivan (1970). *De-Schooling Society*. New York, New York: Harper & Row.

――― (1977). *Disabling Professions*. London: Marion Boyars.

――― (1977). *Medical Nemesis: The Expropriation of Health*. New York, New York: Penguin Books.

――― (1983). Silence is a commons. *The CoEvolution Quarterly*, 40, 5–9.

Ingram, David (1987). *Habermas and the Dialectic of Reason*. New Haven: Yale University Press.

Jackson, Nancy (1989). The case against "competence": The impoverishment of working knowledge. *Our Schools/Ourselves*, 1, 3, 77–85.

Jameson, Fredric (1979). Reification and utopia in mass culture. *Social Text*, 1, 1, 130–48.

――― (1991). *Postmodernism, or, The Cultural Logic of Late Capitalism*. Durham: Duke University Press.

Jansen, Theo and Van der Veen, Ruud (1992). Reflexive modernity, self-reflective biographies: Adult education in the light of the risk society. *International Journal of Lifelong Education*, 2, 4, 275–86.

Jarvis, Peter (1987). *Adult Learning in the Social Context*. Beckenham: Croom Helm.

——— and Peters, John, eds. (1991). *Adult Education: Evolution and Achievements in a Developing Field*. San Francisco: Jossey-Bass.

———, ed. (1987). *Twentieth-Century Thinkers in Adult Education*. London: Croom Helm.

Jay, Martin (1972). The Frankfurt School and the genesis of critical theory. In Dick Howard and Karl Klare, eds., *The Unknown Dimension: European Marxism since Lenin*. New York: Basic Books.

——— (1984a). *Adorno*. London: Fontana Books.

——— (1984b). *Marxism and Totality: The Adventures of a Concept from Lukacs to Habermas*. Berkeley: University of California Press.

Jenkins, Henry (1992). *Textual Poachers: Television Fans and Participatory Culture*. New York: Routledge

Jhally, Sut (1989). The political economy of culture. In Ian Angus and Sut Jhally, eds., *Cultural Politics in Contemporary America*. New York: Routledge.

Johnson, Christopher (1993). Lifeworld, system, and communicative action: The Habermasian alternative in social history. In Leonard Berlanstein, eds., *Rethinking Labor History: Essays on Discourse and Class Analysis*. Urbana: University of Illinois Press.

Johnson, Richard (1983). What is Cultural Studies Anyway? *Department of Cultural Studies*. University of Birmingham, 1–48.

Jones, J. (1986). *Labor of Love, Labor of Sorrow: Black Women, Work, and the Family, from Slavery to the Present*. New York: Vintage Books.

Kahn, P. (1993). Capitalism at work. *The Women's Review of Books*, 11, 25–27.

Kaplan, E. Ann (1987). *Rocking Around the Clock: Music Television, Postmodernism and Consumer Culture*. New York: Methuen.

Katz, M. B. (1989). *The Undeserving Poor*. New York: Pantheon Books.

Kazemek, F. E. (1990). Adult literacy education: Heading into the 1990s. *Adult Education Quarterly*, 41, 53–62.

Keane, John (1984). *Public Life and Late Capitalism: Toward a Socialist Theory of Democracy.* Cambridge: Cambridge University Press.

Kellner, Douglas (1989). *Jean Baudrillard: From Marxism to Postmodernism and Beyond.* Oxford: Polity Press.

―――― (1990). *Television and the Crisis of Democracy.* Boulder, Col.: Westview Press.

Kessler-Harris, A. (1990). *A Woman's Wage: Historical Meanings and Social Consequences.* Lexington, KY: The University Press of Kentucky.

Kitchener, Karen S. and King, Patricia M. (1990). The reflective judgment model: Transforming assumptions about knowing. In Jack Mezirow, ed., *Fostering Critical Reflection in Adulthood.* San Francisco: Jossey-Bass.

Knowles, Malcolm S. (1957). Malcolm Knowles Papers, box 18, October. Syracuse University Archives.

―――― (1968). Andragogy, Not Pedagogy! *Adult Leadership*, April 1968, 350–52, 386.

―――― (1970). *The Modern Practice of Adult Education: Andragogy versus Pedagogy.* New York: Associated Press.

―――― (1975). *Self-Directed Learning.* New York: Associated Press.

―――― (1980). *The Modern Practice of Adult Education: From Pedagogy to Andragogy.* Rev. ed. and updated. New York: Cambridge.

―――― (1986). *Using Learning Contracts: Practical Approaches to Individualizing and Structuring Learning.* San Francisco: Jossey-Bass.

Korsch, Karl (1972). *Three Essays on Marxism.* New York: Monthly Review Press.

Kramer, D. A. (1983). Post-formal operations? A need for further conceptualization. *Human Development*, 26, 91–105.

Kramer, D. A. and M. Bopp, eds. (1989). *Transformation in Clinical and Developmental Psychology.* N.Y.: Springer.

Kuhn, Annette, ed. (1990). *Alien Zone: Cultural Theory and Contemporary Science Fiction Cinema.* London: Verso.

Kulich, J. (1992). Adult education through a rear view mirror: The changing face of adult education over the last 25 years. *Convergence*, 25, 42–47.

Labouvie-Vief, G. (1984). Logic and self-regulation from youth to maturity: A model. In M. Commons, F. A. Richards and C. Armon, eds., *Beyond For-*

mal Operations: Late Adolescent and Adult Cognitive Development. New York: Praeger.

———— and Blanchard-Fields, F. (1982). Cognitive ageing and psychological growth. *Aging and Society*, 2, 2, 183–209.

Lamphere, L., Zavella, P., and Gonzales, F., with Evans, P. B. (1993). *Sunbelt Working Mothers*. Ithaca, N.Y.: Cornell University Press.

Langsdorf, Lenore (1992). The Interpretative focus: A prerequisite for critical reasoning. In Richard Talaska, ed., *Critical Reasoning in Contemporary Society*. Albany: State University of New York Press.

Larrain, J. (1989). *Theories of Development: Capitalism, Colonialism and Dependency*. Cambridge, England: Polity Press.

Lash, Scott (1990). *Sociology of Postmodernism*. London: Routledge.

Lave, Jean and Wenger, Etienne (1993). *Situated Learning: Legitimate Peripheral Participation*. New York: Cambridge University Press.

Lawson, Kenneth H. (1991). Philosophical Foundations. In John Peters and Peter Jarvis, eds., *Adult Education,* San Francisco: Jossey Bass.

Lee, C. (1988). Basic training in the corporate schoolhouse. *Training, 25,* 27–36.

Lefebvre, Henri (1971). *Everyday Life in the Modern World.* New York: Harper & Row.

Leiss, William (1974). *The Domination of Nature*. Boston: Beacon Press.

Leonard, Stephen (1988). *The Recent Work of Jürgen Habermas: Reason, Justice and Modernity.* Cambridge, Mass.: Cambridge University Press.

Levin, Charles (1991). Baudrillard, critical theory, and psychoanalysis. In Arthur and Marilouise Kroker, eds., *Ideology and Power in the Age of Lenin in Ruins*. Montreal: New World Perspectives.

Leymann, H. and Kornbluh, H. eds. (1989). *Socialization and Learning at Work.* Brookfield, Vt.: Gower.

Lindeman, E. (1961). *The Meaning of Adult Education*. Montreal: Harvest House.

Lisman, David, and Ohliger, John (1978). "Must we all go back to school?" The pitfalls of compulsory education. *The Progressive*, October, 35–37.

Little, David (1991). Critical adult education: A response to contemporary social crisis. *Canadian Journal for the Study of Adult Education*, 5, Special Issue, 1–20.

Loder, J. I. (1981). *The Transforming Moment: Understanding Convictional Experiences*. San Francisco: Harper & Row.

Loughlin, Kathleen (1990). A call to action: Women's perceptions of the learning experiences that influenced consciousness-raising—a retrospective study. Unpublished doctoral dissertation, Teachers College, Columbia University.

Lovett, Tom (1988). Community education and community action. In Tom Lovett, ed., *Radical Approaches to Adult Education: A Reader*. London: Routledge.

Lyotard, Jean-François (1984a). *The Postmodern Condition: A Report on Knowledge*. Minneapolis: University of Minnisota Press.

———— (1984b). *Driftworks*. New York: Semiotext(e).

MacIntyre, Alisdair (1981). *After Virtue: A Study in Moral Theory*. Notre Dame: University of Notre Dame Press.

Manchester Guardian Weekly (1993). Pope criticises capitalism. *Manchester Guardian Weekly*, 7 November.

Marcuse, Herbert (1960). *Reason and Revolution*. Boston: Beacon Press.

———— (1964). *One-Dimensional Man*. Boston: Beacon Press.

———— (1969). *An Essay on Liberation*. Boston: Beacon Press.

———— (1972). *Counter-revolution and Revolt*. Boston: Beacon Press.

Markus, Gyorgy (1986). *Language and Production: A Critique of the Paradigms*. Dordrecht, Germany: D. Reidel.

Marsick, V. J., ed. (1987). *Learning in the Workplace*. London: Croom Helm.

Martin, Jane Rolland (1994). Methodological essentialism, false difference, and other dangerous traps. *Signs*, 19, 3, 630–51.

Marx, Karl (1963). *The Eighteenth Brumaire of Louis Bonaparte*. New York: International Publishers.

———— (1968). *The German Ideology*. Moscow: Progress.

———— (1977). *Capital*. 3 vols. New York: Vintage Books.

———— and Engels, Frederick (1975). *Karl Marx Frederick Engels Collected Works. Vol. 3: 1843–1844*. New York: International Publishers.

McCarthy, Thomas (1985). *The Critical Theory of Jürgen Habermas*. Cambridge, Mass.: MIT Press.

———— (1991). *Ideals and Illusions: On Reconstruction and Deconstruction in Contemporary Critical Theory.* Cambridge, Mass.: MIT Press.

McIlroy, John (1990). Border country: Raymond Williams in adult education, part I. *Studies in the Education of Adults,* 22, 2, 129–66.

———— (1991). Border country: Raymond Williams in adult education, part II. *Studies in the Education of Adults,* 23, 1, 1–23.

McRobbie, Angela (1989). Postmodernism and popular culture. In Lisa Appignanesi, ed., *Postmodernism: ICA Documents.* London: Free Association Books.

Merrifield, J. and Bingman, M. B. (1993). Living and learning: Strategies for survival in a literate world. *Proceedings of the 34th Annual Adult Education Research Conference.* University Park, Pa.: Pennsylvania State University.

Mezirow, Jack (1981). A critical theory of adult learning and education. *Adult Education,* 32, 1, 3–24.

———— (1985). Concept and action in adult education. *Adult Education Quarterly,* 35, 3, 142–51.

———— (1991). *Transformative Dimensions of Adult Learning.* San Francisco: Jossey-Bass.

————, ed. (1990). *Fostering Critical Reflection in Adulthood.* San Francisco: Jossey-Bass.

Miller, George A. (1992). Sneaking up on consciousness. *New York Times Book Review,* 4 October, 33.

Muller, Lucienne (1991). Progressivism and U.S. adult education: A critique of mainstream theory as embodied in the work of Malcolm Knowles. Unpublished doctoral dissertation, Teachers College, Columbia University.

Murray, K. (1993). Companies rethink one-shot diversity training as new problems are created. *Chicago Tribune,* 13 September, Section 4, 6.

———— (1993). The unfortunate side effects of "diversity training." *The New York Times,* 1 August, F5.

Nadler, Leonard, ed. (1980). *Corporate Human Resource Development: A Management Tool.* Madison, Wis.: American Society for Training and Development.

Naples, N. (1992). Activist mothering: Cross-generational continuity in the community work of women from low-income urban neighborhoods. *Gender and Society,* 6, 441–63.

Nicholson, L. J., ed. (1990) *Feminism/Postmodernism*. New York: Routledge.

Noble, B. P. (1992). Round two on the mommy track. *The New York Times*, 23 February, F23.

—— (1993a). The debate over *la difference*. *The New York Times*, 15 August, F6.

—— (1993b). Worthy child-care pay scales. *The New York Times*, 18 April, F25.

Noddings, N. (1992). *The challenge to care in schools*. New York: Teachers College Press.

Norris, Christopher (1991). The "end of ideology" revisited: The Gulf War, post-modernism and *realpolitic*. *Philosophy and Social Criticism*, 17, 1, 1–40.

Ohliger, John (1974). Is lifelong education a guarantee of permanent inadequacy? *Convergence*, 7, 2, 47–59.

Okin, Susan (1987). Justice and gender. *Philosophy and Public Affairs*, 16, 1, 42–72.

Palmer, Parker J. (1991) The courage to teach. *The National Teaching and Learning Forum*, 1, 2, 2–7.

Pateman, Carole (1989). *The Disorder of Women: Democracy, Feminism and Political Theory*. Palo Alto: Stanford University Press.

Paterson, R. W. K. (1989). Philosophy and adult education. In Barry Bright, ed., *Theory and Practice in the Study of Adult Education: The Epistemological Debate*. London: Routledge.

Pear, R. (1993). Poverty in U.S. grew faster than population last year. *The New York Times*, 5 October, A10.

Pefanis, Julian (1991). *Heterology and the Postmodern: Bataille, Baudrillard, and Lyotard*. Durham: Duke University Press.

Perelman, L. J. (1984). *The Learning Enterprise: Adult Learning, Human Capital and Economic Development*. Washington, D.C.: The Council of State Planning Agencies.

Perenchio, Yorkin, and Scott (1982). *Bladerunner*. Los Angeles: The Ladd Company (in association with Warner Brothers).

Peterson, S. R. (1984). Against "parenting." In J. Trebilcot, ed., *Mothering*. Totowa: Rowman & Allanheld.

Peukert, Helmut (1984). *Science, Action, and Fundamental Theology*. Cambridge, Mass.: MIT Press.

Phillips, A., Taylor, B. (1986). Sex and skill. In *Feminist Review,* ed., *Waged Work: A Reader.* London: Virago Press.

Plumb, Donovan (1989). The significance of Jürgen Habermas for the pedagogy of Paulo Freire and the practice of adult education. Unpublished Master's thesis, University of Saskatchewan.

———— (1994). Critical adult education in postmodern times. Unpublished doctoral dissertation, University of Alberta.

Polakow, V. (1993). *Lives on the Edge.* Chicago: University of Chicago Press.

Polatnik, M. R. (1984). Why men don't rear children: A power analysis. In J. Trebilcot, ed., *Mothering.* Totowa: Rowman & Allanheld.

Pratt, Dan. (1993). Andragogy after twenty-five years. In Sharan Merriam, ed., *An Update on Adult Learning Theory.* San Francisco: Jossey-Bass.

Pusey, Michael (1987). *Jürgen Habermas.* London: Tavistock Publishers.

Quigley, A. B. and Holsinger E. (1993). "Happy consciousness": Hegemony and hidden curricula in literacy readers between 1977 and 1991. *Proceedings of the 34th Annual Adult Education Research Conference.* University Park, Pa.: Pennsylvania State University.

Radway, Janice (1992). Mail-order culture and its critics: The Book-of-the-Month Club, commodification and consumption, and the problem of cultural authority. In Lawrence Grossberg, Cary Nelson, and Paula Treichler, eds., *Cultural Studies.* New York: Routledge.

Reed, A., Jr. (1992). The underclass as myth and symbol. *Radical America,* 24, 21–40.

Regnier, Robert (In press). *Warrior as Pedagogue—Pedagogue as Warrior: Reflections on Aboriginal Anti-Racist Pedagogy.* South Hadley, Mass.: Bergin & Garvey.

Rockhill, Kathleen (1985). Ideological solidification in university adult education: Confrontation over workers' education in the USA. In Richard Taylor, Kathleen Rockhill, and Roger Fieldhouse, eds., *University Adult Education in England and the USA.* London: Croom Helm.

———— (1985). The liberal perspective and the symbolic legitimation of university adult education in the USA. In Richard Taylor, Kathleen Rockhill and Roger Fieldhouse, eds., *University Adult Education in England and the USA.* London: Croom Helm.

Rogers, Carl (1969). *Freedom to Learn.* Columbus, Ohio: Merrill.

Romero, M. (1992). *Maid in the U.S.A.* New York: Routledge.

Rorty, Richard (1967). *The Linguistic Turn: Recent Essays in Philosophical Method.* Chicago: University of Chicago Press.

———— (1985). Habermas and Lyotard on postmodernity. In Richard J. Bernstein, ed., *Habermas and Modernity.* Cambridge, Mass.: MIT Press.

Rosen, Stanley (1992). Postmodernism and the possibility of crititical reasoning. In Richard Talaska, ed., *Critical Reasoning in Contemporary Culture.* Albany: State University of New York Press.

Ryan, Michael (1982). Deconstruction and Radical Teaching. *Yale French Studies*, 63, 45–58.

Sayer, Derek (1987). *The Violence of Abstraction: The Analytical Foundations of Historical Materialism.* Oxford: Basil Blackwell.

———— ed. (1989). *Readings from Karl Marx.* London: Routledge.

Schemel, Robert Joseph, Jr. (1992). The work of *The Inquiry*: A review, comparison to current adult education thinking and critique. Unpublished doctoral dissertation, Teachers College, Columbia University.

Schied, Fred (1991). *Towards a Reconceptualization of the Historical Foundations of Adult Education: The Contributions of Radical German-Americans to Workers' Education.* Unpublished doctoral dissertation. DeKalb, Ill.: Northern Illinois University.

Schied, Fred and Zacharakis-Jutz, Jeff (1993). Workers' education, social reconstruction, and adult education. *Adult Education Quarterly*, 43, 2, 101–9.

Schmidt and Verhoeven (1987). *Robo cop.* Los Angeles: Orion Pictures.

Schon, Donald A. (1983). *The Reflective Practitioner: How Professionals Think in Action.* New York: Basic Books.

Schor, J. (1992). *The Overworked American.* New York: Harper & Row.

Schwartz, F. N. (1989). Management women and the new facts of life. *Harvard Business Review*, January–February, 65–76.

———— (1992). *Breaking with Tradition: Woman and Work and the New Facts of Life.* New York: Warner.

Selman, Gordon and Kulich, Jindra (1980). Between social movement and profession—A Canadian perspective on adult education. *Studies in Adult Education*, 12, 2, 109–16.

Semin, Gun R. (1990). Everyday assumptions, language and personality. In Gun R. Semin and Kenneth J. Gergen., eds., *Everyday Understanding*. London: Sage.

Shapiro, Michael (1990). Strategic discourse/discursive strategy: The representation of 'security policy' in the video age. *International Studies Quarterly,* 34, 3, 327–40.

Sherover-Marcuse, Erica (1986). *Emancipation and Consciousness: Dogmatic and Dialectical Perspectives in the Early Marx.* Oxford: Basil Blackwell.

Siegel, Harvey (1992). Education and the fostering of rationality. In Richard Talaska, ed., *Critical Reasoning in Contemporary Culture.* Albany: State University of New York Press.

Sinnott, Jan D. (1989). *Everyday Problem Solving: Theory and Applications.* New York: Praeger.

———(1989). Life-span relativistic postformal thought: The methodology and data from everyday problem-solving studies. In M. L. Commons, J. D. Sinnott, F. A. Richards and C. Armon, eds., *Adult Development,* vol 1: *Comparisons and Applications of Developmental Models.* New York: Praeger.

——— (1991) Limits to problem solving: Emotion, intention, goal clarity, health and other factors in postformal thought. In Jan D. Sinnott and John C. Cavanaugh, eds., *Bridging Paradigms.* New York: Praeger.

Sissel, P. A. (1993). Educational scholarship on women: A feminist analysis of two decades of adult education literature. *Proceedings of the 34th Annual Adult Education Research Conference.* University Park, Pa.: Pennsylvania State University.

Sleeper, R. W. (1992). Whose reason? Which canon? Critical reasoning and conflicting ideas of rationality. In Richard Talaska, ed., *Critical Reasoning in Contemporary Culture.* Albany: State University of New York Press.

Sloan, T. S. (1986). *Deciding: Self-Deception in Life Choices.* New York: Methuen.

Sloterdijk, Peter (1988). *Critique of Cynical Reason.* London: Verso.

Smith, J. (1990). All crises are not the same: Households in the United States during two crises. In J. L. Collins and M. Gimenez, eds., *Work without Wages.* Albany: State University of New York Press.

Spady, William (1978). Cited in *Report of U.S. Office of Education Invitational Workshop on Adult Competency Education.* Washington, D.C.: U.S. Government Printing Office.

Stacey, J. (1992). Backward toward the postmodern family: Reflections on gender, kinship, and class in the Silicon Valley. In B. Torne and M. Yalom, eds., *Rethinking the Family*. Boston: Northeastern University Press.

Stalker, J. (1993). Sexual harassment: The dark side of the adult learner/teacher relationship. *Proceedings of the 34th Annual Adult Education Research Conference*. University Park, Pa.: Pennsylvania State University.

Stewart, David (1987). *Adult Learning in America: Eduard Lindeman and His Agenda for Lifelong Education*. Malabar, Fla.: Robert E. Krieger Publishing Co.

Stubblefield, Harold (1988). *Towards a History of Adult Education in America: The Search for a Unifying Principle*. London: Croom Helm.

Suanmali, C. (1981). The core concepts of andragogy. Unpublished doctoral dissertation, Teachers College, Columbia University.

Sullivan, E. (1990). *Critical Psychology and Pedagogy: Interpretation of the Personal World*. Toronto: OISE Press.

Sunstein, Cass R. (1993). *Democracy and the Problem of Free Speech*. New York: The Free Press.

Tawney, Richard H. (1964).*The Radical Tradition: Twelve Essays on Politics, Education, and Literature*. London: Allen and Unwin.

The New York Times (1993). Census figures show a racial salary gap. *The New York Times*, 16 September, A10.

Thomas, Alan (1991). *Beyond Education: A New Perspective on Society's Management of Learning*. San Francisco: Jossey-Bass.

Thorne, B., Yalom, M., eds. (1992). *Rethinking the Family*. Boston: Northeastern University Press.

Tomaskovic-Devey, D. (1993). *Gender Racial Inequality at Work*. Ithaca, N.Y.: ILR Press.

Tomlinson, John (1991). *Cultural Imperialism*. Baltimore: John Hopkins University Press.

Torres, Carlos (1990). *The Politics of Nonformal Education in Latin America*. New York: Praeger.

Tough, Allen (1966). The assistance obtained by adult self-teachers. *Adult Education*, 17, 1, 30–37.

—— (1981). *Learning without a Teacher: A Study of Tasks and Assistance during Adult Self-teaching Projects*. Toronto: OISE Press.

Touraine, Alain (1981). *The Voice and the Eye: An Analysis of Social Movements*. Cambridge: Cambridge University Press.

Tulvig, E. (1989). Remembering and knowing the past. *American Scientist*, 77, 361–67.

Turim, Maureen (1991). Cinemas of modernity and postmodernity. In Ingeborg Hoesterey, ed., *Zeitgeist in Babel: The Postmodernist Controversy*. Bloomingon, Ind.: Indiana University Press.

Turner, Graham (1990). *British Cultural Studies: An Introduction*. Boston: Unwin Hyman.

Usher, Robin (1991). Theory and metatheory in the adult education curriculum. *International Journal of Lifelong Education*, 10, 305–15.

Usher, Robin and Bryant, Ian (1989*). Adult Education as Theory, Practice and Research: The Captive Triangle*. London: Routledge.

Vajda, Mihaly (1972). Karl Korsch's 'Marxism and Philosophy.' In Dick Howard and Karl Klare, eds., *The Unknown Dimension: European Marxism since Lenin*. New York: Basic Books.

Valentine, T. and Darkenwald, G. G. (1990). Deterrents to participation in adult education: profiles of potential learners. *Adult Education Quarterly*, 41, 29–42.

Verner, Coolie (1964). Definitions of Terms. In G. Jensen, ed., *Adult Education: Outlines of an Emerging Field of Study*. Washington, D.C.: Adult Education Association.

Vogel, L. (1993). *Mothers on the Job: Maternity Policy in the U.S. Workplace*. New Brunswick, N.J.: Rutgers University Press.

Vygotski, Lev. S. (1956). *Selected Psychological Research*. Moscow: Izadateltsuo Akademii Pedagoshes Kikh Naul.

—— (1978). *Mind and Society: The Development of Higher Psychological Processes*. Cambridge, Mass: Harvard University Press.

Walsh, M. (1991). Tough new bosses for tough times. *Business Week*, 25 November, 174–79.

Warren, Scott (1984). *The Emergence of Dialectical Theory: Philosophy and Political Inquiry*. Chicago: University of Chicago Press.

Watkins, K. E., Marsick, V. J. (1993). Designing an empirical audit of the learning organization. *Proceedings of the 34th Annual Adult Education Research Conference*. University Park, Pa.: Pennsylvania State University.

Watkins, Karen (1989). Business and industry. In S. Merriam and P. Cunningham, eds., *Handbook of Adult and Continuing Education*. San Francisco: Jossey-Bass.

Watkins, P. (1986). *High Tech, Low Tech and Education*. Geelong, Victoria: Deakin University Press.

Weber, Max (1958). *The Protestant Ethic and the Spirit of Capitalism*. New York: Scribner.

Weil, Susan and McGill, Ian (1989). *Making Sense of Experiential Learning: Diversity in Theory and Practice*. Milton Keynes: Open University Press.

Wellmer, Albrecht (1971). *Critical Theory of Society*. New York: Herder and Herder.

———— (1985). Reason, utopia, and the *Dialectic of Enlightenment*. In Richard Bernstein, ed., *Habermas and Modernity*. Oxford: Polity Press.

Welton, Michael (1987). "Vivisecting the nightingale": Reflections on adult education as an object of study. *Studies in the Education of Adults*, 19, 1, 46–68.

———— (1991a). *Toward Development Work: The Workplace as a Learning Environment*. Geelong, Victoria: Deakin University Press.

———— (1991b). Dangerous knowledge: Canadian workers' education in the decades of discord. *Studies in the Education of Adults*, 23, 1, 24–40.

———— (1991c). Shaking the foundations: The critical turn in adult education theory. *The Canadian Journal for the Study of Adult Education*, 5, Special Issue, 21–42.

———— (1993a). The contribution of critical theory to our understanding of adult learning. In Sharan Merriam, ed. *An Update on Adult Learning Theory*. San Francisco: Jossey-Bass.

———— (1993b). Social revolutionary learning: The new social movements as learning sites. *Adult Education Quarterly*, 43, 3, 152–64.

Westwood, Sallie (1980). Adult education and the sociology of education: An exploration. In Jane Thompson, ed., *Adult Education for a Change*. London: Hutchingson.

Wildemeersch, Danny (1992a). Crossing borders in socio-cultural education with adults. In Danny Wildemeersch and Theo Jansen, eds., *Adult Education, Experiential Learning and Social Change: The Postmodern Challenge*. Driebergen, Netherlands: VTA Groep.

——— (1992b). Ambiguities of experiential learning and critical pedagogy. In Danny Wildemeersch and Theo Jansen, eds., *Adult Education, Experiential Learning and Social Change: The Postmodern Challenge*. Driebergen, Netherlands: VTA Groep.

Williams, L. (1992). Scrambling to manage a diverse work force. *The New York Times*, 15 December, A1, C2.

Williams, Raymond (1977). *Marxism and Literature*. London: Oxford University Press.

Wilson, Arthur (1991). Personal correspondence with Michael Welton. 6 September.

——— (1992). Science and the professionalization of American adult education, 1934–1989: A study of knowledge development in the adult education handbooks. *Proceedings of the 33rd Annual Adult Education Research Conference*. Saskatoon, Saskatchewan: University of Saskatchewan.

——— and Clark, Carolyn (1991). Context and rationality in Mezirow's theory of transformational learning. *Adult Education Quarterly*, 41, 2, 75–91.

Women Employed Institute (1988). *Occupational segregation*. Chicago: Women Employed Institute Study.

Ziegahn, L. (1992). Learning, literacy, and participation: Sorting out priorities. *Adult Education Quarterly*, *43*, 30–50.

Zinn, M. B. (1992). Family, race, and poverty in the eighties. In B. Thorne and M. Yalom, eds., *Rethinking the Family*. Boston: Northeastern University Press.

Zuboff, S. (1988). *In the Age of the Smart Machine*. New York: Basic Books.

INDEX